The Master's Degree in Education as Teacher Professional Development

The Master's Degree in Education as Teacher Professional Development

Re-envisioning the Role of the Academy in the Development of Practicing Teachers

Gary R. Galluzzo,
Joan P. Isenberg,
C. Stephen White,
and Rebecca K. Fox

ROWMAN & LITTLEFIELD PUBLISHERS, INC.
Lanham • Boulder • New York • Toronto • Plymouth, UK

Published by Rowman & Littlefield Publishers, Inc.
A wholly owned subsidiary of The Rowman & Littlefield Publishing Group, Inc.
4501 Forbes Boulevard, Suite 200, Lanham, Maryland 20706
www.rowman.com

10 Thornbury, Plymouth PL6 7PP, United Kingdom

British Library Cataloguing in Publication Information Available

Library of Congress Cataloging-in-Publication Data

The master's degree in education as teacher professional development :
re-envisioning the role of the academy in the development of practicing teachers /
Gary Galluzzo ... [et al.].
    p. cm.
   Summary: "Teacher education is under more scrutiny than ever as standards-based education is becoming more and more the norm. Although much literature is available that addresses developing teacher education, no one addresses how to create and develop a master's level program. Gary R. Galluzzo, Joan Packer Isenberg, C. Stephen White, and Rebecca K. Fox, professors at the highly regarded Graduate School of Education at George Mason University, present a text to help deans and other professionals develop a master's level degree program that meets the standards of the National Board for Professional Teaching Standards. The various sections explain in depth the facets of the program's design, including how to qualify future students answering the call by the National Board, provide researched evidence around Advanced Studies in Teaching and Learning, and lastly, explore what will become the new standards of accountability for teacher education. Using their own experience as they reconceived their own program for a master's degree for practicing teachers, the authors provide first-hand accounts of their own expectations, outcomes, and continual dilemmas to inspire more discussion how teacher education can improve the quality of teaching in America's schools"— Provided by publisher.
   ISBN 978-1-4422-0722-6 (hardback) — ISBN 978-1-4422-0724-0 (ebook)
   1. Master of education degree—United States. 2. Teachers—Training of—Standards—United States. 3. National Board for Professional Teaching Standards (U.S.) I. Galluzzo, Gary R.
  LB1741.5.M37 2012
  370.71'1—dc23
            2011047877

Printed in the United States of America

Contents

Foreword

Read this book! You will be ever grateful that the dedicated team at George Mason University's College of Education and Human Development (CEHD) determined to thoroughly document their steadfast and still ongoing voyage to creating a unique master's degree in education: Advanced Studies in Teaching and Learning (ASTL). It is a program of which the educator preparation profession can be immensely proud. This volume, which describes its development—including the good, the bad, and the ugly—with grace, good humor, and wisdom, will be instructive to all education colleges initiating program redesign responsive to the contemporary demands of practice. As the following pages detail, CEHD took on much more than most redesign efforts—regardless of discipline. Many such attempts are quickly found to be shortsighted and short-lived. The GMU effort, however, was a unique, massive undertaking that has produced a living, organic, ever-evolving education experience and with a built-in process for sustainability. Most importantly, the program results in a credential that connects to the delivery of K–12 educational services in a conspicuous manner.

The George Mason CEHD set out to use the master's degree as a vehicle for strengthening teachers' ability to strengthen the schools in which they work—thus the title, *The Master's Degree in Education as Teacher Professional Development*.

This master's is not for the faint-hearted or irresolute. Its multifaceted framework presents challenging experiences built around a thoughtfully expanded version of the National Board for Professional Teaching Standards (NBPTS) Core propositions. Cohorts of students study and teach in local Northern Virginia schools for an entire calendar year. A major emphasis is placed on gathering evidence, reflection and constant analysis, and portfolio documentation of teaching effectiveness and student learning.

Particularly powerful, I find, is that partner schools are supported in bending the disciplinary curricula of the College of Arts and Sciences to their particular teaching needs. The master's degree now not only serves the traditional goals of advanced knowledge and skills, but also provides a critical mass of teachers in each school who no longer work in professional isolation from one another, or in schools that are unable to support high-impact instructional practice. This new master's makes great strides toward building the essential bonds between pedagogy and content, between education schools and the disciplines, and between the university and schools in their communities.

These authors provide honest insights on how to create a new program given the context of countless university traditions. Their candor alone will be particularly valuable to other education school leaders. You will nod, laugh, and squirm as you read of the discontinuities between the academy and the schools, and how CEHD made the connections to build relationships and organizational structures required to launch its new program.

The release of this volume couldn't be timelier, as education master's degrees are under heavy scrutiny across the nation. Districts and states are reconsidering teacher compensation, promotion, and retention policies, including the granting of automatic pay increases to those who obtain education master's degrees. The ASTL degree is the absolute antithesis of the often criticized "fly-by masters," because this degree can confirm the effect of the degree on actual practice.

Appropriately and purposely, CEHD created this master's program for teachers who plan to remain in the classroom and want to strengthen their practice and hone their skills—not for those simply looking for a pay bump or a ticket to a corporate career after two years' service.

I have stated publicly that some education master's programs do not add value to teaching quality or student learning and should cease to exist—and that the public should not pay for such credentials. I now welcome the reader to the story of, and the facts behind, an exemplar truly worth the money.

> Sharon Robinson, President and CEO,
> American Association of Colleges for Teacher Education

Preface

It has been over a quarter of a century since the 1983 publication of *A Nation at Risk*, by the National Commission on Excellence in Education, the document that arguably started the contemporary revolution in American education. Its influence is still being felt today in the standards movement, the accountability agenda, the professionalization agenda, and the deregulation of education and teacher education. Its fundamental premise, captured by the sound bite, "the education foundations of our society are presently being eroded by a rising tide of mediocrity that threatens our very future as a Nation and a people," (p. 5) launched the need for explicitly stated academic content standards that are now evidenced in all states, as well as in the movement for national curricular standards. *A Nation at Risk* also gave impetus to an accountability agenda that reached its fruition in the No Child Left Behind Act of 2001 that required all states to test its students at a minimum in grades three through eight. The commission's report also spurred a wide collection of education leaders, policymakers, foundation leaders, and others to address the report's attack on the education of teachers and the teaching profession in general. With support from the Carnegie Forum on Education and the Economy (1986), the Task Force on Teaching as a Profession published its response to *A Nation at Risk*, entitled *A Nation Prepared: Teachers for the 21st Century* (1986), thereby initiating a national effort to improve the quality of the teaching force and how teachers are prepared from entry into a teacher education program and throughout one's career. Most notably, and germane to this volume, was its recommendation that if we create standards and accountability for students, then we should have standards and accountability for teachers as well, embodied in the call for a National Board for Professional Teaching Standards (NBPTS). Lastly, with the authors of *A Nation at Risk* challenging the very foundation of public education, we have since seen a deregulation of public schooling to include innovations such as open enrollment beyond school district borders, the invention of charter schools, and both locally and federally funded school voucher programs that allow students to use public funds for a private school education. Indeed, it can be argued that the last twenty-five years has seen more change in American education than was seen in the previous decades of the twentieth century combined.

It has also been more than a quarter-century since the publication of Harry Judge's *American Graduate Schools of Education: A View from Abroad* (1982), a seminal work in the study of the scholarly nature of education schools in which he chides the nation's education schools for choosing to seek recognition as centers of scholarly inquiry at the risk of working closely with their local schools and teachers. While not directly focused on advanced education programs for practicing teachers, in many ways Judge's work opened the doors to wide-ranging discussions of reform in teacher education, including the controversial, yet impactful work of the Holmes Group with its call for more rigor in teacher education (Holmes Group, 1986), greater concern for the growing diversity of the school populations (Holmes Group, 1990), and the need for education schools to follow a path of continuous improvement (Holmes Group, 1995). But the calls for change didn't stop there. Another group of institutions, primarily institutions with founding histories as "teachers' colleges," formed the Renaissance Group, which began a nationwide discussion among its members about teacher education reform at institutions not known as centers of research and inquiry, but as the practice-oriented institutions that prepare the vast majority of the nation's teachers annually. Still numerous other consortia were formed that sought to influence the quality of teacher education, such as the Project 30 institutions funded primarily by IBM, and the National Network on Education Renewal, the brainchild of noted scholar John Goodlad (1990) among many others. Lastly, in this sequence, there is the report *What Matters Most: Teaching for America's Future* (1996) by the National Commission on Teaching and America's Future (NCTAF), which solidified the National Board Certified Teacher (NBCT) as the nation's image of teachers to achieve a future of quality education for all children. In short, the last quarter century has seen so much discussion of reform in education and teacher education that the avenues to change available to education school faculty are as numerous as the possibilities are endless, and there was no lack of opportunity for education school faculty to identify with an agenda and begin to pursue it. It is against this backdrop that we prepare this volume. As a result of all of this ferment, doors were opened to teacher educators to experiment with new ideas and new approaches in educating the nation's teachers, at the outset at the preservice level, and eventually at the advanced or master's degree level. This volume details one college of education's values, designs, expectations, outcomes, and ongoing dilemmas as it reconceived the master's degree for practicing teachers as a convergence of three strands: (1) challenging the scholarly traditions of the academy in more contemporary form; (2) the expectations that education schools can provide opportunities for continuous improvement in teachers' practice; and (3) the development of deeper and richer content knowledge for practicing teachers.

With so many options, and many of them in conflict with one another, for example, field-based, campus-based, standards-based, assessment-based, content-based, theory-based, and the like, we usually look to the research on a topic for guidance in selecting our paths. Unfortunately, and as has been made clear in the three volumes of the *Handbook of Research on Teacher Education* (Cochran-Smith, Feiman-Nemser, McIntyre, & Demers, 2008; Houston, 1990; Sikula, 1996), the AERA Panel volume *Studying Teacher Education* (Cochran-Smith & Zeichner, 2005), as well as the National Research Council's Committee on the Study of Teacher Preparation in the United States report *Preparing Teachers: Building Sound Evidence* (2010), we simply don't know enough about how students become teachers to provide direction, and even less about what contributions master's degrees make to a teacher. As such, we look to prevailing conceptions of the well-educated teacher and what he should know and be able to do to act as effectively as possible in service to his students. These conceptions can be applied to the preservice preparation of teachers or to the continuing professional development of teachers throughout their careers.

More recently, we're seeing Louisiana undertaking reviews of master's degree programs. Kentucky sunset master's degree programs for teachers in 2010 did not meet the expectations of its state professional standards board. Georgia has revised its standards to tie coursework and practice more closely together. Master's degrees, once accepted as a statement of higher accomplishment, are now questioned as tax burdens on local communities that have historically awarded salary increases to teachers who earned them. Times continue to change and new opportunities for experiments and innovations in schools, colleges, and departments of education in the continuing education of practicing teachers will exist.

Our particular interest in this volume most closely relates to the continuing education of teachers in a world of standards, accountability, professionalization, deregulation, and most importantly, change. Having to begin somewhere, the Advanced Studies in Teaching and Learning (ASTL) program was initiated with a memo from the dean of the then-Graduate School of Education (GSE) to the faculty asking for the creation of a new kind of master's degree for teachers that bridges the scholarship on teaching with the new conceptions of program design in teacher education and that is consistent with the five Core propositions of the National Board for Professional Teaching Standards (1989a), particularly with its application of Shulman's (1986) concept of pedagogical content knowledge. What emerged was a conceptual framework of the "Master's degree as continuing professional development," a merging of the idea that the master's degree should be scholarly in its orientation and the idea that teachers should be students of themselves toward their own more robust practice. Some people have called this the "scholar-practitioner" model, although we have not used such terms. Rather, ASTL is a hybrid of many parts, including the skills of inquiry found in most master's degrees and deeper professional knowledge about practice, which we call the "Core," on the one hand, and the study of a discipline the teacher teaches (e.g., mathematics, history, literacy) that gives teachers the depth needed to prepare them for the role of teacher leader, if not teacher as change agent, which is labeled the "Concentration." In this way, the NBPTS' conception of teachers who are both skilled as practitioners and experts in their content area is fulfilled in a master's degree that tries to bridge the long-standing divide of pedagogy and content; and education school and the traditional academic disciplines.

In the ten chapters that comprise this volume, we hope to detail the program from its conceptual framework through its structure, processes, activities, expectations, and the ongoing challenges that require regular attention—sometimes to resolution and sometimes not. In addition, we will demonstrate how the ongoing study of the program is used to improve the quality of the program as well as to understand how teachers continue to grow and develop over the course of the program, and in some ways, beyond the program.

This volume is divided into three parts. The first part is on the tenets of our program's design. In chapter 1 we present the conceptual framework touched upon earlier. In it we describe our fundamental values, how we approached how teachers learn, and how we structured the program to approach the conception of a NBCT. In chapter 2, we discuss the opportunities and challenges of implementing and reconfiguring program design for practicing teachers in a traditional university planning context. In this chapter we address how we overcame university course structures and limitations to provide a welcoming learning environment for teachers. In chapter 3 we face the issues of program design, building coherence, staffing, and learning from our experiences. Chapter 4 completes the first section of the volume and treats the problem of implementation while we're learning and the everyday challenges that presents, from student concerns to institutional barriers and obstacles that can impede learning.

Part 2 is concerned with evidence. Now a fixture in this era of standards and accountability, we focus on the centrality of evidence of our effectiveness on teacher growth and student learning, and how we constructed a research and evaluation agenda around ASTL to study them. In chapter 5 we discuss our use of evidence through the various course-based studies we conduct on each cohort of students that enters the program. Chapter 6 presents how we have translated student-focused research and course-based evidence into evidence of program effectiveness by aggregating our data within and across cohorts, and lastly in chapter 7 we present the concept of program portfolios and performance-based assessment and how they support the conceptual framework of inquiry and reflection on practice across the Core.

In part 3, we devote time to what is new for education school faculty who want to consider leaving the past behind and moving into new conceptions of continuing professional development for teachers. In chapter 8, we explore new dimensions of accountability and where we're heading. In chapter 9, we examine the new roles we have had to learn as faculty. As we hope will be clear prior to this chapter, we have had to learn to behave in new ways, as in many instances we are partners in the learning of our students. And finally, in chapter 10, we discuss what we have learned about teaching teachers in a master's degree program for those who want to remain in the classroom and whom we see as the central agents of school improvement and change.

Our experience in ASTL has already been rewarding beyond words. Those of us who teach in the program see ourselves as a cohort of faculty working with a cohort of students. Our students can see our relationships as we move in and out of their classes. We have evidence that they can see how one course leads to the next. They can see how what we are asking them to do is "Board-like" without being a preparatory course for seeking National Board Certification. But most importantly, we have learned a great deal about designing a master's degree program that has merit in what it teaches and has worth in that many of our graduates go on to become leaders in their schools, or NBCTs, or both. It is our hope that this volume stimulates more discussion among teacher educators about what education schools can do to improve the quality of teaching in our nation's schools.

Gary R. Galluzzo
Joan P. Isenberg
C. Stephen White
Rebecca K. Fox

1

Tenets of Program Design

Programs for teachers in this era of accountability must stand for something. They must be grounded in what some might call a conceptual framework to which the parts that make up the whole are tied. In these opening four chapters we walk the reader through our earliest efforts to create a master's degree program for teachers who want to remain in the classroom that is enriching, is expansive, teaches the value of reflection, and develops additional content expertise. These four chapters strive to provide some insight into how to accomplish the goals of the program in the context of countless university traditions. By the end of chapter 4, the reader will have a sense of the discontinuities between the academy and the schools and how we strived to build the many bridges needed to launch a new program.

1

The Tenets of a New Kind of Master's Degree in Education

Act I: The challenge was clear. Enrollments in the master's degree for practicing teachers suffered significant annual declines as the education faculty spent almost ten years implementing a Holmes Group–inspired preservice program that replaced undergraduate teacher education with a fifth-year program culminating in a master's degree and conducted in professional development schools. In many ways, George Mason University's Graduate School of Education was fulfilling the call for more robust and more intellectually rigorous preservice teacher education. As a result of the time and energy to a radical change in preservice teacher education, the old master's in curriculum and instruction for practicing teachers was neglected: it was "dying on the vine," and had few "owners" of the program. Its moribund status had already opened the door for a competing program for this "market" of teachers outside the graduate school of education that had earned support across campus with the exception of the graduate school of education.

A new dean with a different conception of the role of the master's degree arrived. Within a few months a group of faculty was asked to design a new program, one that would be grounded in the conception of the "accomplished teacher" promulgated by the National Board for Professional Teaching Standards (NBPTS), which contemplated inviting the faculty members in the then-College of Arts and Sciences to become partners in the process of the continuing professional development of teachers in the academic disciplines. All assumptions about credits, design, format, use of faculty time, and so on were open for discussion. The only expectation was that the new program would be consistent with the NBPTS' five Core propositions, but not a training program for National Board Certification.

Act II: How do you take those five propositions and turn them into curriculum? How do you structure the program such that it has fidelity with what is taught in the field of education and with the academic disciplines? How do you get a historian or mathematician to care about the continuing education of teachers? What do you do about someone seeking a master's degree in education that requires graduate coursework in an academic discipline when the student may not have an undergraduate degree in that discipline, but teaches it every day to young children? How do you negotiate the stark reality that there was a master's degree for teachers already successfully operating elsewhere on campus? The new dean, working in a university that valued programs that competed for students if they could sustain enrollments and income, was now leading an education school that offered no master's degrees for teachers, and who included in his vision for the college that it aligned with another national initiative, like Holmes, but this time, NBPTS. In this way, the college would have implemented the Holmes fifth-year model of preservice teacher education and a master's program grounded in the NBPTS' Core propositions. At the time these changes were seen as current in the field and possible.

Act III: Two worlds, long separated by mutual disinterest. The new education dean addresses the department chairs in the then-College of Arts and Sciences. Foreign territory. What could he say to them that would interest them? He was there to invite them into a partnership on a master's degree for practicing teachers that would strengthen teachers' knowledge of content, in addition to enhancing their pedagogical skills and understandings. A few of the department chairs stared vacuously at him as he spoke. Some pursued other work. Two chairs, though, immediately became excited about such a possibility to reach into schools and be part of student achievement. And a third chair wrote a twelve-page paper to the dean using ten-year-old citations bashing teacher education and ridiculing the idea as the selling of undergraduate knowledge for graduate rates.

A strange admixture of academic politics, interpersonal relationships, and the uncertainty of attempting what no institution had yet accomplished: design a master's degree program for practicing teachers that met the five Core propositions of the still nascent NBPTS. Innovation requires vast amounts of faith.

THE ANTECEDENT CONDITIONS

As this opening suggests, many factors led to the creation of the Advanced Studies in Teaching and Learning (ASTL) program. The College of Education and Human Development (CEHD), as a member of the Holmes Group, moved to a fifth-year teacher education program with professional development schools. The faculty at the time devoted all of its energy to building a state-of-the-art program for preservice teacher education. As a regional state university, but not a normal school, the history of the university, and the education programs had a decidedly practical orientation aligning with the extant state regulations. Joining in the Holmes agenda, it was moving from what Feiman-Nemser (1990) would describe as a "practical orientation" to one that would maintain its practical orientation but would also adopt a more academic orientation.

George Mason University has a history of encouraging risk-taking in program design and delivery. It encourages academic units to blur the lines that often divide them and even to encourage multiple units offering competing programs. As the college's faculty implemented the Holmes agenda, the master's degree program was left virtually unattended. In that vacuum, a new program was created and a new unit to support it outside the college (Sockett, DeMulder, Lepage, & Wood, 2001), entitled the master's in new professional studies. This degree program was based on a distinct philosophical orientation of reflective practice and organizational transformation in education. With the arrival of a new dean who had previous experiences with NBPTS, it was proposed that the college breathe new life into the largely untended master's in curriculum and instruction, and create a master's degree that was aligned with NBPTS, and by virtue of this alignment, reintroduced the traditional academic disciplines into the graduate education of teachers.

THE MASTER'S DEGREE AS TEACHER PROFESSIONAL DEVELOPMENT

The conditions associated with the creation of master's degree programs for teachers who want to remain in the classroom have changed over the years. At one time, the master's degree was an option chosen only by some of the teachers who enrolled in the programs to learn "advanced" professional content and skills. As years passed and salary schedules rewarded teachers for earning a master's degree, enrollments expanded, but the content remained rather static: more advanced methods. With the rise of accountability in education generally, and in teacher education specifically, all teachers are now held to new professional standards set by national, state, and local regulatory agencies, to new emphases on teaching content, and to new professional expectations for practicing teachers that they demonstrate a professional commitment to the continuous improvement of practice. These influences have provided education schools with the opportunities to reconceive their models of continuing education for teachers offered through master's programs (Blackwell & Diez, 1998; Galluzzo, 1997, 1999; Putnam & Borko, 2000; Tom, 1999), and to make them more meaningful and impactful concerning student achievement and school renewal. The contents of this book are derived from these forces that impelled the faculty in the CEHD at George Mason University to design a master's degree program that strengthens teachers' skills as reflective and analytic professional practitioners, that deepens their understanding of the content they teach to their pupils, and that develops their skills as classroom-based agents of school change. This master's degree program for practicing teachers was entitled the Advanced Studies in Teaching and Learning (ASTL) program.

The design and the contents of the program are drawn from many highly visible reports, such as *Toward High and Rigorous Standards for the Teaching Profession* (National Board for Professional Teaching Standards, 1989a), *What Matters Most: Teaching for America's Future* from the National Commission on Teaching and America's Future (NCTAF) (1996), and *Teacher Quality: A Report on the Preparation and Quality of Public School Teachers* (National Center for Education Statistics, 1999) have anticipated a critical shortage of qualified PK–12 teachers and have consistently concluded that a qualified teacher in every classroom is essential to helping all students learn. According to NCTAF (1996), the key to improving and transforming schools is to improve and transform the continuing education of practicing teachers. The work of the commission is based on the following three assertions:

1. What teachers know and can do is the most important influence on what students learn.
2. Retaining good teachers in the classroom is central for improving America's schools.
3. School reform must focus on creating conditions in which teachers can teach and teach well.

This new context of both accountability and professionalism has propelled education schools to turn their focus to master's degrees for teachers on thoughtful professional development rather "than on continuing education, or license renewal" (Galluzzo, 1999, p. 8) to retain a cadre of highly qualified teachers (Darling-Hammond & Cobb, 1996; Murray, 1996; National Center for Education Statistics, 1999). Additionally, Blackwell and Diez (1998), analyzing the needed changes for master's degrees for practicing teachers, suggests that framing advanced degrees around NBPTS' five Core propositions helps focus the degree on the ongoing professional development of teachers.

One purpose of this volume is to expose how one faculty decided to discard old conceptions of the master's degree as "more of the same" and how it chose to create one that is more connected to how teachers learn, what they need to know and be able to do, and to prepare them to lead from the classroom.

THE ASTL PROGRAM

The ASTL program, as a substantiation of these contemporary views on the future of teaching as a profession, is a master's degree program for practicing teachers. Created in 1998, the program is aligned with the NBPTS' Core propositions. The central purpose of the ASTL program is to provide practicing teachers with learning experiences and activities that simulate the requirements for National Board Certification, while explicitly not serving as a "training" program for National Board Certification. Rather, the program is grounded in the conception of a National Board Certified Teacher (NBCT) and uses "Board-like" activities of video analysis, lesson study, differentiated instruction, child study, reflection on practice, and outreach beyond the classroom as course assignments. We employ the five Core propositions of NBPTS, which are delineated in Figure 1.1. NBPTS defines accomplished teaching through its five Core propositions.

After a great deal of faculty discussion about grounding the new program in these five Core propositions, the faculty designers chose to add three more they felt were not emphasized directly enough by NBPTS. As a result, ASTL students are expected to demonstrate knowledge, skill, and dispositions in the following three areas listed in Figure 1.2, which serve as Core propositions 6–8 for ASTL.

---

1. Teachers are committed to students and their learning;
2. Teachers know the subjects they teach and how to teach those subjects to students;
3. Teachers are responsible for managing and monitoring student learning;
4. Teachers think systematically about their practice and learn from experience; and
5. Teachers are members of learning communities.

Source: www.nbpts.org

Figure 1.1 The core propositions of the National Board for Professional Teaching Standards.

6. Teachers account for the needs of culturally, linguistically, and cognitively diverse learners;
7. Teachers are change agents, teacher leaders, and partners with colleagues; and
8. Teachers use technology to facilitate student learning and their own professional development.

Figure 1.2 Additional ASTL core propositions.

Combined, these eight statements are ASTL's Core propositions that serve as the stated program learning outcomes and provide the conceptual framework for the program, the courses, the learning activities, and the outcomes to which we hold our students accountable.

In addition, there are other programmatic features or attributes that mark ASTL. These attributes are described in the next section to provide a sense of how we view the continuing education of teachers. We begin with the structure of the program and its features and then describe others that seek to tie the Core propositions to the structure to conceptions of appropriate learning environments for teachers.

The Structure of the Program

The ASTL program has both structural and conceptual features (Feiman-Nemser, 1990) that provide its boundaries. They are drawn from our interpretation of what it would take for our university to offer a master's degree that strives to achieve the vision of the teaching profession as articulated by NBPTS. These features are what our campus environment could support—that is, there were procedures and regulations in place that would allow for cross-campus participation in a graduate degree program in education; it had a scheduling system that could, up to a point, facilitate the use of cohort programs (in fact, the School of Management had been using this model for many years prior to the creation of ASTL); and it offered a budgeting system that allowed deans to experiment with new revenue streams and would hold them harmless until there was evidence about their viability. These are important preconditions for establishing this kind of program because they "put on hold" the issues of assigning credits for full-time equivalencies for a period of time.

There are five specific features that define the ASTL program: (1) the two components of education and content, called the "Core" and the "Concentration," respectively; (2) a commitment from the faculty in the traditional academic disciplines who collaborate with ASTL; (3) partnerships with local school districts who can shape the nature of the Concentrations to advance their own plans; (4) admitting students into the Core in cohorts that stay together for one calendar year; and (5) the option to earn a university-based certificate rather than a master's degree, either in the Core or in the Concentration, which allowed initially for budget flexibility as Northern Virginia school districts were simultaneously embracing National Board Certification for their teachers. This last feature allowed these school leaders to support teachers to experience "Board-like" coursework on their way to certification, or to support teachers to gain deeper knowledge in a discipline of value to the school district. In the early years of ASTL, many school districts partnered with ASTL to prepare teachers to use instructional technology in new and improved ways. Shortly thereafter, the Commonwealth of Virginia embraced improved reading instruction for all children at all levels, and some school leaders partnered for the literacy concentration. In this way, at any time all five features or some of them are available to school leaders who see what ASTL has to offer as a way to facilitate school improvement.

The Core and the Concentration

To accomplish the program's eight Core propositions and to achieve our desire to have ASTL be a partnership with various academic disciplines around the university, there are two distinct components of the program: (1) a sequence of courses taught in the CEHD, labeled "the core," and (2) the Concentration taught in the student's chosen discipline.

The twelve credits in the Core are divided among five courses as presented in Figure 1.3.

The "Concentration" is the other component half of ASTL. Its eighteen to twenty-one credit hours of study enables the teachers to develop an area of academic expertise, such as, mathematics, history, literacy, or the arts, and is grounded in Shulman's (1986) concept of pedagogical content knowledge. Figure 1.4 includes the Concentration options.

The successful completion of these two program components and their requirements results in the completion of the master's degree. Because this degree program values teacher content knowledge, the Concentrations include the active participation of colleagues from other colleges in the university where they are taught, after a recent university reorganization in what are now the College of Science, the College of Humanities and Social Sciences, and the College of Visual and Performing Arts. The key faculty members in these colleges are actively involved in increasing and refining, through the use of state and national content standards, the content knowledge of both

EDUC 612 Inquiry into Practice (2): In this first course in the Core, the students experience using research skills to foster systematic and thoughtful inquiry into classroom practice. They explore issues in their classroom practice through critical writing, action, and research with an emphasis on cultural diversity and gender.

EDUC 613 How Students Learn (3): This course delves deeply into the study of learning based on research and theory from different disciplines. The students focus on increasing their pupils' learning through study of different learning systems, and understanding each learner in context of the learning process itself.

EDUC 614 Designing and Assessing Teaching and Learning (2): In this course, the students explore the design and development of curricular, pedagogical, and assessment strategies responsive to needs and interests of their pupils. They investigate the factors that affect teaching and learning, and examine the multiple ways of knowing that teachers and pupils bring to classroom.

EDUC 606 Education and Culture (3): In this course, the students learn the cultural inquiry process (CIP) to acquire cultural, social, and language-related perspectives on educational processes. They also learn the skills to analyze educational settings and expand strategies to address puzzlements in their own practice.

EDUC 615 Educational Change (2): In this course we examine the influences on educational change at classroom, school, community, state, and national levels. The students analyze these influences and factors, and reflect on their own experiences as the recipients of change initiatives. This course seeks to provide them with the skills to become agents of change.

Figure 1.3 The ASTL Education Core (12 credits).

elementary and secondary teachers, such that they have deeper understandings of the content they teach to their pupils and that they can provide richer and more meaningful examples during instruction. This is a major commitment of the program and consistent with NBPTS' expectations that "teachers know the subjects they teach and how to teach those subjects to students."

Campus-wide Commitments

As suggested in the opening vignette, the ASTL program would not reach its ideals without the participation of departments around the university. In key

Art Education	Literacy
Early Childhood Education	Mathematics
Elementary Mathematics	Physical Education
Foreign Languages: French & Spanish	Science
Gifted Child Education	Special Education
History	Teacher Leadership
International Baccalaureate	

Figure 1.4 ASTL concentrations (18–21 credits).

disciplines that relate to the public school curriculum (e.g., mathematics, history, the arts, world languages), we have cultivated partners who see ASTL as a vehicle to increasing teachers' knowledge in at least one discipline they teach. With this campus-wide commitment to improving the practicing teachers' quality of instruction in both content and pedagogy, we are well-positioned to pursue our desire to prepare teachers who have the knowledge and skills to be agents of school change who lead others in advancing the academic skills and abilities of hundreds of children over their careers. For them to do this, they require much greater depth in their own knowledge of academic content and pedagogy, and a solid understanding of how to study their schools, identify problems, and identify, create, and implement solutions. Moreover, they require a more enriched sense of themselves as teachers, how they teach, how they can improve their teaching, and how to lead others to improve themselves. The ASTL curriculum is geared toward these important instructional and school reform goals. It is a partnership among CEHD, the College of Science, the College of Humanities and Social Sciences, the College of Visual and Performing Arts, and the local school divisions in Northern Virginia.

Of course, we have not addressed the ongoing problem that is posed by elementary teachers who teach many subject areas, and their lack of expertise in any of them. The program offers them the opportunity to specialize in one traditional academic discipline that will allow them to become "lead teachers" in that discipline at their grade levels or in their school building. For example a teacher may choose to take the Concentration in mathematics and to become an informed teacher leader in math instruction to elementary school children. They would lead their peers in the design and development of the math curriculum and in identifying appropriate instructional practices. This outcome is consistent with the ASTL core propositions of teachers knowing their discipline and how to teach it, as well as teachers being agents of change.

In Partnership with Local School Districts

A second key feature of the design of ASTL is that much of the student recruitment is conducted in partnership with local school districts. As school
districts identify their goals, ASTL is used as a vehicle for developing the
teachers needed to reach those goals. Since the program's inception, the
ASTL program faculty has worked collaboratively with the school districts
in Northern Virginia to provide master's degree programs with specific concentrations in content areas such as history, instructional technology, literacy,
teacher leadership, and gifted education. The school districts in Northern Virginia work in partnership with ASTL to provide master's degree cohort programs for their teachers in support of school district goals, such as improved
literacy or instructional technology. Fourteen cohort programs have been
offered by ASTL through contracts with individual school divisions, placing
the master's program as a supportive partner in school district initiatives. As
designed, the teachers in the Core, and in some instances in selected Concentrations, work together during the day and study together in the program.

In an effort to reach out to all the school districts in the region and to
cross district boundaries, the ASTL program offers specific Concentrations
such as literacy and Core coursework at any of the four regional campuses of
George Mason University. In this way we strive to provide access to teachers in different parts of Northern Virginia who are interested in pursuing a
Concentration outside their school district's interests. Efforts to improve the
program include school district participants meeting once a semester in an
advisory capacity to provide feedback on program content, structure, coursework, and assessments. The advisory group structure has been used in other
ASTL concentration areas such as literacy where school representatives have
successfully met with university faculty to provide feedback and suggestions
on proposed program and course revisions.

A Cohort Approach

As has already been intimated, the students are admitted in cohorts that remain
together for the twelve-credit-hour core, which typically takes one calendar
year to complete. Over the last eight years of ASTL, we have found the cohort
approach to be particularly powerful in teaching teachers how to break down
the isolation that characterizes teaching by creating "critical friends" groups,
peer reviewing of video, practicing lesson study, and writing and reviewing
each other's work. Additionally, through the cohort approach connected with
the school district partnership described previously, ASTL provides to local
school districts a cadre of teachers who have developed advanced expertise in
a concentration, for example, literacy or gifted education. At the conclusion

of the program, the partnering school district now has perhaps twenty teachers who are prepared to advance its goals, who have already established themselves as a learning community, and who have become unafraid of being "public" about their teaching because it was scrutinized in coursework throughout the core and, in some instances, the concentration. This is a very powerful form of teacher education wherein the master's degree now not only serves the traditional goals of advanced knowledge and skills, but also provides a critical mass of teachers in a building or district who can begin to create and lead change because they no longer work in professional isolation from one another. We have strived to teach teachers to learn to work together toward improved student achievement, thus addressing the core proposition that "teachers are members of learning communities."

Certificate or Degree

As noted previously, ASTL is a partnership of four colleges at George Mason University. While a program designed by the faculty of the CEHD, it has always existed as a partnership for improving teachers' content knowledge and pedagogical content knowledge in a traditional academic discipline, such as mathematics, science, and history, or in providing teachers with greater depth in a field traditionally found in a school, college, or department of education, such as literacy, early childhood education, or gifted education. The English department has never become a partner, but for many years it has offered an active program for the region's teachers of writing. Through a package of eighteen credits of content in a traditional academic discipline, for example, we strive to provide practicing teachers with deeper and richer knowledge of a discipline and how to teach it to children. An interesting phenomenon in ASTL is that an elementary teacher does not have to have an undergraduate major in mathematics to take the Concentration in mathematics in ASTL. The courses in the selected discipline are informed by what competent and qualified teachers of that discipline need to know to teach it effectively. At the end of a cohort, we return to our school division partners a number of elementary teachers who not only will have deeper knowledge of that discipline but, who through the education Core of the program, will become more like the accomplished teachers envisioned by NBPTS and who will have the skills to initiate and lead educational change in their school settings.

In the original design of ASTL, there was another option for the students. They could choose to pursue the Core, the Concentration, or the master's degree, depending upon their goals. ASTL offered potential students the opportunity to earn a university-awarded certificate and left the door open for teachers to choose to enroll in only a concentration. For example, a teacher who is only interested in advancing his professional knowledge and skill or who wants the support in preparing for National Board Certification can apply to and enroll in the Core and learn and study with a cohort of degree-seeking teachers for the year. Or, a teacher who is only interested in developing richer content knowledge is free to apply to and enroll in a concentration and complete those courses. Either choice culminates in a university-approved "certificate." George Mason made extensive use of certificate programs in many disciplines beyond education, and ASTL participated by dividing the program into two parts and allowing teachers to shape the path that best fit their goals. This was arranged not to accomplish any particular Core proposition, but to demonstrate that choice was a key feature of teacher learning and to model the possibility of curricular flexibility for our students to emulate in their own settings.

As the program grew, we found that students who enrolled in either the Core or the Concentration eventually decided to complete the full degree program. In addition, our university conducted a review of certificate programs throughout the campus and determined that it wanted to eliminate most, except for particular instances, one of which applied to ASTL. As of fall 2011, only the literacy concentration retains the option to pursue only the Concentration. All other Concentrations are now fully incorporated into the master's degree program.

Operational Attributes

In addition to the structural attributes described previously that are designed to reconfigure teacher learning and the development of teacher expertise, five conceptual and operational attributes contribute to meaningful teacher learning toward our Core propositions. They are similar to the conception of teacher learning described by Hammerness, Darling-Hammond, and Bransford (2005). The first is seeing teachers as much more than empty vessels waiting to be filled with readings and assignments that may not add up to changes in practice. The second is our belief that too many master's degree programs treat teachers' classrooms as something apart from learning to improve. In contrast, we see the classroom as a living laboratory waiting for measured experimentation and analysis. The analysis that we encourage in the classroom laboratory leads to our third operational attribute, reflection on actions—one that is commonly found in the literature and in practice. The fourth operational attribute for the program is that professional development is cumulative within courses and experiences and across the program. To accomplish this cumulative record of growth we require the students to develop a professional portfolio and to present it as a requirement for graduation.

During the presentation of the portfolio, which is detailed in chapter 7, the students are expected to reflect on the Core propositions where they believe the evidence suggests they have grown the most and the Core propositions where they believe they still have work to do and have thought about a plan for continuing their professional growth. Lastly, the fifth conceptual attribute is that graduate programs for teachers should develop their capacities as teacher leaders who become disposed to become agents of school change. Each of these is described in the following.

Teachers as Connected and Constructing Knowers

Arguably most central to ASTL is the conception of practicing as the "connected" and "constructing" knowers described by Belenky, Clinchy, Goldberger, and Tarule (1986) rather than as students in a graduate program that has little connection to them, their work, and their countless relationships as practicing professionals. In their volume, *Women's Ways of Knowing*, they describe these ways of knowing as active and interactive, engaged, collaborative, thoughtful, self-regulated analysts of the world around them. In many ways, instruction in ASTL is premised on teachers as these kinds of learners: people, regardless of gender, who actively engage in meaningful work solving myriad problems on a daily basis and who see themselves as active co-investigators in professional practice, performing what Bruner (1996) has called, intersubjectivity in the study of teaching and learning. In this way, we strive to achieve the proposition that teachers learn systematically from practice in learning communities of professional practice. This idea of teachers as having active minds is consistent with the NBPTS proposition and Hammerness, Darling-Hammond, and Bransford's (2005) assertion that teachers are members of learning communities. ASTL is structured to build upon connected and constructed knowing through two other attributes that are central to the program. The first one is that students are admitted in cohorts that stay together for the Core component of the program. The second one is the intensive reliance on "read-and-reflect" and "act-and-reflect" assignments in each course and across the program as will be discussed and detailed in other chapters in this book.

The Classroom as a Living Laboratory

The program asks the teachers who enroll to treat their classrooms as laboratories for trying new skills and content by drawing on their existing knowledge and experiences as well as on theoretical and empirical research to support their effectiveness in the classroom and their positive influences on

PK–12 student learning. Most class assignments require the ASTL students in the program to return to their classrooms and test out a teaching skill, and then to gather evidence systematically, via an action research model, and then to draw some observations and reflections on how well the students responded. In other words, professional knowledge and skills are not inert; they are not something learned in a course for some later date. Rather, they are to be tested, reflected upon, shared with peers in the cohort, and considered again. In this way, we hope to help the ASTL students develop an approach to their teaching where they experiment with new ideas that meet the needs of the learners, who change from one year to the next. Teacher learning is active learning.

Reflection on Actions

As it is with most teacher education programs, reflective practice is central to ASTL. The teachers who enroll learn quickly that they will be asked to reflect on their personal and professional histories, on their students, on their instruction, on the skills to test in their classrooms, on their growth and development throughout the program, and on their accomplishments at the end of the program. To accomplish our goal of teaching the value of reflection, the ASTL students respond to four reflection prompts during the program presented below in Figure 1.5.

Portfolios and Performance Assessment

ASTL was created prior to the national concerns about teacher content knowledge. It was created by an education school faculty that was already committed to developing teachers in both content and pedagogy in partnership with key academic departments around campus, for example, mathematics, sciences, and history.

To keep a close link between the program's intentions and its outcomes, all teachers must build, edit, and maintain a record of their accomplishments in a program portfolio. The ASTL Professional Portfolio is a performance-based document that provides concrete evidence of teacher professional development throughout the ASTL program and links the ASTL program requirements with national, state, and institutional professional standards. The portfolio provides program participants the opportunity to synthesize and reflect upon their own growing, learning, and teaching practices as they make important connections between program coursework and daily encounters with student learning in the context of school-based experiences. The contents of

**FOUR PROGRAM REFLECTION PROMPTS
IN ORDER OF COURSE SEQUENCE**

EDUC 612/613: In this section, you will focus on how coursework, related readings, and products in EDUC 612 and EDUC 613 have led you to think more deeply about *the learning process and your own students, as well as your own learning*. Please reflect on your own learning and your growth and change at this point in the Core. In your reflection, please address any of the applicable eight program learning outcomes and the ways in which the performance assessments included thus far in the Core provide evidence of this knowledge.

EDUC 614: In this section you will focus on how coursework, related readings, and products in EDUC 614 have led you to focus more carefully on *the teacher as designer of curriculum and assessment and how you are incorporating technology into your teaching practice* and your Core experience. Please reflect on your own learning and your growth and change at this point in the Core. In your reflection please address any of the applicable eight program learning outcomes and the ways in which the performance assessments included in this section provide evidence of this knowledge.

EDUC 606: In this section you should focus on how your coursework, related readings, and products in EDUC 606 have led you to focus more deeply on *teachers as researchers with a cultural perspective*. Please reflect on your own learning and your growth and change at this point in the Core. In your reflection please address any of the applicable eight program learning outcomes and the ways in which the performance assessments included in this section provide evidence of this knowledge.

EDUC 615: In this section, you will focus on how coursework, related readings, and experiences in EDUC 615 have led you to think about yourself as a *teacher leader in your school and learning communities*. Please reflect on your own learning and your growth and change at this point in the Core. In your reflection, please address any of the applicable eight program learning outcomes and the ways in which the performance assessments included in this section provide evidence of this knowledge.

Figure 1.5 ASTL reflection prompts.

the professional portfolio provide program participants with a forum for the presentation of their knowledge and practice as articulated by the NBPTS.

The ASTL Professional Portfolio serves two purposes. First, it encourages the teachers to develop their teaching practice to the highest level. This is accomplished through evidence of targeted reflection, presentation of pedagogical and content-based knowledge, action research skills as they inform teaching practice and a synthesis of professional knowledge and skills. Secondly, it provides performance-based evidence of the degree to which program goals have been met. As both a formative and summative document, the portfolio articulates the NBPTS Core propositions and the three additional ASTL propositions, and other content-specific standards in the Concentration, as appropriate.

The ASTL Professional Portfolio is a requirement of the ASTL program, but is only one of several factors considered in determining successful program completion. Since the ASTL program is comprised of two distinct components, the Core and the Concentration, the evaluation of the portfolio takes place at two junctures during the program, at midpoint and at program completion. ASTL participants may choose to take the Core and the Concentration in any order. However, the final evaluation takes place at the completion of the program and is comprised of a formal presentation to faculty and peers. The portfolio is evaluated according to a preestablished rubric. This final portfolio presentation is integrated with a specially designated program exit session whose date will be announced for each cohort.

As we strive to present in chapters 5–7, ASTL has proven a viable vehicle for developing teacher pedagogical expertise and content expertise. The local school divisions have supported whole cohorts of teachers in previous years. The design of the program allows teachers to use their classrooms as laboratories for testing ideas and strategies learned in the program and to seek feedback from faculty and peers. The requirement that the ASTL students reflect on their practice is consistent with the spirit of NBPTS and serves them well as their own formative assessments of their growth and development as professionals.

Leading from the Classroom

As suggested earlier, ASTL is predicated on teachers as leaders who develop the disposition to become agents of change in their school settings. The fourth reflection for the program focuses on teachers thinking about their growth as change agents in their schools. In the class Educational Change, the students confront how schools are defining change, how public policies are shaping change, how to work with peers toward initiating and supporting change, and how to seek grant funding to make local change happen. The prompt for the fourth reflection is "In this section, you will focus on how coursework, related readings, and experiences in EDUC 615 have led you to think about yourself as a teacher leader in your school and learning communities. Please reflect on your own learning and your growth and change at this point in the Core. In your reflection, please address any of the applicable eight program learning outcomes and the ways in which the performance assessments included in this section a provide evidence of this knowledge." As a program with its fundamental value of advancing the knowledge and skills of teachers who want to "lead change from the classroom," ASTL is designed so that the graduates become leaders among peers and change agents within the school.

CONCLUSION

In this introductory chapter, we set the stage for the many foundational, conceptual, and operational dimensions of ASTL that will be described in greater detail in the ensuing chapters. It is a program dedicated to moving beyond the master's degree as advanced preservice teacher education, making up for any shortcomings therein. It is premised on helping teachers become seekers of their own development. It is hoped that for many it will serve as a stronger foundation for their future development, even as we fully acknowledge that almost all of them will not pursue another degree. It is our hope that accomplishing the eight Core propositions sets the stage for their own ongoing renewal as professionals such that they can chart their own course for continuous growth and development.

2

Reconfiguring Programs in the University Context

The dean of Mason's Graduate School of Education (GSE) had a vision for what a master's degree for practicing teachers should look like and created a new position, Director of Advanced Professional Studies, to help carry out that vision. With that appointment, the dean charged the new director to work swiftly with the faculty to reconfigure a master's degree for practicing teachers according to the four key questions outlined in Act II of chapter 1 of this volume and to do so in an academic year. The questions related to (1) structuring the degree with fidelity to developing accomplished teachers; (2) engaging faculty in the Core disciplines to support the need for appropriate content courses for teachers; (3) helping teachers and faculty understand why this master's in education degree would require graduate courses in an academic discipline; and (4) negotiating the reality of creating a new degree when one already existed for practicing teachers.

The director's first challenge was to create a faculty committee to carry out this charge. The new director used the May faculty meeting to share the charge and invited volunteers to work with her throughout the year. Five volunteers, representing five education disciplines, answered the invitation and made a commitment to work diligently and collaboratively to reconfigure this degree. The director subsequently met with the director of the other existing master's degree program for practicing teachers and asked him to invite one of his faculty members to serve on the design committee.

With the design team in place, work began. Initially the team dealt with mechanical aspects, such as reviewing the charge, preparing a timeline, scheduling regular meeting times and dates, and establishing our approach to complete the work that would meet our different work styles.

Next we addressed the substance of the degree. We faced challenging and often controversial questions such as: What are the Core values of this degree and how can we make them transparent? What will the content of the Core and Concentrations be? What will the structure look like? How should we divide our thirty credit hours and why? How can we ensure coherence across the whole degree so that all elements of the Board's principles are integrated throughout? How do we address social problems and issues of culture both in and out of school? After many unfocused discussions that suggested multiple ways of re-design, we had the hard conversation about creating a new program from the ground up that looked nothing like what we have ever done or knew of anyone else doing, and agreed that because of the timeline and commitment we made to serve on this team, to focus our energy on the greater good of the degree, examine diligently and carefully the Board's propositions, and keep on our personal and professional biases in the conversation but not let them drive our decisions. Eventually, we had difficult conversations about content, including those with faculty in the academic Core disciplines and structure, including talking with our school partners who convinced us to have an eighteen-hour concentration that would afford teachers more professional opportunity for growth and development and eligibility for teaching that content at the community college level. The team was also challenged by how to divide the education Core to achieve coherence, infuse board-like activities and assessments, intentional reflection, while having the learning outcomes drive our planning, instruction, and assessment at the student, course, and program levels. Finally, we were challenged by how to engage the faculty in the Concentrations, wherein the director talked one-on-one with department chairs in the disciplines to have them and their key faculty on board with us and how to address technology knowledge, skills, and dispositions within the program.

As described in chapter 1, the emphasis on higher, more rigorous standards for teachers, new expectations for practicing teachers to engage in continuous improvement of practice, and the increasing accountability of teacher education programs propelled the reconfiguration of a master's degree program for practicing teachers at Mason. In designing this degree, faculty from a variety of disciplines in CEHD, that was at the time known as the GSE, engaged in intentional reflection, conversation, and study to meet the challenges associated with creating a master's degree that was relevant to the needs of practicing teachers while increasing both their content and pedagogical content knowledge (Galluzzo, 1997, 1999; Putnam & Borko, 2000; Tom, 1999). Our design team worked together voluntarily, intensely, and continuously for one academic year to develop a master's degree that challenged old ideas. Such challenges included struggling with reframing our thinking about master's degrees for practicing teachers, teasing out agreed upon key elements of program design, arriving at consensus about the curriculum, creating new delivery and staffing options, and assessing program impact. These challenges will each be discussed in this chapter.

CHALLENGING OUR THINKING ABOUT MASTER'S DEGREES

Mason's faculty took the work of the NCTAF (1996) seriously in rethinking the professional development of teachers. That work asserts that what teachers know and can do is the most important influence on what students learn; retaining good teachers in the classroom is central for improving America's school; and focusing school reform on creating conditions in which teachers can teach and teach well is essential. These assertions, coupled with framing advanced degrees around the NBPTS' five Core propositions and our own additional three ASTL propositions, shaped the nature and quality of our redesign. They were used as conceptual organizers for decisions about courses, assignments, and opportunities for structured reflection. We adopted the Board's research-based principle that teachers are expected to demonstrate research-based, ethical, professional judgment in a variety of teaching situations and worked to develop a degree that enabled teachers completing the ASTL program to act accomplished, make effective and sound professional judgments about students' learning and best interests, and increase their depth in a content area.

To reframe our thinking about structuring this new master's degree with fidelity to the NBPTS' Core propositions, the work of the NCTAF (1996), and the teacher quality literature (Ball & Cohen, 1999; Cochran-Smith & Lytle, 1999), the faculty engaged in deep conversation and intentional reflection about the meaning, implementation, and documentation of what standards-based, coherent, authentic educational experiences for teachers across grade levels can and should look like. We were challenged into collectively shaping learning for PK–12 teachers in the required, foundational Core, a new phenomenon to most faculty accustomed to teaching a narrow range of teachers in their discipline and at either the early childhood, elementary, or secondary level. We read Board portfolio materials, analyzed the nature of Board assessments, read and discussed research on teacher professional development (Guskey, 1994; National Staff Development Council, 2001), and used our own personal and professional experiences with teachers to address vast challenges and hurdles.

CHALLENGING OUR THINKING IN PROGRAM DESIGN

Our faculty design team represented a variety of content areas and teaching levels ranging from early childhood education to educational research. That said, we agreed to rise above our individual comfort zones and examine the commonalities of good program design that are important for all PK–12 teachers regardless of content area. We began to "think outside the box" as we grappled with what Board-like activities and assessments would look like as part of a master's degree coursework. Challenged by the research on what constitutes good professional development, we embedded those principles into creating a new program—one that could meet the challenges for today's teachers and classrooms.

The new program would be driven by the identified learning outcomes and enable all practicing teachers to engage in and demonstrate intentional reflection on their practice, have frequent opportunities to set their own learning goals, communicate their understandings with their peers, engage in inquiry-based learning in their own classrooms, and create classroom learning environments that are conducive to inquiry. We then developed a conceptual framework that focused on the following key elements: pedagogical content knowledge, teacher reflection, teacher collaboration, school-based and community learning experience, and technologies. These elements would thread through the fabric of the Core and the Concentrations and be the hallmarks of this degree.

Pedagogical Content Knowledge

Pedagogical content knowledge (PCK) includes what teachers know and believe about teaching, learning, and learners that cross disciplines. Professional development experiences that deepen teachers' pedagogical content knowledge should be grounded in actual teaching practice, enable teacher collaboration and reflection, and reflect the expanding scope of teacher responsibilities expressed in National Board Standards (Interstate New Teacher Assessment and Support Consortium, 1992; Putnam & Borko, 1997; Shulman, 1987).

Educational research has identified multiple kinds of knowledge (e.g., disciplinary, content, cultural, social) and skills (e.g., communicative, diagnostic) that teachers must possess to be effective in the classroom (Burroughs, Schwartz, & Hendricks-Lee, 2000). The emerging image of the professional teacher is one who thinks systematically about her practice in the context of educational research and the experience of others, and will work creatively and collaboratively as a member of a learning community. In ASTL, our assignments to teach reflective thinking, for example, all use the same criteria, language, and rubrics for reflection across all courses in the Core to achieve coherence and meet the program outcome of reflective thought.

Teacher Reflection

The ASTL courses offered in the Core are designed to provide teachers with the critical knowledge, skills, and dispositions necessary to develop pedagogical expertise through the practice of reflection in action research, problem-based learning, and self-inquiry. These courses provide systematic opportunities for candidates to inquire about their practice, provide evidence of student learning for all students, design and assess their teaching and learning, and develop a knowledge and understanding of culture and education and educational change processes. They encourage teachers to wonder, explore, and try alternatives in their own classrooms. As a faculty we are committed to having teachers deepen their reflective ability and become increasingly committed to school and pedagogical reform, increasingly conscious of their own efficacy as teachers (Cochran-Smith & Lytle, 1999). All of these outcomes are measured, in part, by the teacher's ability to engage in deep reflection.

From the outset, the faculty scaffolded teachers' ability to engage in critical reflection through the use of a common rubric and common language. As the Board requires, we asked teachers to reflect on their practice at three different levels: description, analysis, and synthesis. In each Core course, students end their learning with a written reflection, addressing each of the levels of reflection that is then evaluated with the same rubric. These reflective entries are used as data to measure the teachers' growth in their abilities to reflect at higher levels, and to determine further planning, instruction, and assessment in the coursework across the Core.

Teacher Collaboration

Currently, increasing attention is given to viewing teachers as members of learning communities and to using professional learning communities as a vehicle for deepening teachers' pedagogical knowledge (Dufour, Dufour, Eaker, & Many, 2006; Tom, 1999). Most master's degree candidates seek out ideas and programs with the capacity for increasing student learning and are inclined to inquire into their professional practice to increase this capacity. Thus the university classrooms in which the coursework occurs must be intentionally community and collaboration oriented to engage teachers in learning. Providing the context for learning as a member of a community means providing stability via classroom norms; ensuring emotional, physical, and intellectual safety; making intellectual camaraderie and healthy attitudes toward learning; building on the learning of others; fostering excitement in learning; and promoting connections to the outside community (Bransford, Brown, & Cocking, 1999; Maslow, 1999). Grounding teachers' learning experiences in their own practice by conducting activities at their own school sites and largely in their own classrooms makes it likely that what they learn will indeed influence and support their teaching practice in meaningful ways (Putnam & Borko, 2000).

How should we get there? Do we have a single course or do we embed and build the skills of collaboration across the courses? If so, what attributes should we address and how can we ensure that it happens systemically and not just at the passion of a particular faculty member? To infuse notions of collaboration and community across courses so that teachers could experience these attributes and have a basis for transferring them into their own classrooms, we looked carefully at the attribute of learning community. One assignment that relies heavily on this attribute is our learning theorists assignment in which groups become responsible for learning about and then educating the others about the concepts, theory, and application of a particular learning theorist. To tie this assignment directly to the outcome of learning community, we explicitly focused part of the assignment to examine the process and elements of collaborative learning and its relevance to living a learning community.

We recognized that our assignments and assessments needed to be respectful of each teacher learner and that they needed to be connected to the real world of the teacher's practice. We also recognized that our learning outcomes had to be crystal clear, that there were appropriate levels of challenge, and that there needed to be different groups for projects and assignments based on interests, learning profiles, grade levels, and other groupings of choice to ensure that teachers felt safe and comfortable to learn. With many opportunities to participate and share ideas, thoughts, and questions, we wanted to teach the important role teachers have in their own learning and that of the group, and to be able to take the academic and social risks needed to improve their practice.

School-based and Community Learning Experiences

Professional development for practicing teachers must be grounded in school and community environments that allows for, indeed requires, professional consultation, collegiality, and collaboration. To develop meaningful learning experiences for their students, teachers must understand the community from which their students and families come. "Such collegiality and collaboration should be part of the workplace of every teacher and include ongoing work on immediate problems of practice, as well as teacher studies and projects regarding curriculum and student issues, and teacher participation in activities like the development of authentic assessments" (Interstate New Teacher Assessment and Support Consortium, 1992, p. 17).

Technology

From the outset, the faculty design team was guided by a technology outcome. To meet this outcome, we created a matrix of technology skills we wanted teachers to develop across the Core and show competence in and not be expected to repeat the same competence in each course. Such competencies included e-mail, PowerPoint presentation, and evaluating research retrieved online. Faculty teaching all five modules in the Core received the matrix identifying in which course each of these technology skills would be demonstrated.

The Core aspires to create communities of teacher learners who will apply their learning to their own specific educational context and setting. To this end, we rely on learning experiences that encompass both individual and social perspectives (Vygotsky, 1978) and a better understanding of the processes of learning, conceptual development, problem solving, and communication from both cognitive and social science (Greeno, Collins, & Resnick, 1996; Okada & Simon, 1997).

Research shows that teacher conceptions of teaching and learning in particular subject areas can be transformed through their observations and analysis of what goes on in classrooms (Wilson, Floden, & Ferrini-Mundy, 2001, 2002). Much recent research has documented some of the important ways that teachers' knowledge of the subjects they teach shapes their instructional practice. They report that the more deeply teachers grasp the content they are teaching, the more they "tend to emphasize conceptual, problem-solving, and inquiry aspects of their subjects, whereas less knowledgeable teachers tend to emphasize facts and procedures" (Putnam & Borko, 1997, p. 1232).

Some researchers have found serious problems with the typical subject matter knowledge of teachers, even of those who have completed majors in academic disciplines. Lacking fundamental subject matter understanding impedes good teaching, especially given the high standards called for in current reforms. Research suggests that changes in teachers' subject matter preparation may be needed, and that the solution is more complicated than simply requiring a major or more subject matter courses (Wilson, Floden, & Ferrini-Mundy, 2002). Thus, our solution to this dilemma is to require a concentration in a discipline to focus on depth in knowledge apart from the Core.

CHALLENGES WITH THE CURRICULUM

What is now known as Mason's master's degree program in ASTL involved several controversial conversations to transcribe the lofty goals and vision to which we were committed. From the beginning, ASTL faculty read literature on teacher learning, advanced master's degrees, and the ever-changing nature of education reform. Our readings, dialogue, and individual knowledge and experience helped to redesign a degree program that has integrity and enriches the advanced preparation of PK–12 teachers. We knew that we were forging new territory; our research had revealed that there were no other university models like this one to examine and to guide our work.

Conceptualizing the curriculum for the Core, developing new syllabi framed around our eight learning outcomes that included NBPTS' five Core propositions, and preparing a full program proposal for review by school and university-wide curriculum approval bodies required steady work. Our bimonthly meetings included faculty feedback on the content of the syllabi, on the authenticity of the activities and assessments, and the realistic goals proposed within the time allotted for the course. Learning to be a "critical friend" and provide constructive, targeted feedback that aligned the content of each syllabus with learning outcomes was often sensitive and challenging. To ensure fidelity with the Board, we used NBCTs to review the syllabi, to ensure accuracy and authenticity in our assignments and readings.

Candidate outcomes are aligned with NBPTS propositions and Virginia's Standards of Learning (SOL) and are tailored to meet the specific needs of Virginia professional educators. Through study and learning experiences in this degree program, experienced teachers expand and demonstrate their knowledge, skills, and dispositions in eight areas, specified in the five NBPTS (1989a) Core propositions and the additional three ASTL outcomes listed in chapter 1.

The complexities of designing curriculum from the outset presented new challenges. While we read and discussed our readings, we struggled with how to have the appropriate learning outcomes for each of the syllabi in the twelve-credit-hour Core cover the five modules and intersect with the knowledge, skills, and dispositions we hoped to develop in our teachers. Our struggles with how to develop syllabi that mirrored board-like instruction and assessment and how we would teach this to others continued. To the surprise of some faculty on the design team, there was difficulty in completing the syllabi that rang true to our goals. We had to address the gaps that the NBCT reviewers raised and came to rely on the NBCTs who reviewed the syllabi for us. While program development and syllabi development are basic faculty endeavors, we had to address our new roles as learners and collaborators for this program. Even though we were not board certified, we knew well how to teach new strategies and ways of thinking to teachers based on our own research, scholarship, and professional experiences.

ASTL has as its core value "excellence in teaching and learning." Its belief is to develop professionals who think, act, and teach like NBCTs. To that end, the ASTL program is committed to engaging teachers in meaning-ful analysis of teaching and learning, improving and deepening their content knowledge, and aligning its curriculum with published standards. ASTL's student-centered program has a strong emphasis on teacher action research that emphasizes the professional as a reflective practitioner. Our faculty were proud of their accomplishments but were clear about the need for adequate support to make our work on curriculum a reality. The director had several conversations with the dean to ensure that adequate support would be in place to implement this innovative curriculum and achieve the potential they envisioned.

CHALLENGES WITH DELIVERY

Central to the curriculum was the decision to offer a coherent, innovative configuration of coursework and teacher-friendly schedule to provide teachers with the critical knowledge, skills, and dispositions necessary for high-quality teaching. Creating a structure that would ensure coherence challenged our plans about accomplishing this within the confines of the academy. We settled on the notion of one twelve-credit-hour course chunked into learning modules that we named as five different courses and to which we assigned credit hours to be aligned with university procedures and to make it easy for students to register. In this way, we could ensure in our own minds that the yearlong experience would indeed be that—that teachers would commit to a yearlong experience as a cohort, that we could thus ensure coherence, that it would be systemically sound, and that teachers' skills were being developed across the Core—in reflection, technology, cultural awareness, self-assessment—and were indeed embedded and measurable. In the Core, all teachers are expected to examine their practice, provide evidence of student learning, design and assess their teaching and learning, develop knowledge of understanding of cul-ture and education, and think about themselves as educational change agents.

The Core is an intensive program of professional development that focuses on analytical thinking and writing around ASTL's eight propositions. It fea-tures cohort-based learning, innovative scheduling, courses taught by NBCTs, alignment with the Board's propositions and standards, and extensive use of technology. To illustrate, teachers told us that they wanted to spend time in the summer to start on their degree. ASTL summer scheduling involves sixty hours of coursework associated with a case study project, which ASTL students work on in their own classrooms throughout the fall semester. As a result, from the opening of the Core coursework, teachers' classrooms serve as laboratories for conducting action research on their own practice and on documenting student learning. These features align well with what is known about reinventing master's degrees for experienced teachers, such as a commitment to quality, coherent program requirements, a participatory culture, and interactive learning (Blackwell & Diez, 1998; Lytle, 2000; Tom, 1999).

The Concentrations, developed by faculty in each discipline, are based on the needs and interests of teachers and the appropriate professional standards. We began with history, mathematics, and science because those were the disciplines with which we had the strongest relationship. Each had at least one faculty member who believed that teaching content knowledge to all PK–12 teachers was a worthy and necessary endeavor; each also believed that these concentrations would result in better prepared undergraduates coming to them for college level work in that discipline. So, the integrity of the discipline and the belief that they, too, had a high stake in teacher education were the two main points that helped us gain the support of these faculty members at our institution.

Delivery options continue to be challenging even after nine years of operation. With our "out of the box" teacher-friendly schedule, we are constantly bumping against an unfriendly, university schedule that operates in traditional undergraduate scheduling blocks and room assignments. Campus space is at a premium and allocated in traditional scheduling blocks. Consequently, we have had to create an internal infrastructure to find classroom space that accommodates our teachers in nontraditional time blocks and that often varies from semester to semester. Because ASTL has grown from fourteen students in 1999 to almost three hundred students in 2011, scheduling issues have added another layer of administrative work for our directors.

CHALLENGES WITH STAFFING OPTIONS

Staffing also continues to be a challenge for the ASTL faculty. We are committed to using NBCTs as adjuncts, where possible, and to keep our adjuncts with us for multiple semesters. This lofty goal, however, has been hard to sustain. We have found that some of our NBCTs are not up to the quality of teaching adults, although they are outstanding in their own classrooms with elementary and secondary students. No longer do we assume that all NBCTs can teach adults the required course content. As we ourselves have grown and learned, we are now relying more on our own doctoral students who regularly meet with the faculty, are supported in their teaching of teachers as part of their teacher education internship, who learn how to help teachers develop the inquiry and reflective skills that are the foundation of the ASTL curriculum, and who keep the appropriate learning outcomes in front of them as they teach the different modules.

CHALLENGES WITH TECHNOLOGY

With the rapid influx and use of new technologies, such as visual, media, and technological literacy, school systems in our area quickly began preparing teachers for these new literacies. Our state and local school systems began adding them to their standards to improve student learning and to become an active part of the school reform agenda. Consequently, teachers were coming to our classes already using electronic communications such as discussion boards, blogs, and chat rooms and conducting research using the Internet with online libraries, WebQuests, and databases.

In this context, the faculty faced two primary challenges to move beyond what teachers knew and could do and facilitate using technology and the Internet for professional development. These challenges were (1) locating, evaluating, and applying Internet websites and the information retrieved online and (2) using technology to improve the learning of diverse student populations. Helping teachers see the value in staying current in the field, where teachers can read and evaluate journal articles that keep them current in their fields. While there are many exemplary sites, faculty were challenged as to how best to help teachers locate, evaluate, and apply the content they were reading. Yet, at our university, the faculty continue to struggle to keep up with the teachers in part because of inadequate faculty resources and support.

CHALLENGES WITH PROGRAM IMPACT

Evidence of program impact was a goal from the outset of the redesign. ASTL faculty were, and still are, committed to finding out how well the program is meeting its goals, how well ASTL students are meeting the program's stated learning outcomes, and what effect the ASTL experiences are having on teachers' continuing professional development, their practices and student outcomes. Creating the kinds of assessments that would provide these data created yet another series of conversations and consensus building to keep the assessments authentic, reasonable, useful, and credible. Finally, our design team agreed to a two-phased assessment system. We first looked to evaluate the structure of the degree and make the necessary adaptations based upon the data. Following that, we decided we would find ways to evaluate the program and the teachers' self-reported change in their practice and their professional growth.

As a result, ASTL has a two-pronged assessment/evaluation system that recognizes the belief that both the program and the candidates each need continuous assessment and evaluation. First, the ASTL program evaluation model provides a systematic means of collecting data from candidates and faculty on where we are meeting program outcomes and where we need to make modifications. Data are used for program improvement.

During the pilot year, we collected formative data from instructors and students in the program through questionnaires and focus groups that provided information on the content, pacing, assignments, and relevance of the Core experiences. Faculty also provided input regarding course adjustments such as the number and quality of the assignments. This formative process led to changes in the second year and to the realization of the need for a more systematic means of evaluating the ASTL program.

ASTL has an ongoing candidate assessment plan for students at admission, midpoint, end point, and follow-up after graduation, as described in chapter 1. We use a comprehensive program portfolio requirement, aligned with NBPTS processes, at both the mid-point and end point of each candidate's outcomes.

CONCLUSION

The ASTL master's degree program began with a vision to change professional development for experienced PK–12 teachers. The faculty still remains challenged by the realities of maintaining program integrity and fidelity with NBPTS principles at a time of increasing demand for more alternative, less rigorous degree programs. Our monthly meetings continue to focus on program development and ways to make our work public through presentations, research, and scholarly writing. The faculty in ASTL continues to center its teaching, research, and program evaluation on a search for the salient attributes of the program that enable our graduates to teach like NBCTs.

It is the continuous feedback through our teachers, our portfolio assessments, our course-based and individual assessments, our scaffolding, and the intentionality of our faculty conversations about this program that keeps ASTL alive and dynamic. In reality, the faculty are a professional learning community and they model that to our teachers. In difficult times, when faculty are feeling overwhelmed and stressed by the usual requirements of the academy to publish, to teach well, to engage in service, and to be a good citizen, it is easy for the program attributes themselves to take a back seat. Yet this is not the case with ASTL, with the flexible structure and the board-like focus, excellence in teaching is still the focus of ASTL's future agenda.

3

Dilemmas with Program Design

During our ASTL faculty program design meetings, we were driven by the belief that the Board assessments reflected the highest standard of what teachers should know and be able to do. Our goal was simple—to teach teachers to address those standards within the context of their own classroom situations. We wanted them to write to the standards, to be specific, and provide relevant examples. Of utmost importance to our faculty was for the teachers to show clear and convincing evidence in their practice. We expected them to demonstrate how and why the evidence they presented met a standard through student work samples, written reflections or commentaries, video analyses, and impacted student learning.

Our discussions focused on the essential evidence-based practice, as defined by the Board and to reach consensus on the meaning of the term. We had to decide what constitutes evidence and how its various forms were to be assessed. More importantly, we had to align our learning experiences and ensure that they could embrace the complexity and uncertainty that exist in teachers' work. We knew that teachers' knowledge is influenced by what they learn from practice, which may or may not be grounded in systematic data collection and analysis.

Our journey with program design was one of discovery and learning. We began with a narrow focus in mind, intending to address the redesign, on which we had spent considerable time thinking and developing, to advance teachers' content and pedagogical knowledge in an evidence-based program. But at almost every turn, we encountered barriers. The more we wrestled with the dilemmas we faced, the more we came to understand the potential for evidence-based practice to transform the program design with our faculty peers and practicing teachers. Once we grasped how to advance teachers' content and pedagogical knowledge through evidence-based practice, we worked hard to be open to different ways of thinking about the needs of teachers and to consider alternatives for mobilizing knowledge and faculty on their behalf.

In the first two chapters, we outlined the tenets of a new master's degree and the challenges we faced in reconfiguring programs. In this chapter, we review the historical context in which ASTL was created, and then we focus on the dilemmas faced as we developed a "professional practice-oriented, experiential degree program" (Blackwell & Diez, 1998, p. 12). We explore five challenges we faced with program design: (1) a content focus, (2) using the classroom as a laboratory for learning, (3) evaluation, (4) communication, and (5) staffing and professional development.

HISTORICAL CONTEXT

ASTL was started in 1998 at a time when you could count on one hand the number of education schools that began to align its programs with the Core propositions of the nascent NBPTS. It was thirteen years after Lee Shulman's 1986 presidential address to the members of the American Educational Research Association (AERA) in which he presented his concept of pedagogical content knowledge as one of several dimensions of teachers' knowledge. As Shulman describes it, pedagogical content knowledge is that specialized knowledge that includes, "the ways of representing and formulating the subject that make it comprehensible to others" (p. 9). His work spawned countless researchers to begin to expand our understandings about the knowledge teachers need to enact high-quality instruction by re-inserting into the conversation a long-accepted, but not well understood notion that both content knowledge (the substance of teaching) and pedagogical knowledge (the skills and abilities to bring content to the students) were necessary but not enough to develop both beginning and practicing teachers. There were "unique representations" of content within each discipline and that, it could be speculated, each one had many ways in which to make content within each discipline more accessible to the students dependent upon age, the complexity of the content, and other factors distinct to each classroom. In essence, Shulman presents a new way of looking at teaching that went far beyond the "general methods classes" and even "content methods classes." He elevated teaching, inside Schön's (1983) conception of the reflective practitioner, to more nuanced thinking about the intersections of the curriculum, the teachers' knowledge of content, their skills, the classroom contexts, and the specific subject matter the students were expected to learn, and how to design instructional explanations that increase the likelihood that the students will profit from the teachers' decisions about how to teach it.

Over the ensuing years, many other scholars developed the concept of pedagogical content knowledge (Cochran, DeRuiter, & King, 1993; Hashweh, 1987; Ma, 1999; Wilson, Shulman, & Richert, 1987; Wineburg, 2001). Simultaneously, in 1987, NBPTS was founded. Borne of the Carnegie Forum on Education and the Economy's panel report, *A Nation Prepared: Teachers for the 21st Century*, this report included a recommendation that, in response to the landmark 1983 *A Nation at Risk*, prepared by the National Commission on Excellence in Education, the Carnegie report argued that if standards for students were to become the norm, then the nation would also need standards for teaching. That recommendation led to another recommendation: that the nation's interests in education would best be served by a national board of teachers to uphold the standards of the profession, as is practiced in medicine and law. The term "standards" was altered to become the five Core propositions of NBPTS, from which specific standards for each certificate would be derived.

Influential in the work of NBPTS during its early years was Lee Shulman, whose work on the study of teaching and teacher assessment, including his aforementioned presidential address was one piece. In a seminal paper, entitled *A National Board for Teaching? In Search of a Bold Standard* commissioned by NBPTS, Shulman and Sykes (1986) outlined an entire teacher assessment system that was based on the work of the Teacher Assessment Project at Stanford that Shulman headed. In their monograph, Shulman and Sykes outlined a teacher assessment protocol that began the day an aspiring teacher declared an interest in pursuing teaching as a career, and one that would continue periodically throughout a teacher's life in the profession. Clearly implicated in their framework was the observation that teaching had become a national profession that was still regulated by the states, especially at the level of preservice teacher education, and what was also implied was that teaching was establishing a new career path for teachers, especially for those who wanted to remain in the classroom. The framework, as logical as it was for promoting teaching as a self-regulating profession, was not a workable idea in many policy arenas because it would remove the licensing authority and power that the states have held so closely. The best placed application of their framework and the Core propositions was to be found in building an infrastructure for "accomplished teaching," which was the sum of Core propositions. NBPTS published *What Teachers Should Know and Be Able to Do* (1989b), its first public statement of its conception of teaching which also suggested a career ladder for teachers. The document presented a rationale and foundation of a vision of accomplished teaching.

Within a few years of the National Board's statement regarding accomplished teaching for practitioners with a minimum of three years of teaching experience, the Council of Chief State School Officers began its own standards-setting process, through its initiative, the Interstate New Teacher Assessment and Support Consortium (INTASC). The INTASC panel prepared its own publication, *Model Standards for Beginning Teacher Licensing, Assessment, and Development: A State Resource for Dialogue* (1992). While NBPTS Core propositions could be applied to preservice teacher education programs, with the 1996 publication of *What Matters Most: Teaching for America's Future* by NCTAF, these two sets of standards for teaching were appropriated to the two levels of teacher education: preservice and continuing professional development. The NCTAF report denoted the INTASC standards for guiding preservice programs and NBPTS Core propositions for practicing teachers with at least three years of experience. At the same time, the standards for the accreditation of teacher education upheld by the National Council for Accreditation of Teacher Education (NCATE) (2001) adopted the INTASC principles for the review of preservice teacher education programs and NBPTS Core propositions for the review of advanced degree programs for practicing teachers.

Our purpose in briefly reviewing this history of national standards setting in professional education is to provide a foundation for the decisions made by the designers of the ASTL program. ASTL is not merely "aligned with NBPTS," rather, it has attempted to adopt, adapt, and accommodate much of the intellectual foundations of the standards-setting process. In the particular case of ASTL, that included introducing the content teachers teach to children into the continuing professional development of teachers seeking a master's degree in education, performance assessment, and deep reflection on one's teaching. As noted earlier in this volume, this intentional decision was made in stark contrast to a moribund and lightly enrolled master's degree that was built primarily on the traditional foundations of education, advanced methods classes, and emerging issues in education. The vision for ASTL was to reenergize the master's degree as continuing professional development where the classroom was the laboratory for testing out new ideas, recording them in a journal or on video, reflecting on the implementation of the new ideas taught in the program, and assessing one's skill development along the way.

Content Focus: Breaking the Mold

The original vision for ASTL content focus (what we called Concentrations) was to offer coursework in the four core disciplines represented in Virginia's then-new SOL assessments, specifically, English and language arts, mathematics, history, and science. It was our intent to develop teacher leaders who would become both richer in their knowledge of one of these content areas and be better able to teach them. We envisioned, for example, a third grade teacher who studied the eighteen-credit-hour math concentration and who would then become a team leader in her elementary school in math curriculum and instruction. For middle and high school teachers, who often have an undergraduate major or minor in the subjects they teach, we envisioned the ASTL program as preparing them for leadership roles in their schools and their departments. The same premise underlay all four of the first disciplines on which ASTL was founded. Tying the Core and the Concentration together, our goal was to use the master's degree as a vehicle for strengthening the school and not just the teacher through the study of oneself, and one's teaching, and how to lead others in change coupled with greater breadth and depth in a discipline. It should be noted here that we always hope our graduates will feel prepared to stand for National Board Certification, but that has never been a stated objective of the program; we may encourage National Board Certification, stress our belief in its process and worthiness, but we've never seen this program as a "preparation program" for it.

As might be expected, the first step in the process was building relationships with the College of Arts and Sciences, in which all four disciplines were then housed. It is important to remember that our college's relationships with the College of Arts and Sciences and these four departments was distant due to the fact that in 1988, our college took up the program format promulgated by the Holmes Group (1986) and moved preservice teacher education to a graduate-level preparation program. In the ensuing ten years, there was little need for coordination between the two colleges beyond grant-specific activities. Relations were not strained, but they were left fallow. New deans in each of these colleges in 1997 opened the door to new relationships, of which ASTL was the first.

The two deans met on a series of occasions to talk informally about expectations, and eventually to form an action plan. The dean of the College of Arts and Sciences, himself a mathematician and the former chairperson of his department, was enthusiastically supportive of the chance to provide more content to teachers in a degree program format. Identifying the incentives for the faculty to design new courses and then to teach them to teachers was the next task. In its first few years, ASTL was seen and presented as an off-campus program than as a campus-based program. Under our university's model, an incentive exists for programs that serve the broadest community possible by delivering courses at local sites around Northern Virginia. It has historically been a rather lucrative arrangement for the colleges that perform this kind of instructional outreach. A ratio was negotiated between the two colleges wherein the departments in the College of Arts and Sciences could create a new revenue stream that would build their own financial resources. It was at this point that the dean from CEHD met with the department chairs in the College of Arts and Sciences to invite their participation in the program. The incentives were outlined and the request of four eighteen-credit-hour Concentrations was made. Much to our satisfaction, the history department and the mathematics department signed on immediately and quickly produced six-course packages for teachers who teach content to students, but who lack an undergraduate major in that particular discipline. Over time, and due to some rather strong relationships associated to grant work in the sciences, we eventually had a third Concentration in science. The lone department of these four that did not choose to participate was the English department. For the last twenty years, the English department at George Mason has actively reached the area's English and language arts teachers through its Northern Virginia Writing Project. And lastly, as noted in the opening to chapter 1, one department chair, leading a department that would likely never be asked for a Concentration, wrote a twelve-page paper using fifteen-year-old citations on why selling undergraduate knowledge for graduate credit, especially for teacher education was both an affront to academia and a sign that teacher education was not worth further investment by the institution. He had few supporters and the discussion of a new degree founded on a partnership between the two colleges was pursued.

As one might expect, each of the four departments chose its own path, which meant that the new ASTL director had to work with departments with varying levels of commitment and infrastructure to make such a nontraditional move into teacher education. The history department's faculty identified six courses in their collection that tied directly to the content tested on the Virginia SOL exams. Typical titles included Themes in American History, Themes in World History, and Approaches to Modern World History. The faculty immediately delivered them off campus. The mathematics department designed six new courses for elementary teachers to give the teachers much deeper knowledge in numeracy and to deepen their conceptual mathematical knowledge for teaching students more effectively (Ball, 1991; Hill, Rowan, & Ball, 2005). The mathematics Concentration was the closest to Shulman's (1986), Ma's (1999), and Thames and Ball's (2010) conceptions of pedagogical content knowledge. In the sciences, there were well-established relationships around grants to improve science teaching. Because of this, the science Concentration most closely approximated Shulman's conception of pedagogical content knowledge by borrowing on the many professional development opportunities afforded university science faculty. As a result, the science concentration used a format of two nine-credit courses that combined content and pedagogy. With these three, ASTL admitted its first cohort of students, who met our program entrance requirement of a minimum of three years of teaching experience. We chose this entrance requirement for two reasons. The first is that we believed to be reflective toward changing and improving one's teaching teachers need to have taught the curriculum more than once or twice. They needed greater conceptual and factual understandings of the content, as well as enough distance from their teaching to be willing to explore it in some depth. The second reason is that we were trying to align expectations with NBPTS, which also had a three-year minimum.

With the structure of the partnership established, it was time to address the logistics of delivering the program. Based on input from teachers in the field and the ASTL faculty, we decided to offer the ASTL Core in a twelve-month timeframe that began in June and finished the following May. The courses were systematically held on the same evenings, thereby leaving maximum flexibility for the courses in the Concentrations to be offered on other weeknights. With no Core courses offered in the summer, there was also room for the Concentrations to offer courses in the summers, which had its own attractive financial incentive structure in our university. Within one year of the dean proposing to the faculty that we should pursue this program, the first courses were offered about forty miles from our campus. ASTL was up and running. Within five years, both deans had stepped down, but by then ASTL was graduating about fifty students per year with that number increasing annually.

The Classroom as a Laboratory

Given that a major goal of ASTL is to ground teachers' learning in the practice of their own classrooms, a term now referred to as "situated learning" (Wei, Darling-Hammond, Andree, Richardson, & Orphanos, 2009; Whitcomb, Borko, & Liston, 2009), the faculty design team wrestled with issues related to our stated outcomes to ensure (1) reflection, (2) coherence across the program, and (3) evidence-based practice. Our team structured its decision-making around one central question: In what ways can this advanced master's program open teachers' eyes to what works in the classroom and why? As we know from the literature, "the content of professional development is most useful when it focuses on concrete tasks of teaching, assessment, observation, and reflection" (Wei, Darling-Hammond, Andree, Richardson, & Orphanos, 2009, p. 3). We also know the value "of placing core practices at the center of teacher learning experiences . . . in which the development of pedagogical skill in interactive aspects of teaching is addressed by university-based teacher educators" (Whitcomb, Borko, & Liston, 2009, p. 209).

Our first task was to unpack the meanings of the terms reflection, coherence, and evidence-based practice and then develop criteria for them. Having consensus on what these terms would look like would be necessary to syllabi development. Even though a critical component of accomplished teaching is teachers' ability to reflect on their practice, to explain what they do and why they do it, most practicing teachers struggle with what this looks and sounds like. Our dilemma was how to teach that skill, thread it throughout the program, and evaluate its development. We used the Board's guidelines of description, interpretation, and synthesis as the three levels of reflective thought to define.

To ensure intentional and consistent expectations of reflection across all courses, we agreed upon the following descriptors for each level of reflection. We defined *description* as telling what is; *analysis* as applying and interpreting "what is" and telling how or why; and *synthesis* as telling what one might do differently, think about and reconsider, and examine impact, and answer the question, "So what? To elaborate, analysis concerns motives, reasons, and meaning-making to oneself and connects back to description whereas synthesis coherently puts together ideas from the general to the particular, carefully examines ideas, and considers seriously the influence of these ideas on oneself, actions, and beliefs.

In addition to agreed-upon descriptors, the faculty wanted reflection to be cumulative across all courses and culminate in a final portfolio. The course reflections were to provide a focused, intentional, consistent framework for writing about how coursework, readings, and projects led to deep reflection about learning for both the student and the teacher. This perspective is clearly aligned with the Board's view of accomplished teaching—one that requires ongoing inquiry into practice as they perfect their craft throughout their career (Blackwell & Diez, 1999) and is integral to advanced study that leads to improved teaching and learning.

To ensure coherence, the faculty wanted experienced teachers to use their advanced study to expand and demonstrate their knowledge, skills, and dispositions in relation to ASTL's eight program outcomes. We used Buchmann and Floden's (1992) definition of coherence, the ability to form a unified whole that allows for many kinds of connectedness, in addition to the Board's propositions and assessments, as benchmarks for developing the course projects. To that end, the faculty developed a framework for the Core that focused its work on the outcomes, courses, performance-based assessments, and their relation to NBPTS-related assessments. This framework structured faculty thinking and planning, and provided a quality control mechanism for integrity across the Core and across all faculty members who would be teaching those courses. Appendix A lists the ASTL principles and candidate outcomes, the

ASTL courses, the performance-based assessments, and the related NBPTS assessment activities for the Core.

To ensure evidence-based practice, we decided to create performance-based assessments with accompanying rubrics for each signature course project and use the descriptors for reflective practice to provide systematic feedback. The performance-based assessments and rubrics were to reflect the language of the Board for evaluation for portfolio entries across each rubric. All rubrics were developed on a four-point scale listing the assignment, the maximum number of points for that assignment, and descriptors for little or no evidence, clear evidence, clear and consistent evidence, and clear, consistent, and convincing evidence. An example of a rubric from the course, EDUC 612, Inquiry into Practice that ensures evidence-based practice in a Multigenre Assignment can be found in Appendix B.

Once we had unpacked and agreed on parameters for reflection, coherence, and evidence-based practice, our second task was to develop syllabi for each of the five courses in the Core. Each faculty member on the design team took lead responsibility for one course and served as partner on another so that we could move quickly toward development, obtaining constructive feedback, vetting syllabi with NBCTs and other interested faculty to go through the required course approval process both at the college and university level.

The following three sample projects illustrate how our assignments require teachers to (1) use evidence through performance-based assessments to study their practice, (2) apply reflective thinking in their own settings, and (3) share their findings with peers from other schools and disciplines. We discuss here the case study, video analysis of teaching, and professional portfolio to demonstrate a focus on reflection, coherence, and evidence-based practice.

Integrative Case Study

In the three-credit course, EDUC 613, How Students Learn, the outcome is "Teachers are committed to students and their learning," and the signature course assignment is a case study of a learner. It is designed to deepen teachers' knowledge and skills in monitoring and managing student learning in their own classrooms. To portray a rich, meaningful picture of one learner, teachers must synthesize all information that they have collected on that learner. This performance-based assessment is designed to help teachers better understand how a student thinks, learns, and views the world by focusing on what arouses that student's curiosity, motivation, and interest. The integrative case study assignment includes three parts: (1) a descriptive discussion of the learner with relevant background information, (2) an analytic discussion of the learner that draws on the descriptive data that were collected, and (3) a reflective evaluation regarding the process and outcomes of the case study. The rubric used to evaluate the final integrative case study can be found in Appendix C.

Recorded Lessons and Analyses

To develop an inquiry toward teaching stance during EDUC 614, Designing and Assessing Teaching and Learning, the signature assignment in this course is a teacher's video of two class sessions of a content lesson to identify what took place and to explain why it occurred. This particular assignment was designed to support the outcome "Teachers know the subjects they teach and how to teach those subjects to students." By studying one's own teaching, one can assess responsiveness to the needs and interests of learners and, in particular, classroom contexts.

In the performance assessment for analyzing video-recorded lessons, teachers describe their classrooms and create classroom maps. In the first video-recorded lesson, the teacher describes and analyzes classroom inter-actions. In the second video, the teacher describes changes that occurred in student engagement, practice, and student-teacher interactions or student understanding using a specific lesson in which the teacher has altered some practices based on the first video analysis and reflection. This assignment aligns clearly with current research that recognizes the importance of video analysis as a "tool for teacher development because of its ability to depict the richness and complexity of classrooms and to capture aspects of classroom life that a teacher might not notice in the midst of carrying out a lesson" (Sherin, Linsenmeir, & van Es, 2009, p. 214). Moreover, video analysis continues to be used as a springboard for rich discussions about classroom in-teractions related to student learning, level of content, and reasoned practice.

A Professional Portfolio

The ASTL professional portfolio is a performance-based document that pro-vides concrete evidence of teacher professional development throughout the program and supports the Board's proposition, "Teachers think systemati-cally about their practice and learn from experience." The portfolio also links the ASTL program outcomes with national, state, and institutional profes-sional standards. Because the ASTL program has two distinct components, the Core and the Concentration, the portfolio evaluation occurs twice—once at midpoint and once at program completion. The final evaluation comprises a formal presentation to faculty and peers. As with all ASTL assignments, the portfolio is evaluated with a preestablished rubric.

The faculty intended for the portfolio to be a systematic way for teachers to use their course-based work and reflections as evidence of their growth over their degree program, making visible their practice by examining reasons for their choices, and keeping the requirements meaningful but not too controlling. In 1999, the use of portfolios for the assessment process in this program was a pioneering effort for our faculty. Grounded in the ASTL program design, the performance-based assessments, student work samples, and other evidence are a combination of required and self-selected representations of the knowledge, skills, and dispositions that participants gain throughout the program. Teachers in the program systematically compile and assemble an evidence-based record of their professional knowledge and skills, professional growth throughout the program, professional teaching practices, and leadership skills throughout the program (Fox & Ritchie, 2003). Teachers may also use the portfolio as a tool for self-assessment or as part of a school-based professional development plan.

To help teachers achieve a cumulative record of their growth, each teacher in our program presents a portfolio as a requirement for graduation. During this presentation, all teachers must identify and reflect on the Core propositions that show their greatest growth and on the Core propositions that show they still have work to do. They also share publicly with colleagues their plans for continuing their professional learning. Reflections for the portfolio are written to prompts at specified points during the coursework sequence; however, the required reflections are not evaluated nor are they a specific part of the coursework. For example, at the conclusion of the course, How Students Learn, ASTL students write to the Reflection Prompt 1 that focuses on

> how coursework, related readings, and products . . . have led you to think more deeply about the learning process and your own students, as well as your own learning. . . . In your reflection, please address any of the applicable eight program learning outcomes and the ways in which the performance assessments included thus far in the Core provide evidence of your knowledge.

Similarly, at the end of the course, Designing and Assessing Teaching and Learning, all teachers write to the Reflection Prompt 2 that focuses on

> how coursework, related readings, and products . . . have led you to focus more carefully on the teacher as designer of curriculum and assessment and how you are incorporating technology into your teaching practice and your Core experience. . . . In your reflection, please address any of the applicable eight program learning outcomes and the ways in which the performance assessments included in this section provide evidence of this knowledge.

At the conclusion of both the Core and the Concentration, teachers write a synthesis reflection that demonstrates their growth and change over the course of the entire program. In the synthesis prompt, ASTL students

> address how the applicable eight program learning outcomes and the ways in which the performance assessments included in your coursework provide evidence of your growth and development as a professional as well as *specific examples* of how you are impacting student learning in your educational setting and what you will do to continue your professional development.

The portfolio provides all teachers in the program the opportunity to synthesize, reflect, and connect program coursework to what their own students are learning in their classrooms.

Evaluation from the Outset

ASTL was created based on a conceptual framework that teacher education for practicing teachers should blend graduate-level content in a specialization with professional education that is grounded in teacher problem-solving, that teachers' classrooms are their learning laboratories, and that teachers are agents of change. Any evaluation of ASTL would have to attend to our theory of practicing teacher growth and development along our theoretical lines.

In keeping with the concepts of continuous improvement and increased accountability for students, teachers, and teacher educators, our faculty chose to build in a model for program evaluation from the inception of the program. The faculty focused specifically on the program aspects of: (1) how well it was meeting its stated outcomes in terms of deeper understanding of one's teaching; (2) how the program was achieving coherence through carefully developed assignments that were linked to the teachers' classrooms as well as across the program; and (3) how well it was meeting the teachers' needs through course content, structure, and delivery modes.

Our first decision was to determine how well we were meeting our program outcomes. During the pilot year, we collected formative data from instructors and students across the program through questionnaires and focus groups that provided information on the content, pacing, assignments, and relevance of the Core experiences for each student. Faculty also provided input regarding course assignments, such as the number and quality of the assignments. This formative process led to changes in the second year and to the realization of the necessity for a more systematic means of evaluation for the ASTL program.

During the second year of the program, we hired an outside consultant to help us develop a program evaluation model in which students and faculty provided the same quantitative and qualitative input on every course across courses, commented on the relevance of assignments and on instructor feedback, and made recommendations for course improvement. All instructors evaluated the opportunity for their students to learn the course outcomes and commented on the formative evaluation measures they used and how they used them to make changes in their courses. This collaborative, iterative, and interactive process has been a major catalyst in keeping ASTL current and dynamic.

In addition to quantitative data, the faculty found more in-depth qualitative information about student learning, relevance of assignments, instructor feedback, and facilitating and limiting factors. In the first years, we obtained these data by using an open-ended questionnaire with a few questions:

- How did the assignments help you meet the course objectives? Please explain.
- How were the assignments relevant to your practice?
- How relevant was the instructor's feedback in helping you meet the course objectives?
- How might this course be improved?

We analyzed the data annually and used the analysis to make changes in the program structure, assignments, and sequence. What we aspired to but did not achieve at the outset was an evaluation model that explicitly examined how teachers were developing the knowledge, skills, and dispositions needed for accomplished teaching, a system for examining teachers' development over time, and the influence of our program on teachers' abilities to articulate and provide evidence for what their students were learning. We also found that we still needed to find an evaluation means that centers on the salient attributes of the program that enables our graduates to seek and achieve Board certification.

The Role of Communication: Embracing Ambiguity

As noted previously, designing a program that is outside traditional thinking requires vast amounts of investment in communication, a sort of shuttle diplomacy. Once the deans agreed, and the work became that of the faculties in the two colleges, there were many issues to be settled, including design and delivery of the courses and the incentives for partnering.

With the exception of science, as noted earlier, the faculties in history, and to a lesser degree, mathematics, were not as aware of the work in the study of teaching, where a concept like PCK, had become a foundational dimension of the assessment of teaching. While early discussions helped these committed faculty members understand designing a program where PCK would be prevalent in the Concentrations, these faculties proposed new courses for teachers who are expected to teach content in which they may be weak. The new courses were a mix of the content found in Virginia's SOL for PK–12 students and some meta- or thematic courses that situate the content at the graduate level and are accessible to students who likely did not major in the field as an undergraduate aspiring to teach. Both the faculty in the discipline as well as the faculty liaisons with the ASTL program reviewed the courses. As with any institution of higher education, curriculum review was conducted at the university level to be sure that the courses met the expectation for graduate credit. We cannot say that our content colleagues know the Core propositions of NBPTS, nor can we say that, in these three areas, there is the kind of PCK you might find in courses taught by discipline-based teacher educators. What we can say is that our goal of introducing content into a master's degree for teachers was accomplished and students enroll in these Concentrations annually.

Beyond the substance, however, many other issues had to be addressed, including locating a reliable faculty advisor in each discipline, identifying a critical mass of discipline faculty who were interested in working with teachers, and developing an ongoing commitment to support an education program in the disciplines. The teachers taking the ASTL program would need advisors. Each department identified a liaison who would serve as the Concentration advisor for ASTL.

We also had a goal of reaching down into these departments to engage more faculty members, to avoid ASTL students becoming an afterthought in comparison to the master's level students who aspire to emulate their professors as discipline experts. In the early years, progress on this front varied among the three disciplines. The sciences and mathematics had a handful of faculty in each discipline who would teach these graduate courses to teachers. In history, where the commitment of the department chair and a faculty member was arguably the highest among the three leaders, one faculty member served multiple roles and multiple courses. We discuss this further in the following.

This placed the director of ASTL in the position of serving as a de facto advisor in the disciplines who guided students through the courses in the Concentrations when the infrastructure for student advisement was still in its nascent stages. Communication within an academic program is often a challenge, and across two colleges with multiple departments, it remained one of those implementation issues that continued to take up the time of a director of a new and innovative program that continues to this day, as will be discussed in chapter 4.

Staffing and Professional Development

A final dilemma in this particular program design concerned staffing. While we had a critical mass of faculty to teach the Core courses and a few committed content experts to teach the Concentration courses, we also sought to employ NBCTs as adjunct faculty experts. Recognizing that each group of faculty had different qualities and would bring different but important dimensions to all the coursework, we tried to sort out the faculty qualities we hoped our students would experience throughout their master's degree program. With these lofty goals came the realization that we needed a plan for hiring, training, and sustaining faculty quality across the entire ASTL program. As a first step, we developed very broad conceptual statements that would guide the selection and placement of what we hoped for in our faculty.

First, we expected all faculty members not only to hold the necessary credentials for the courses they would teach but also have a commitment to the ASTL program and its goals. For example, in our Concentration courses, all faculty must hold a degree in that content area as well as have a commitment to improving teachers' content knowledge in that area. For faculty teaching in the Core, we expected them not only to have the credentials to teach the pedagogy associated with a particular course but also be committed toward the fundamental values and beliefs of the new degree program. And for NBCTs, we used their knowledge, skills, and expertise to vet syllabi and assignments so that we remained grounded in classroom practices that aligned closely with what the Board sought in accomplished teachers.

Second, we expected all faculty members to provide meaningful learning activities that required reflection, job-embedded learning, and deep thought about classroom practices and student learning. We knew from the literature then, as well as now, that job-embedded learning was central to teachers' professional development and learning (American Educational Research Association, 2005; Chappuis, Chappuis, & Stiggins, 2009; Knowles, 1973; Sparks & Hirsch, 1997; Wood & Killian, 1998).

To accomplish these initial staffing goals, we looked to the college for resources to help us get started. The dean provided funding for faculty to be trained at the National Board Facilitators' Institutes so they could understand the expectations of National Board Certification. The college also provided a $500.00 stipend for NBCTs who serve as adjunct faculty in a degree program to validate their expert knowledge as teaching faculty. And the faculty began the ASTL program knowing that there was much left to do but anxious to launch the newly designed degree program.

CONCLUSION

Having the vision for this master's degree guided the dilemmas we faced in our decision-making and program development. Early on in the development process, the faculty realized the complexity of transformative change. We knew that this master's degree "must be sufficiently flexible so that it can respond to differences in teachers, students, curricula, and contexts while maintaining consistency with the intended design features and Core principles" (Whitcomb, Borko, & Liston, 2009, p. 211). We also knew that sustainability would depend greatly on how we specified our outcomes, principles, learning experiences, and assessments so that the degree would always comprise a dynamic set of learning experiences in both pedagogy and content.

4

Addressing Dilemmas and Sustained Challenges—
Implementing the Big Ideas

As faculty members change, so do the challenges we face as a program of maintaining coherence across our college and with programs in other units across the university. We have worked carefully from the outset with faculty teaching Concentration coursework outside the College of Education to establish a clear rotation of content area classes. For ten years, one particular Concentration has provided instructors who are knowledgeable about PK–12 classrooms. The professor in charge of coordinating their Concentration scheduled the courses in such a way that they have avoided the evening when the Core classes meet. This department has also maintained a workable yearly course rotation schedule that offers at least one course per semester, one that we established together. Recently, the professor left the university. It was several months before it came to our attention that not only were a few problems surfacing, but they were escalating. We began to receive an increasing number of student complaints that we had never had before; some were about instructors, some were about course scheduling, while others were concerned about the disconnect between the curriculum and its application in the classroom. Then, the class schedules for two semesters in a row conflicted with the Core, with one semester almost resulting in course cancellation due to low enrollment.

The directors scheduled a meeting to discuss these new developments and initiate solutions to the problems. As we talked with the faculty member who was now coordinating the ASTL courses, we came to realize that he had basically been handed the task of scheduling these classes and didn't have any background knowledge about the ASTL program; nor was he aware of any of the parameters for course rotation or scheduling. It was an important conversation; once we were able to explain the program and combination of the Core and Concentration components, he began to understand what the enrollment problems and the growing complaints from the students were all about. He has grandchildren himself who are in elementary school, and he talked about the importance of content knowledge for teachers at all levels. He made the connection right away among the courses in his department, advanced pedagogy, and the connection to PK–12 teachers and their classes. Now back on track with a working schedule and more PK–12 connected faculty, we can breathe a bit more easily. Walking away from the meeting that afternoon and watching the changes several months later, we had a renewed awareness that consistent dialogue is essential, and we fully realize that program implementation is never static and never over.

This chapter focuses on the ongoing challenges the ASTL program has encountered since its inception more than ten years ago. We organized the chapter using the challenges and dilemmas encountered during program design and implementation, as described in chapters 2 and 3. These challenges: curriculum design, program delivery, staffing, and measuring programmatic impact have all been addressed in different ways as the ASTL program has grown and changed. ASTL continues to maintain a flexible structure, Board-like focus, and teaching excellence despite rapid growth that at times has exacerbated the challenges addressed when the program was originally designed. For example, we continue to offer courses in cohorts both on and off the main campus, which has presented management issues, such as securing and supporting additional part-time instructors or finding viable locations for the off-site courses. The primary goal of this chapter is to share how we have addressed the ongoing challenges to ensure sustainability.

DILEMMAS OF CURRICULUM DESIGN

Content Focus

A significant content challenge has involved working with an increased number of faculty and administrators both within and outside of GSE as we have an additional fourteen Concentrations since the original three were established. The three original Concentrations—history, mathematics, and science—involve content area coursework delivered by faculty outside CEHD in the College of Arts and Sciences. Art education, foreign languages, and geography (also a state add-on license endorsement) are newer Concentrations, also taught by faculty in other areas.

Within the college, as well as with other units of the university, we have developed other new Concentrations. Incremental additions of new Concentrations have allowed the program to meet the needs of many content specializations for PK–12 classroom teachers. For example, the literacy Concentration, the first to be added, aligns with Virginia's requirements for those seeking a reading specialist license. This Concentration provides classroom teachers with an opportunity to become literacy specialists in their schools. Gifted child education provides courses that lead to a state add-on license, or endorsement. Other Concentrations added since the inception of the program include early childhood education, physical education, teacher leadership, and special education.

Ongoing communication regarding revision and sequence of courses within and across colleges has been critical to the development of content expertise for ASTL students. For example, we continue to work with faculty in different content areas such as art education, history, and mathematics to develop effective methods for assessing content knowledge as part of accreditation requirements for CEHD and the university. While the faculty in other units provides content expertise, a significant challenge remains how to communicate effectively our needs for developing key performance-based assessments and performance rubrics, implement and validate the performance assessments, and maintain data collection for program accreditation. These performance-based assessments are also important because they become part of the ASTL students' required portfolios as evidence of their content knowledge. Effective communication across the units that is consistent and open to discussion remains an ongoing challenge as faculty positions change and department chairs rotate in and out of leadership positions.

Classroom as a Laboratory for Learning: Situated Learning/Pedagogy

As described in chapter 3, the faculty worked from the outset to ensure that the three principal elements (1) reflection, (2) coherence across the program, and (3) evidence-based practice were embedded in the Core syllabi. As faculty developed each syllabus and aligned it with the eight program learning outcomes, they also incorporated experiences to expand and deepen teachers' understanding of and capacity for critical reflection. Teachers' classrooms served as laboratories for conducting research, where they apply new knowledge from coursework and make personal connections between research and their practice. Reflection was the element that faculty embedded across all learning experiences; reflection thus served as a pedagogical approach to support the teachers' learning.

From its inception, ASTL has remained faithful to its commitment to engage teachers in research-based practice anchored in their classrooms. The case study of a learner, the video analysis of teaching, the culturally based action research study, and the grant proposal all directly relate to teachers' own educational settings. These key performance assessments ask teachers to apply knowledge from course readings and provide evidence of the degree to which they have understood and can now apply their newly acquired coursework knowledge. Teachers have found learning that is situated in their classrooms to be concrete and applicable in their daily teaching practice. Recently, however, challenges have emerged concerning ready access to research in the schools. Requirements for parental and administrative permissions have increased in specificity in the school districts. Consequently, the faculty has had to become more flexible in requiring how teachers complete classroom assignments that involve their students.

An example of adhering to school-based administrative constraints regarding the use of PK–12 student data emerged recently concerning the video-recording analysis assignment in EDUC 614, Designing and Assessing Teaching and Learning. One school indicated that its teachers were not granted permission to show, discuss, or analyze their videos in a collaborative setting. Our requirements for group analysis should be flexible, while maintaining the integrity of the assignment. As a solution, faculty asked the teachers to describe the content of the recorded lesson, conduct the analysis, and then share only the results of the analysis with a critical friends' group. Although upon discussion, faculty found this substitution to be somewhat successful; however, since teachers were unable to engage in the full discussion and analysis in collaboration with other cohort members, this alternative caused a break in the established group analysis process, thus limiting the ability of the group to provide fully contextualized input to this teacher. As teachers are called upon to situate their learning in the context of their classrooms to challenge their expanding knowledge base (Ball, Thames, & Phelps, 2008), program faculty should also be aware of the contextual barriers individual teachers may face and understand possible existing constraints during corresponding coursework.

Reflection: An Underlying Element across the Program

Supporting ASTL students' growth and development in reflective capacity remains both a key focus of the program and one of the greatest challenges. One consistent challenge we face has been helping ASTL students reach the three levels of reflection as defined by NBPTS. To meet this challenge, faculty members have systematically engaged in research to determine how to best meet the needs of the individual teachers who enter our program, teachers who come from varying backgrounds, who teach in different schools and school districts, and who also differ in years and scope of classroom teaching and other educational experiences. We have strategically incorporated changes in readings and in-class experiences, and embedded reflection into the assignments and readings, always with the idea of this work being based in teachers' classroom laboratories. By then studying the results of these changes, we have determined what has (and has not) achieved the desired results.

The following example illustrates how we have approached this type of challenge over time with solutions that are providing positive results. We have explained that while each course across the Core addressed specific pedagogical content, our goal simultaneously was also to build and strengthen teachers' critical reflective skills so that they could become researchers who were leaders in their schools and were able to share multiple perspectives. Supporting teachers in reaching the three levels of reflection (i.e., description, analysis, and synthesis) as defined by NBPTS has been, and remains, both our expectation and our goal because teachers should develop capacity and effect purposeful change in their classrooms.

To meet this challenge, we have consistently promoted the centrality of structured critical reflection during each course so that it includes analysis and interpretation of teaching and classroom events with the goal of promoting teacher learning and development (Shulman & Shulman, 2004). We have also continually exercised and tested our belief that helping teachers engage in metacognitive reflection could enhance their capacity for growth by situating their experiences in their own classrooms. As ASTL students see their classrooms as laboratories, their inquiry stance can help them become more conscious of their decisions and actions by considering the results on learners.

The faculty also carefully selected readings for each course and created reflection prompts to challenge the teachers' thinking about how they were applying theory to their classroom practice. The ASTL students' reflective writings have also helped the ASTL faculty identify which readings the teachers found the most meaningful or which reflection prompts helped them delve below the surface to engage in more critical levels of examination of their practice. The practice of examining ASTL students' reflective data to inform decisions about readings or in-class discussion topics has proven to be an iterative process for the faculty. That is, we continually challenge ourselves to base our decisions for change on the reflective data, initiate change, examine the results of that change, and begin the process again.

Research, and particularly research involving the investigation of the ASTL students' growth and learning, provides the faculty with opportunities to better understand teacher change. It enables faculty to connect its work with the broader literature and consider results in the context of the teacher development research literature. However, systematic research is time-consuming, particularly when faculty are teaching new cohorts of teachers and examining the results of previous research findings on the teachers' learning. Finding time to examine teachers' reflections, discuss the results of program decisions, and consider new directions for program updates remains an ongoing challenge for faculty. This lack of time is a particular challenge during the course of the ongoing academic year as faculty rotate teaching courses in the current cohort. One solution has been to approach our process as ongoing research to provide faculty with opportunities to incorporate the results of our examination of reflection data into conference presentations and publications.

At the opening of the coursework sequence, we ask ASTL students to write a reflection to a prompt. They also complete a self-assessment questionnaire (see Appendix D). As faculty read these reflections and studied the self-assessments, we determined that most of the teachers began the program reflecting at a description-only level, which was counter to our assumption that teachers would enter the program as active reflective practitioners. On the self-assessment questionnaires, teachers generally indicated that they reflected on their teaching. The faculty was surprised to realize that some teachers viewed reflection as the description of classroom activities and events or reporting what wasn't going well. We found that even experienced teachers who had been in the classroom for many years did not reflect systematically, critically, or purposefully. Thus, while most ASTL students could describe puzzlements or present problems, they were not thinking beyond a descriptive level. If teachers were to achieve the levels of reflective thought defined by NBPTS, the program faculty determined that we would need to refine our approach and scaffold learning differently during the first program course to help ASTL students reach a more critical level of reflection.

The changes made in the first course were designed explicitly to help teachers understand critical reflection and to help them move toward a higher level of reflection. Specifically, we incorporated selections from Dewey (1933, 1938, 1944), Schön (1983), and Brookfield (1995) into weekly readings. We also included readings that addressed the concept of reflection having multiple levels (Rodgers, 2002), or the importance of incorporating multiple lenses to provide a deeper perspective (Fendler, 2003). We simultaneously incorporated collaborative thinking in "critical friends groups" (Hole & McEntee, 1999) and introduced the development of new lenses focused on cultural perspectives through readings, a cultural autobiography reflection, and critical conversations. As a result, teachers came to better understand additional ways that their reflections could move beyond description. What made the reflection process real to the teachers was the ability to draw their puzzlements and questions from their own classroom settings. That is, they were reflecting on actual scenarios drawn from their personal experiences and school contexts, making the thought process visible to themselves for examination and problem solving.

Aligning with Shulman and Shulman's (2004) work in scaffolding teacher reflective capacity, the cohorts of teachers developed communal reflectivity which, in turn, served to broaden their understandings and form additional connections. We discovered that it was necessary for faculty to provide structured in-class opportunities for teachers to deliberate collaboratively on the instructional questions they posed and to seek actions or solutions. These opportunities were facilitated by critical reflection protocols, such as the process identified by Hole and McEntee (1999) or by posing questions and asking our ASTL students to respond in class and connect their responses to specific readings. In-group reflective activities provided scaffolded learning through distributing expertise and solution building capacity among the cohort members. The results of these efforts become apparent during the final course when students write a grant proposal. This culminating learning experience required the students to reflect on the results of their own classroom research and apply those results to support the needs assessment used to justify their grant. Thus, students were asked to identify specific funding needs by anchoring their grant proposals to the contexts of their individual classrooms and schools, and in many cases to base the proposal on research they had conducted during earlier Core courses. Our faculty continue to study the ways that our students establish connections between the content of their professional development coursework and their students' learning (Wei, Darling-Hammond, Andree, Richardson, & Orphanos, 2009; Whitcomb, Borko, & Liston, 2009), and then use this information to propose solutions.

DILEMMAS OF DELIVERY

Coherence across the Program

In addition to building reflective capacity and supporting the development of teachers' research skills, other elements of the program structure have served to provide programmatic coherence. The challenges in maintaining coherence across the program involve addressing both the academic coursework sequence and the organizational structure as numbers of ASTL students have increased and cohorts spread across locations. The eight program learning outcomes, the cohort structure for students and development of a programmatic research agenda are three ways that the ASTL program responds to these challenges.

Continuing Focus on Program Learning Outcomes

First, continuing to focus the Core coursework discussions around the eight program learning outcomes has helped the faculty consider any proposed program changes. Performance-based assessments informed by the program outcomes provide evidence of the degree to which the ASTL students have met the outcomes. The faculty continue to discuss proposed changes in consideration of the anticipated impact on ASTL students' coursework experiences or their relevance to coursework experiences. Because a change in one course has potential impact on other courses in the sequence, when program faculty implements any change, it is also implemented across current cohorts to maintain consistency. In this way, the learning outcomes not only provide a foundation, but they also continue to provide a guiding structure for considering changes to coursework experiences.

Cohort Structure

Second, the ASTL students enroll in the Core as members of a cohort that moves through and completes the coursework together. The ASTL Core is designed to be a community of learners and to facilitate the establishment of a peer network whose task is to co-create knowledge "through collaborative learning and experiential knowing" (Lawrence, 2002, p. 83). Some ASTL students enter the Core sequence knowing others in the cohort; however, the majority begin as strangers who only have the common goal of earning a master's degree. We found that the common goal of wanting a master's degree does not automatically create a cohesive community. Therefore, from the outset of the courses, the faculty work systematically to take steps during the opening class meetings and throughout the coursework to create and develop ongoing opportunities for collaboration. The cohort model has become a primary avenue to build coherence across the coursework.

The practice of working together in peer groups occurs throughout the Core and is supported by the initial time taken to establish community during the first course. Those initial peer groups do not remain static; rather, the students regroup regularly throughout coursework. For example, early in the Core, faculty creates the first critical reflection groups based on ASTL students' responses to questionnaires about years of experience, grade level and subjects taught, or experience in teacher research. Other groups are formed in the second course when they research specific learning theories and then become "expert presenters" of a particular learning theorist assigned to their peer group; they then regroup later in that course to provide peer feedback during the time that they gather data and write a case study of a learner in their classroom. Each time a new peer group is created, its members have the opportunity to work with some new cohort members while building on the relationships already established with other group members. Participation in experiences with different cohort members is designed to provide in-depth experiential learning, opportunities to consider new and diverse perspectives, and develop critical reflection.

Two aspects of the program, size and culture, created challenges for the cohort structure. In recent years, as the university has encouraged increasingly larger master's degree classes with twenty-five or more students per class, the resulting size of our cohorts presents an ongoing challenge, particularly if the program has to schedule two cohorts at the same time. The faculty has recently discovered that larger cohorts were resulting in less time for individual support and interaction between faculty and students and consequently decided to limit the class size to less than twenty. We have also determined that cohorts can sometimes develop their own communication patterns or cultures. The result is that groups can sometimes adopt a tone or a perspective that does not honor multiple perspectives during discussions of course content or genuinely engage in developing the program's strong emphasis on reflection and inquiry. For example, one cohort that was comprised largely of teachers from one concentration from the same school district challenged our ability to bring multiple lenses and ideas into peer discussion and feedback. Groups would at times seem to fixate on one particular approach or arrive at a solution that would have benefited from other points of view and other solutions. At these times, it has been particularly important that faculty members bring in additional articles and research to infuse new ideas into the discussion. As a result, we recently made a concerted effort when forming the cohorts to include ASTL students from multiple school districts, concentrations, and grade levels to create more diverse critical research groups and encourage more multidimensional discussions.

Researcher Approach

Third, helping teachers develop capacity to take a researcher's approach to solving classroom dilemmas is another area that guides our efforts to maintain program coherence. From the very first class, teachers are asked to provide information about their experiences in teacher research. This information serves to form the first sets of working groups based on common experiences. Collaborative approaches teach research skills, and we consistently emphasize the application of these skills to teachers' classrooms.

In EDUC 606, Education and Culture, the completion of a culturally focused action research study is the course performance assessment. This assignment is supported by carefully selected readings about culture and critical discussion on culture and the role it plays in our schools and in students' learning. It also helps ASTL students work on new ways to work with learners in culturally and linguistically diverse classrooms. Small group discussion, coupled with weekly reflective writings, helps teachers delve below the surface as they tackle questions about the various cultural challenges faced on a daily basis. The safe and open environment established earlier in the coursework is an important aspect of the group culture that allows teachers to recognize and question some of their own assumptions. Teachers can then discuss their questions and issues honestly and without fear of judgment because their larger learning community has been in place since the outset of the program.

Evidence-Based Practice

Just as a major goal of the program is to ground teachers' learning in the practice of their own classrooms, the program faculty has also taken an inquiry stance on their work with the program. A continuing challenge has been to maintain a consistent inquiry focus while instructors move in and out of teaching different classes and full-time faculty members are not always able to devote time to the programs' ongoing research agenda. Despite these challenges, our work has been guided by questions such as: Which readings do the teachers find meaningful and engaging? What learning activities help teachers pose meaningful questions about their classrooms and their learners? Which practices help teachers move from more superficial reflection to a deeper, more critical view of their classrooms and their teaching practice? How can faculty support teachers to develop an inquiry stance on their classrooms? How can faculty support the use of research to inform their classroom decisions? How does the faculty implement backward design so that it serves to support student learning? Commitment to research-based practice is consistently taught and modeled by the faculty and continues to support an inquiry focus across the program. By using performance-based evidence about teacher learning, the program continues to maintain its commitment to use data to inform course- and program-level decisions based on the compiled evidence.

DILEMMAS OF MEASURING IMPACT

Evaluation from the Outset: Evaluation Plan to Program Research

Maintaining a viable evaluation plan that extends beyond the normal range of evaluation approaches that use course evaluations and post-program survey data has been an ongoing challenge. What originally began as a course-level program evaluation plan has evolved into a full line of longitudinal programmatic research. Several faculty members have engaged in multiple years of research and data collection on teacher learning. This work has resulted in research presentations and papers, case studies, book chapters, and ultimately theory development about what comprises meaningful professional development and the growth of reflective practice in teachers. The third section of this book will present examples of this research in greater detail. By conducting consistent annual research that examines the results of recent programmatic decisions, we can maintain consistency in the efficacy of the program while continuing to make informed changes based on research data.

We continue to encounter additional challenges, such as managing the data, finding time to focus on analyzing the data, and allotting time for faculty to discuss the results and implications of the results for program structure and policies. While we have addressed these challenges by recruiting graduate assistants to participate in data collection and analysis, we still struggle to prioritize our research agenda when demands of the day-to-day operation of the program compete for our time. We have conducted several studies employing multiple measures that add to the literature on programs that are "developing assessment tools for gauging their candidates' abilities and their own success as teacher educators in adding to those abilities" (Darling-Hammond, 2006, p. 120). This research has helped promote a "culture of evidence and inquiry" (Cochran-Smith & Boston College Research Team, 2009) in the ASTL program to support research-based discussions among faculty members. As teacher education faculty, we have considered multiple measures that help us evaluate what teachers learn during professional development coursework and, in turn, understand more about the effectiveness of their new knowledge on their teaching settings.

DILEMMAS OF STAFFING AND PROFESSIONAL DEVELOPMENT

Addressing Growth

From under thirty students at the program's outset to now nearly three hundred in various phases of their coursework, managing the different facets of the program, maintaining program integrity, and communicating with students, faculty, school districts, and university administrators have posed multiple challenges. The program began with one director, an assistant director, and one program support staff who worked together to oversee all aspects of program scheduling, implementation, and marketing. Once the number of applicants increased and enrollment stabilized, it became necessary to move the management of the program from another office in the college to self-administration by program faculty. As school divisions sought program courses and we established cohorts in different off-campus locations, the need to maintain the program's own scheduling and payment for off-campus course delivery required the establishment of an "in-house" infrastructure. Revenue generated from off-campus courses created a need for more support and infrastructure for the off-campus cohorts resulting in an increase in support staff to include a full-time office program manager and two part-time staff who assist with the fiscal, marketing, and admissions aspects of the program. As of fall 2011, one faculty member serves as director and, along with the support staff, oversee all academic programming and course scheduling; they also work with faculty within our unit and other units of the university and teach in the Core, as well as various Concentrations.

Managing the Different Facets of the Program

The on- and off-campus delivery options for Core and Concentration coursework are major aspects of managing the different program facets. The ASTL program office processes off-campus student registration and payment because off-campus students register with different procedures than on-campus students. Consequently, the director and staff maintain detailed records of course scheduling, student admissions, academic progress, and matriculation and financial aspects of the program. The revenue generated from courses offered off-campus has enabled us to become financially self-sustaining and maintain a presence in multiple school divisions. The program administrator and faculty continually work with both full- and part-time faculty to coordinate teaching assignments and address details such as locating classroom space in school districts, monitoring course syllabi, and supporting part-time faculty.

Maintaining Program Integrity and Quality

As the program has grown, different faculty have assumed leadership and teaching responsibilities in other programs and the university has placed additional restrictions on hiring instructors who do not hold doctoral degrees (including NBCTs) to teach Core classes. Consequently, maintaining program integrity and quality continually challenges us as we partner with part-time faculty who require mentoring and support while teaching Core classes. To ensure a consistent voice of NBPTS and maintain fidelity to the Core propositions, the program identified an NBCT with a doctorate who serves as a consultant. This individual contributes both a NBPTS and classroom-based perspective to the program by attending faculty meetings when available, teaching courses, and participating in particular program research studies. The faculty and director continue to adhere to collaborative decision making in regard to program decisions concerning policies, procedures, and course content (assignments, readings, and assessments). The faculty also continue to address the challenge of working effectively with the intricate and complex nature of a program that spans multiple content areas in PK–12 grade levels in the Core classes. As we address program integrity and quality challenges we can see how essential it was that a year was spent on program planning that was anchored solidly in the literature on effective professional development for practicing teachers.

Communication

Effective communication with different constituencies, such as current and former students, faculty, school districts, and university community, is an ongoing challenge. With the increasing number of students in on- and off-campus cohorts, we now provide multiple modes of communication through face-to-face group meetings, individual meetings, and e-mail. The availability of support staff such as an outreach coordinator to answer student questions about program admission, course registration and scheduling, and graduation procedures has been critical for maintaining consistent and accurate responses to student queries. We recently established an Alumni Advisory Council comprised of former students representing multiple cohorts who meet twice yearly as a formal method of bringing graduate perspectives into the program decision-making process. An overarching purpose of the advisory group is to obtain feedback from former students about the current program and possible changes in course content and structure that the faculty are considering. We have also begun to systematically collect feedback electronically from our students after they complete their coursework. As mentioned previously, the director use monthly faculty meetings to structure consistent communication with faculty regarding coursework planning and revisions, the program performance-based assessment system, changes in college and university academic policies and procedures, and program evaluation.

We continue to improve effective communication with large school districts in our region through maintaining contacts with individuals responsible for professional development or specific content areas such as foreign language or gifted education. Similar to our communication with students we use multiple strategies to communicate with particular school district administrators such as individual meetings and e-mail. The ASTL outreach coordinator actively communicates with individuals in school districts to facilitate student recruitment and address questions about the program. We also maintain consistent communication about course scheduling and advising with units outside the college. Periodic changes in administration of departments outside the college have been challenging and required face-to-face meetings with administrators who are unfamiliar with the purposes and structure of the program. For example, program administrators have met with department heads from outside the College of Education who may not have prior background or experiences related to graduate professional development for teachers. We have also met systematically with administrators such as new deans and associate deans in CEHD to explain program goals, structure, and accomplishments. As other programs in the college have grown in a similar fashion, it has been periodically necessary to provide justification for program expansion efforts such as hiring additional part-time instructors, hiring support staff, and purchasing equipment and materials. Communication regarding these justifications has been supported and enhanced by the data we've collected and analyzed on student performance and program evaluation.

CONCLUSION

The ASTL program has expanded the scope of its offerings while sustaining the original vision for this master's degree. While we attend to ongoing challenges that all programs face, such as the changing nature of the student population and changing financial support at the university level, we continue to rely on the flexible nature of the program to attract students as well as on the original specification of our outcomes, principles, learning experiences, and assessments. Despite tremendous growth in the number of students we serve, the number of faculty teaching classes, and the addition of support staff who assist in managing the program, we have addressed the accompanying challenges by employing a number of strategies described in this chapter. A most effective strategy has been studying the program through systematic data collection and analysis of data sources relevant to our students' performance, our students' learning and professional growth, and our own success as teacher educators in contributing to our students' learning and growth (Darling-Hammond, 2006).

II

Evidence of Effectiveness

How do we know that our work with teachers is effective? In what ways are teachers applying their new knowledge in their classrooms? In what ways can research conducted by teachers in their educational settings help teacher educators meet teachers' needs so that PK–12 students meet their potential? And, in what ways can research at both the course and program level inform teacher educators about the results of our work with teachers? These questions and others are being investigated through the research that has been and continues to be embedded in ASTL's program and evaluation process. In this section, we focus on several examples of the research we've conducted at the course and program levels.

Research in every teacher education program offers the potential for a deliberate and cumulative improvement of teachers' professional learning at the course level. Evidence-based practice is not only integral to coursework, but also a conscious approach incorporated at all levels of our program to better understand the complex dimensions of teaching and learning. Research provides evidence that can help faculty better understand the results of coursework learning experiences. Course and program data collected and analyzed at multiple levels can inform the changes that better meet the needs of the teachers, and ultimately the students in their classrooms. In the ASTL program, research-based practice is at the core of our work.

5

Evidence of Course Effectiveness

Elaine grew up in the western part of the United States; she was educated there and completed her teacher certification and her first years of teaching in her home state. She moved to our area looking for a temporary change of lifestyle and, more specifically, to pursue her master's degree in the ASTL program. Her specialization area in the program was in literacy, and having completed that coursework, she was now enrolled in the Education Core. In an e-mail exchange with her instructor at the outset of the Education and Culture course, Elaine wrote that she was excited about learning more about culture but thought that when she returned home "there just wouldn't be much cultural diversity there." As the course unfolded, she shared several insights via the weekly "exit reflections" the teachers wrote in each class. After the third week's discussion, she wrote at the end of this class that her new understanding was that culture wasn't about "just other ethnicities like I thought, but there is culture everywhere, and even my family and church have our own culture. I don't think I ever saw my own culture as a culture before. I see now that my students have their home culture, and my classroom has its own culture, too." Each week she shared new thoughts, such as "I didn't realize that we as teachers share a culture that other people like my students' parents might not understand. I think our school culture could be hard for some immigrant parents to understand. Hmm. I wonder how parents think about us as teachers and I wonder what assumptions they have about our schools." After another class, her "aha" was that she really had many English language learners (ELLs) in her class but thought that they were "all caught up" once they had finished the ESL program and started in her class. She later wrote that one particular reading helped her to see that even teachers' language and their approaches to working with parents can have cultural bearing on families' relationships in the school.

Elaine's final reflection as part of her culturally focused action research study was particularly revealing and showed how Elaine was making connections across the program from its beginning through the new content in this course. The CIP (Jacob, 1999) is the approach used to help teachers develop a critical stance on the role that culture plays in their educational settings. This process and the action research it supports are a central feature of this course because it provides thoughtful sets of questions in strands that teachers can examine as they attempt to study various perspectives on their puzzlements.

> This CIP research study really taught me the importance of reflective thinking in conjunction with research. One of Dewey's criteria for reflection is it must be a "systematic, rigorous, disciplined way of thinking, with its roots in scientific inquiry" (as cited in Rodgers, 2002). Before conducting my case study [in EDUC 613] and this CIP research study, I believe the majority of my reflections weren't critical reflections, rather a "stream of consciousness or uncontrolled coursing of ideas running through my head," as Dewey described. I often reflect on my puzzlements but before didn't conduct the research necessary to answer my questions or concerns. The CIP study taught me to go beyond surface reflection and conduct action research to address the puzzlement. I have been reflecting on Marco's progress all year. Before this study I continually discussed his progress with my colleagues and tried some strategies but didn't feel confident in my efforts and there wasn't a result . . . [the study] prompted me to collect and analyze data, discuss findings with colleagues and critical friends, and test interventions. I feel confident we can help Marco now because our strategies and interventions are driven by data. . . . Literature and class discussion prompted me to step back from my usual perspective to see a broader picture. Unfortunately, I can't change the politics or pacing guides driving our educational system. However, I can find ways to bring my diverse students' experiences and languages into the classroom in positive ways. No matter how much my professional environment influences the curriculum, I have control over my beliefs. I have the power to be culturally responsive.

While this is the type of realization, or "aha" moment, that we as teacher educators long to read in our students' reflections, not all teachers reach this level. Some reflections show that a teacher may still be at a less engaged level of reflection than Elaine, so by asking teachers to include a closing reflection on the process, we as faculty can better understand more about teachers' thoughts. This information helps us see which readings, which learning experiences, or which critical conversation prompts were the most meaningful from the teachers' perspectives. This information supports our understanding of the degree to which our candidates are meeting the learning outcomes, particularly the diversity and systematic inquiry outcomes in this course.

Each of the course assignments in the Core has an added reflection, which in turn, provides faculty with an additional snapshot of the teachers' perceptions and connections beyond the completion of the course assignment itself. In Elaine's case, we were able to also understand from her reflection that she took this study to another level when she shared how she brought together many school specialists who represented English for speakers of other languages, special education, and literacy, as well as the classroom teacher and the assistant principal. As they problem-solved together to see what could be done to serve Marco, Elaine saw the full circle of how collaboration that we have been doing in the Core classes could also occur in her own school setting. She was so excited that she had to e-mail me right away that Marco had been identified for special child study, and "it was because of my research and because I pulled a team together to collaborate." This example aligns with the ASTL learning outcome that addresses teachers as members of learning communities. Here, Elaine was a member of our program's learning community, but she was also applying it to her school setting.

Just as evidence-based practice has been incorporated as a cornerstone of ASTL's program, faculty have also adopted an inquiry approach at the course level to more deeply understand teacher learning through the lens of research. Although a large body of research exists in the preservice domain (Brouwer & Korthagen, 2005) on teacher development, empirical research supporting the sustained results of professional development with in-service teachers is still needed. By taking a critical approach to the learning that occurs in our courses in the Core, as faculty we have opportunities to make meaning from the results of our teaching. Specifically, we have challenged ourselves to take a critical look at the courses we are teaching and consider the results of our endeavors. Overall, both individual research and required performance-based assessments identified for each course have helped us determine the effectiveness of our courses on teacher learning. These results are used to portray what teachers are learning and to make necessary changes in the courses. Research has been embedded in the coursework to help teachers actively incorporate a systematic approach to monitoring PK–12 student learning, and we do the same thing. As the teachers in the program are learning to understand the effectiveness of their work with PK–12 students through a case study (EDUC 613), a video-recorded analysis of their teaching (EDUC 614), and an action research study (EDUC 606), so have we come to better understand the impact of our courses on their thinking. Our programmatic inquiry provides important data for us to make changes and explore the impact of our coursework on teachers' practices.

By taking an inquiry stance on what teachers learn as a result of the individual courses we teach in the Core, we better understand what our teachers are thinking and the connections they are making in their PK–12 classrooms. We have also been able to study changes in what our teachers know as a result of some of these changes. From this, we have gained greater insight into the kinds of professional development being emphasized in our surrounding school districts and can support teachers as they make important instructional decisions and consider the results in their classrooms. Course-based research helps answer the question, "How do we know that we have been effective in our courses, and where do we need to make changes to make teachers' learning more meaningful?"

This chapter provides evidence of the course-level research we are conducting as part of ASTL's overall research design. We provide summaries of two areas of research at the course level and conclude the chapter by identifying new areas for programmatic change that have emerged as a result of this research. The first study investigates the growth of teachers' cultural knowledge as a result of their action research studies in EDUC 606, Education and Culture. The second study examines teachers' development of self-efficacy and change agency as a result of their participation in the final class, EDUC 615, Teachers as Change Agents.

EVIDENCE OF TEACHER LEARNING AT THE COURSE LEVEL

How we as teacher educators come to understand the growth of teacher knowledge is a key element in helping us provide robust learning experiences for teachers that can filter down to affect K–12 learners. As teacher education faculty, we are well aware that helping teachers deepen their knowledge is far more than providing rote skills or a set of workshops. While we may have a strong idea of what new knowledge practicing teachers require to deepen their practice, we should differentiate our instruction in ways that tap into our ASTL students' prior knowledge and support their building of new understandings to connect to their classrooms. For example, we know that teachers' knowledge and understanding of the teaching cycle is built over time. In seeking ways to help teachers get inside of the complex interaction of teacher, learner, content, and context, we have to translate our knowledge about the complexity of this cycle to ways that can scaffold teacher learning meaningfully. To accomplish this, teacher educators should also systematically and critically examine the results of our work. This premise lays the foundation for the research that is found in multiple levels in our programs.

Teachers' initial learning about pedagogical content knowledge begins during their preservice education. We have talked about how teachers in our program come to us with varying sets of skills and experiences, from different preparation programs, and multiple types teaching settings and school districts. First understanding their background knowledge will be useful in helping them apply theory to practice in their classrooms. Also knowing which coursework experiences provided the most meaningful learning opportunities and which ones require adjustments is key to the process. Thus, it becomes essential for program development to have not only a holistic picture of the degree to which program participants meet the program goals, but we should also look inside the program itself to determine the robustness of course-level learning. The old adage of a chain being only as strong as its weakest link applies here. By examining the effects of individual courses and course experiences and then considering the ways that these support teachers' attainment of course and program learning objectives, we can learn which experiences have the greatest effect on teachers' thinking and which ones require revamping or complete change. We next present two examples of course-level research in which we have been engaged for a few years. One of our next steps in ongoing program development is to examine the impact of other Core courses on teacher learning.

EVIDENCE OF THE GROWTH OF TEACHERS' CULTURAL COMPETENCE

Teachers' understanding of diversity and their growth of cultural competence are essential to our ASTL program. Diversity is not only one of our program learning outcomes (outcome six) but also education for social justice is one of the five Core values of our CEHD. With the rapidly changing demographics we are experiencing in the United States, teachers are being increasingly called to meet the needs of culturally and linguistically diverse students in their classrooms. A recent report indicated that by 2020, more than 50 percent of the U.S. public school population will be classified as students of color—that is, African, African American, American Indian, Latino, and Pacific Islander students (National Center for Educational Statistics, 2006, as cited in Ball, 2009, p. 46). Moreover, the first language of a large percentage of these students is not English.

Local classroom populations in our area parallel the demographic changes occurring nationwide. At the same time that these changing demographics are creating culturally and linguistically complex classrooms (Ball, 2009), many teachers in highly diverse schools feel inadequately prepared to teach students from multiple backgrounds (Knight & Wiseman, 2005). This is exactly the case with the teachers in our program who report that they do not feel as prepared as they should be to work effectively with the students in their classrooms. We know that teachers need meaningful professional learning opportunities to build on their classroom experiences and to increase their knowledge and skills, with the goal of increasing their capacities for advocacy, change agency, and efficacy concerning their work with diverse student populations (Delpit, 1995; Sleeter, 2001, 2008).

There is still a great deal to be known about what makes teachers effective as they interact with students in multiple settings, and most studies have focused on preservice teacher education (Cochran-Smith, 2004; Knight and Wiseman, 2005). Teachers may hold biases and assumptions about cultures different from their own (Sleeter, 2001) or stereotype students based on race, ethnicity, or other aspects of their identities. In addition, teachers may be uncomfortable talking about how diversity affects learning contexts or recognizing its significance within classroom interactions (Florio-Ruane, 2001). Race, culture, poverty, special needs, and social justice should be addressed in ways that help teachers recognize their own perspectives and engage in meaningful experiences to develop and expand their cultural competence, which is exactly the course content we address in EDUC 606. The culturally focused action research studies and teachers' reflections are the course-level evidence that have brought us to understand how teachers learn cultural concepts during the ASTL Core and how our ASTL teachers apply these concepts in their classrooms. Data from this course provide the research on what teachers learn about language and culture and what the effect of this knowledge is in their classrooms and in their teaching practice.

The focus of research in EDUC 606, Education and Culture, is on the growth of teachers' knowledge about the role of culture in their classrooms. We use a rubric to evaluate the culturally focused action research study that the teachers conduct (see Appendix E), but we took a step back to study the cohort results and examine ASTL students' learning with regard to our goals as a program. Investigating how teachers developed cultural understanding through the process of teacher research, Wiseman and Fox (2010) explored the nature of teachers' learning during EDUC 606 as they engaged in a culturally focused teacher research study whose goals are to help the teachers acquire cultural, social, and language perspectives on educational processes. An accompanying course goal is to help teachers expand the strategies they can use to improve the effectiveness of their work with diverse learners. The principal question we posed in the study was: In what ways does a graduate-level course with a dual emphasis on developing cultural understanding and inquiry skills through teacher research affect how in-service teachers conceptualize and address culture in their educational settings? Data from multiple cohorts have indicated changes in teacher learning as a result of new readings and new discussion prompts designed to engage teachers in critical conversations, as seen in the following summaries.

The following four main course experiences have been designed for teachers to learn and build knowledge: (1) defining and understanding ideas about culture; (2) developing and reflecting on individual cultural autobiographies to inform individual perspectives and their influence on classroom practice; (3) experiencing and considering culture through simulation; and (4) researching a culturally based, relevant topic in their educational settings that involved questioning, data collection, and reflection. In addition to the initial study, subsequent data have been analyzed from other cohort years that have helped faculty determine the results of the changes and, in turn, identify additional areas of inquiry among the teachers where new readings and discussion prompts were necessary.

In "Supporting Teachers' Development of Cultural Competence through Teacher Research," Wiseman and Fox use qualitative research methods to analyze in-class discussions and conversations, online and written reflections, and the teachers' studies, particularly the types of questions teachers asked. Table 5.1 provides an overview of the foci of the teachers' studies they examined in study one.

Seven of the thirty-four studies focus on males, or groups of males, whereas ten focus on the females; the remainder focuses on mixed gender groups. Eleven of the studies involve ELLs or language acquisition topics, mostly as they pertained to lack of overall academic achievement or failure to "succeed" at grade level; African American vernacular was the focus of a twelfth study that also included language questions. Student behavior, which also included motivation, was a topic addressed in sixteen of the studies. Research about special needs learners, including autism (two studies), and gifted learners (two studies) was a central focus of six studies. Literacy needs, particularly in the area of writing skills, were addressed in nine studies, and four studies involve inquiry about math. In nine of the studies, teachers focus on their classroom cultures from a teacher's perspective, whereas four particularly sought to understand cultural mismatches between home and school culture, including parental involvement (or lack thereof).

As can be seen in Tables 5.2 and 5.3, in subsequent years faculty have seen changes in the foci of the teachers' studies, which have prompted discussions about how classrooms were changing in our area and helped faculty consider new ways to support the teachers' cultural competence. Thus, we

Table 5.1   Foci of ASTL Teachers' Inquiries in Study One

Foci of Puzzlements Found in Cultural Action Research Studies Conducted in EDUC
606 during Study One (Cohort n = 34)

Topic	Detail	*Number of studies in which this topic was included*
	Male	11
Gender focus of the participants in the	Female	10
classroom study	Mixed	13
	And/or language acquisition	11
English Language Learners	questions	1
	African American Vernacular	
Behavior	Includes motivation & male	16
Special Needs learners	Includes autism & gifted	6
Literacy	Note: Some particularly focused on the need for writing skills	9
Math	General instructional practice and homework	4
Classroom culture	From teachers' perspectives	9
Cultural mismatches	Particularly home-school	4

have incorporated new course readings and created new discussion openers
to be more responsive to these changes in the school populations. The results
of these efforts are then to be investigated as part of our programmatic work
during the next academic year as a new cohort engages in the coursework.

Summary of the Findings

Three principal themes emerged as significant findings from the data analysis
of the first study. First, we observed teachers using course readings, discussions, and their own teacher research studies to explore and develop their
understandings of culture through the semester. Second, we found that the
process of conducting research in their own classrooms and developing interventions to test with their learners supported teachers' cultural understanding
and professional practice and created knowledge *for* practice (Cochran-Smith
& Lytle, 1999). Finally, we discovered some teachers were resistant to concepts related to culture and diversity. The following paragraphs elaborate
briefly on each of these three themes.

Table 5.2 Foci of Puzzlements Found in Cultural Action Research Studies Conducted in EDUC 606 Study Two during 2009 (Cohort *n* = 43)

Topic	Detail	Number of studies
Gender focus of the participants in the studies	Male	8
	Female	13
	Mixed	22
English Language Learners & Foreign Language	Language acquisition questions in mainstream classes	13
Behavior	Including motivation & homework	4
Special Learners	Includes gifted & special needs	7
Literacy-focused studies	Including Literacy Circles	
	Some particularly focused on need for writing skills, reading and vocabulary building	16
	English Language Learners & Literacy	
Physical Education	Particularly with motivation	7
Classroom/School culture	From teachers' perspectives	10
Cultural mismatches	Particularly home-school with parents	5

Growth of Cultural Understanding

A key understanding that emerged as the semester progressed was teachers' increased reflection on the complexity of culture and how it is embedded in classroom interactions. It is extremely difficult for one to "see" one's own culture from the inside. Some people don't have the concept of having a culture, such as we saw in Elaine's reflection in the opening vignette. For many of the teachers, a cultural autobiography (Okun, Fried, & Okun, 1999), in which they identified two or more influencing cultures in their lives and then characterized how these cultures influenced their understanding of the world, has become an important aspect of supporting their growing understanding and helping them identify assumptions.

Table 5.3 Foci of Puzzlements Found in Cultural Action Research Studies Conducted in EDUC 606 Study Three during 2011 (Cohort = 35)

Topic	Detail	Number of studies
Gender focus of the participants in the studies	Male	5
	Female	4
	Mixed	26
English Language Learners & Foreign Language	Language acquisition questions in mainstream classes	15
Behavior	Including motivation & homework	10
Special Learners	Includes gifted & special needs	4
Literacy-focused studies	Including Literacy Circles	12
	Some particularly focused on need for writing skills, reading and vocabulary building	
	English Language Learners & Literacy	
Physical Education	Particularly with motivation	4
Classroom / School culture	From teachers' perspectives	10
Cultural mismatches	Particularly home-school with parents	8

As we read the chapter opening, Elaine was extremely surprised to discover that her family and its religious practices were not understood by everyone; she was also surprised that she lived in a cultural environment that others might not completely understand. Her perspectives on life, learning, and schooling were influenced by these perspectives, and she came to understand that not everyone knew those perspectives. Another example from Melissa came in a midsemester reflection which captured well the idea of how some teachers' conceptualizations of culture might evolve:

I'm seeing that Culture is not quickly defined. There is just so much there beyond physical features. I have not thought about my home culture before, or the influences and messages from church, work, or school that have had powerful influences on my life. Or how that might affect the way I see the world or understand my students or respond to their needs. I know that I need to be more aware of my actions and responses to students to increase self-esteem and achievement!

This quote represents not only how Melissa referenced her own experiences to understand her interactions in the classroom but also exemplifies the type of reflections of many of the teachers. Melissa made an important connection from her own cultural identity that illustrated the complexity of culture, recognizing her own position as an important aspect of understanding.

Many teachers were surprised that their questions about classroom dynamics and learning contexts could be related to cultural factors. For instance, Tracy, a fifth grade teacher who described herself as "so jaded with students not doing their homework," decided to investigate her own homework policy in her action research study where she examined how her students responded to homework. Through her study, she realized that homework was related to her classroom culture, and students' timely completion of homework was highly connected to the students' cultures. She was surprised to learn that students' attitudes about homework were inextricably linked to the role that school played in their lives, and as a result of her findings, she had an open discussion with her students and then adjusted her expectations about homework to better fit those of her students. Tracy's study represents the way that many teachers investigated their own assumptions to understand their personal role in classroom dynamics and consider ways to support their students.

Teachers also reported and discussed the connections between their students' home cultures and classroom learning, using this information to design and implement classroom interventions or actions. Throughout several course sessions, we discussed students' home culture and how it influences children's behaviors and understandings at school. In the action research studies, we noted that four of the teachers specifically investigated home–school cultural connections; cultural mismatches comprised nine of the studies.

One teacher reflected, "I do know for sure that I am going to be putting more attention on this culture dynamic and how I participate within it." She went on to explain that she realized that, "I made the mistake of thinking that others are like me" and she elaborated on why understanding home culture vis-à-vis school culture is essential in helping students be successful learners.

Teacher Research as Cultural Understanding

The data also revealed that the process of identifying their own cultural questions and then conducting research in their classroom settings was significant to teachers' professional understanding about culture. When we juxtaposed the concerns and reflections from teachers' school contexts to explore the topics of their practitioner research, we saw that their teacher research studies connected questions about practice to theories and concepts from class in specific ways. An example occurred with Anna, who focused on linguistic diversity and investigated the slang language used in the classroom by her alternative education students. Her initial approach to slang was to "simply discourage or forbid it" within her classroom, but as she conducted her research, her ideas about slang changed as is evidenced by this reflection:

> Students' culture is so important to them and they need to feel respected as individuals. Modification of language does not need to be punitive, and I understand that now. It can be done in a positive manner that still honors the student as unique and valuable and enables them to learn skills that they will take with them beyond my classroom. I had no idea that culture was such a complex entity or would be one of the answers to really helping my students start to walk a bridge to positive learning outcomes as a life skill.

This quote illustrates how Anna questioned her assumptions and ultimately changed her teaching practice in a way that supported students' language use through her research. It was significant to us that she moved beyond a deficit paradigm and toward understanding the complexities of linguistic diversity. There was a direct link between her inquiry, her understanding of diversity, and her pedagogy. In this way, the action research study provided a cultural bridge that fostered new understanding between the teacher and her students.

Yet another educator who applied the concept of culture to her own teaching context was Stacy. Her professional environment was unique in comparison to the rest of the class because she worked at a rural school system and commuted more than an hour to attend class, whereas most of the teachers in this class worked in urban or suburban settings. Stacy researched teachers' attitudes regarding academic acceleration in a rural school system and expressed to us that, "I believe that the greatest value in [teacher research] is that the research question comes from an educator; it develops from his or her teaching experiences and observations." In her research on academic acceleration, Stacy used a survey and observations and found that the teachers in her district needed more information about different students in their classroom and a protocol for understanding how to accelerate students. As a result of her study, Stacy began conducting information sessions and actually developed a protocol to support teachers in their assessment and placement of students. She reported that she needed to "monitor the results" and then make changes. In her case, and for some of the other in-service teachers, she was able to expand her knowledge base and enact change in the schools she worked in as a result of her research. She was also taking an inquiry stance on her own protocol implementation, which provided program faculty with evidence of systematic inquiry of practice (ASTL outcome four).

Challenges

Some of the teachers' conversations and reflections centered on the theme of resistance, including their own queries about what entailed resistance. It was evident in the ways they identified it in their observations and interactions with the teachers. Despite the fact that many teachers critically engaged in inquiry and met the program's diversity outcome solidly, we realized that some teachers maintained a deficit perspective regarding to their views on culture. We noted that as Hyland and Noffke (2005) found in their work with culture and preservice teachers, so was it with certain in-service teachers in our course who also appeared to operate from a deficit paradigm. These teachers seemed to struggle or perhaps resist the idea of recognizing culture, and voiced a belief that assimilation was a goal that would contribute to student success.

There were teachers who did not appear as engaged in the process of considering the implications of culture, and their reflections and classroom discussions even demonstrated a deficit view of students' backgrounds or experiences. One example of a deficit perspective was how teachers might have attributed differences to descriptors such as "work ethic" or "values." For instance, Lucy described how she learned that "not everyone has the same beliefs and work ethic as me" but she felt that "I still believe that students in my classroom and their families need to adapt to the culture of my classroom and how I set the rules." There were also a few instances of denial of racism and racist structures in schooling and society because some teachers refused to believe that these practices were still in place in today's classrooms. For instance, in an online discussion, Holly responded:

> It is frustrating to me with all the hard work that I do as a teacher, that now I
> have to worry about whether or not I accidentally offend someone when trying
> to determine their needs and what I can do to better their education.

Holly's aversion, and her actual resistance to the importance of culture, reflected the idea that some teachers appeared frustrated or overwhelmed with the idea of attending to culture or changing their practice for equity in the classroom.

The initial study of cultural perspectives provided faculty with additional insight into how data from teachers' weekly reflections can provide evidence about the growth of teachers' thinking and perceptions about culture in response to the changes in readings and classroom discussion prompts. In the past four academic years, cohorts have written increasingly about the effect of the changing demographics in their PK–12 classrooms and the inadequacy they feel as they work to meet the individual needs of their learners. The ASTL faculty has increased the amount of information included in EDUC 606 about ELLs and second language acquisition. Elaine's story at the outset of this chapter provides one example of how some ASTL students are engaging in leadership from their classrooms by calling together teams of resource teachers at their schools to provide students with the most comprehensive help possible.

The changes in teachers' awareness of and dispositions toward change showed that there was resistance in some of the teachers. As a result, several changes have been implemented that include the incorporation of specific discussions regarding cultural assumptions earlier in the coursework sequence to support the development of more culturally focused teacher perspectives that foster deeper reflective capacity. For example, the cultural autobiography that was traditionally part of the EDUC 606 has now been moved to the opening course. We did this to initiate discussions about culture early in the Core coursework and to heighten the teachers' awareness about the role of culture in the classroom setting. We also added a cultural perspective to support the development of teachers' critical reflective capacity from the outset. We have made additional changes in some of the readings in the EDUC 606 course itself to include the latest literature in second language acquisition (e.g., Goldenberg, 2008) and different perspectives, such as those presented by Hollins (2008), Kohl (2002), and Purcell-Gates (2002).

Results of the research in which faculty have been engaged on EDUC 606 have suggested that culturally based action research, when carefully scaffolded and accompanied by critical readings, has the potential to support the growth of cultural understanding in our teachers. Through the interventions the teachers developed during their action research studies, both the teachers and faculty explored the resultant pedagogical applications of their new knowledge on learners. There is more to learn about the effectiveness of certain interventions that ASTL students have implemented in their PK–12 classrooms and about how the monitoring of these interventions might inform changes in our ASTL students' pedagogical practice.

As a result of introducing cultural perspectives in the first course in the Core, we have also asked that ASTL students consciously consider cultural perspectives and assumptions that might be present when they conduct their case study of a learner during EDUC 613. Our plan is to continue to engage in course-level research to examine the development of cultural knowledge and consider the results through teachers' reflections, course performance assessments, self-analyses, and post-program interviews. In the next study, you will find evidence of ASTL students' growth regarding educational change.

EVIDENCE OF TEACHER GROWTH
REGARDING EDUCATIONAL CHANGE

A second body of course-based evidence explores educational change. ASTL learning outcome seven states that "teachers are change agents, teacher leaders, and partners with colleagues." This learning outcome is addressed in several course assignments during the Core, but it is primarily addressed during the final course, EDUC 615, Educational Change. In their study, Lukacs, Horak, and Galluzzo (2010) examined ASTL students' self-efficacy as it occurred at the end of the program coursework, and specifically during the seven week, two-credit course, the culminating course in the program. This course focuses particularly on the problems, issues, and possibilities associated with bringing change to education. During their portfolio presentations, students usually talk about how important they have found this course to be and how much it has influenced their thinking about their role as leaders in their schools. The course really challenges the ASTL students to consider their roles as teacher leaders and agents of change in their educational settings. The faculty have found that many of the ASTL students, and particularly the early career ASTL students, have not considered prior to this course the effect their leadership can have beyond their own classrooms.

In this study on learning, thirty-six ASTL students were asked to investigate the influences on the education system from the national, state, community, school, and classroom levels, and further explored these influences with specific regard to their effects on school improvement. Lecture, group discussions, videos, simulations, and other activities during eight class sessions comprised the course delivery. Faculty begin the course with a discussion that helps ASTL students put the current era of educational reform into context by asking them to analyze the history of related national policy. Policy is also not a topic that the teachers have often considered as being relevant to their teaching. Next, the ASTL students engage in an analytical decision-making process designed to rank the competing priorities of their school culture according to their seriousness, urgency, and potential for growth. At this point, ASTL students are also introduced to the fundamental elements of grant writing. One component included in the fundamentals of grant writing is an emphasis on encapsulating and articulating ideas in such a way as to be clear and memorable to potential funders who may or may not have experience within the field of education. The importance of professional communities and collaborative expertise (learning outcome five) are also emphasized as essential elements of successful grant writing.

Teacher Change Agent Scale

The Teacher Change Agent Scale (TCAS) (Lukacs, 2009), a fifteen-item scale designed to measure teachers' willingness to be change agents within their school context, was administered both before the course began and at the end of the course. Given that the majority of the ASTL students ($n = 36$) at this point in their program coursework were taking only this course and were working in different schools and school systems, faculty felt it was reasonable to assume that the course would be the "cause" of any results obtained, especially given that students enter this class with high levels of uncertainty about their ability to be agents of change (Galluzzo & Hilldrup, 2005). In other words, because there were no outside influences (such as another course or a school-based professional development workshop), we interpreted any whole group changes in responses to the TCAS to be the result of participation in the course.

Results of the Study

The results suggest that there is both good news and bad news for teacher educators who wish to help teachers become agents of change. On the one hand, a course specifically designed to analyze and reflect on the problems, issues, and possibilities associated with bringing change to education made a difference in increasing teachers' willingness to "take a chance" and to express their ideas to their colleagues. In addition, it would seem that a course on change also made it possible for teachers to realize their abilities to influence and motivate their colleagues. In other words, it can be said that teachers' feelings of self-empowerment, motivation, and ability to take risks, all of which are vital for school improvement to be successful (e.g., Day, Elliot, & Kington, 2005; Muijs & Harris, 2003), can be increased in a teacher education course.

The findings also suggest that these ASTL students were hesitant to use their newfound skills. For example, while fostering students' beliefs in the abilities of teachers in general to initiate change, this course appeared to make no difference when it came to helping them feel more positive about their specific school context and colleagues. As a result of this course, these teachers felt that teachers can and should work together, but with regard to their own personal teaching situations, they continue to remain less willing to rely on others and prefer to work in isolation. As such, although they are prepared to take risks and to "speak out," these teachers are unlikely to realize their abilities to be change agents because they may also feel influenced by their own school's context.

The idea that "context matters" is a thorny one for teacher educators who want to help their students become agents of change because it is highly unlikely that a faculty or program could accurately predict what skills or abilities will be needed in each of the various possible contexts in which students might find themselves. However, if the faculty hopes to have teachers capable of being more than pedagogical experts with strong classroom management skills (Goodlad, 1998) by working in their schools to initiate school improvement efforts, it appears as though they need assistance in learning how to identify "change friendly" contexts and colleagues.

Many questions remain as a result of this work. Are ASTL graduates as confident in their abilities to be agents of change a year after taking the course? In two years? In five? Do they go on to pursue school improvements on their own initiative once the course is over? If they reported feeling hesitant to work with others, what specific aspects of their school context do they find most stifling? Do the results of this course vary according to whether the teacher is an early career or experienced educator? A programmatic study following this one (Fox, White, Muccio, & Tian, 2011) investigated early career and experienced teachers' learning during advanced professional learning. Is the length of this course really long enough to be able to measure change in teachers, or should we measure growth over a longer period and consider the changes that might be the result of the entire program? Regardless, as teachers are called to become more active in school reform and as teacher education programs become more active in helping them do this, we feel that we have taken an important first step at understanding the potential obstacles that may have to be addressed as we attempt to teach teachers how to make a difference in their schools.

In response to the final question posed in the preceding paragraph, faculty decided to administer two teacher efficacy measures previously administered only during the last course of the education Core during the first course in the Core sequence. In this way, we would like to measure teacher efficacy pre-Core and then again during the final course of the Core. This way faculty can consider if, and which types of, changes might occur over a broader period. The results of this study will allow us to continue to build our theory on how to best scaffold learning for practicing teachers, both early career and experienced. When we seek to understand the results of our efforts, we are also engaging in critical reflection that emphasizes potential ways that "theory and practice dialogue both within and without the classrooms" (Fecho, 2004, p. 41).

IMPLICATIONS OF COURSE LEVEL EVIDENCE-BASED
RESEARCH FOR THE PROGRAM FACULTY

Conducting course-level research using performance-based evidence has provided us with data not only from a faculty perspective but also from the perspectives of the ASTL students. Through the evaluation of performance assessments, the faculty began to determine what ASTL students have learned
as a result of coursework and to identify some of the challenging aspects of
the program that remain. Our course-level research coupled with analysis of
performance-based evidence provide both general and specific information
about the efficacy of course content, feedback on faculty teaching within and
across courses, and feedback on our teachers' learning.

The evidence from research and course-level performance assessments has
provided data for our consideration and dialogue to support the suggestions
we determine for change. We could see from the course level data what was
and was not working. We will see if future cohorts of ASTL students are
similar to or different from current students in the program, and research on
their learning will serve to validate these changes or inform additional course
changes.

There is no doubt that the successful implementation of performance-
based assessments in any program requires an organized approach and
implementation process. It's true that this is time-consuming and requires the
investment of a program's faculty, but it enables us to consider the results of
individual courses and then look at them in light of the program as a whole. It
is this culture of inquiry that comes alive for us during research discussions.
This approach requires a commitment to formative evaluation to inform
change. For us, the iterative process we have used to achieve research-based
implementation of a successful programmatic performance-based assessment
system has taken time, but it has provided honest data about our program and
our coursework.

Program inquiry at the course level has now become central to our work.
In the next chapter, you will see how embedded inquiry contributes to the
program level research that we have been conducting. In conclusion to this
chapter, we share with you a reflection by Fecho (2004) that captures the essence of this aspect of our research within the program:

> I have come to see learning as a mesh of transactions. Classrooms are places
> where these transactions occur. It is important to realize or remember that trans-
> actions occur in all classrooms, that we shape and are shaped by the stories,
> people, patterns, sounds, and other contextual items present in all classrooms,
> no matter what the pedagogy. What is significant in a critical inquiry classroom
> is that these transactions are not only acknowledged, but inquired into. (p. 143)

Our ASTL classrooms provide laboratories for studying teacher learning. Our decisions about teaching are shaped by the ASTL students, their needs, their dialogue, and their stories. By continually engaging in critical inquiry ourselves, we maintain one of our program goals, that of implementing inquiry-based learning in our program.

What are our next steps in course level research? These are two courses where we have systematically conducted research. We would like to incorporate this approach to course-based research in each of the courses. We need to nurture these studies and then continue to build capacity. We've invested a decade in developing the research approaches, and with each cohort, we learn about what changes we think are necessary and yet we need to move forward with additional lines of inquiry that will tell us more about what teachers need and what the impact of their professional learning is on the students in their PK–12 classrooms.

CONCLUSION

By understanding the individual learning components that are part of each course's experiences, faculty can make changes, consider the effects of these changes at the end of the course, and examine their results at the conclusion of the Core, the program, and beyond. This approach to course-level research has added important data from inside the program coursework to support our understanding of program results and consider learning trends in our program-level research.

In the vignette opening this chapter, Elaine shared her perceptions about how her ability to reflect had changed since the outset of the program. Course-level research in the growth of reflectivity and teacher efficacy has helped us to understand aspects of ASTL students' growth and change during the program that overall program evaluation and end-of-program summative data may not reveal. The research approach we use in the ASTL program, as described in this chapter, helps frame a recursive approach to program renewal (Cochran-Smith & Lytle, 1999) that is part of our program's and our college's goal of continuous improvement. Course-level research allows us to get inside the workings of program learning to better understand the incremental pieces that comprise the pathway toward achieving the program's eight learning outcomes. By acknowledging the learning that occurs in individual courses, critical inquiry into the learning that occurs in that course can create many opportunities for program faculty and ASTL students to be both teachers and learners. All teachers' classrooms are laboratories, and in ASTL, our course-level inquiry provides a laboratory for investigating aspects of course effectiveness.

6

Evidence of Program Effectiveness

Roberta, a lead teacher in a private preschool, began the ASTL Core classes after completing the first three of six early childhood concentration classes. In her early childhood classes she easily related to the content and quickly established connections with her fellow students. When she began the Core coursework it was an adjustment for her to work with teachers outside of early childhood and she was hesitant to speak up in large groups. Before the first Core class she rated her level of understanding of each of the ASTL learning outcomes as moderate to strong on almost all of the outcomes. For instance, in describing her strong understanding of the learning outcome student learning, she wrote, "This is one of the main reasons I became a teacher in the first place and my commitment has only grown over the years." However, Roberta also acknowledged room for growth in her practice, as when she commented about her moderate understanding of the outcome systematic inquiry of practice, "I often do learn a lot from experiences, but I don't always take the time to reflect." She commented on how her teaching has affected her students' learning when she shared, "My teaching has increased young children's love of learning, hopefully. My classroom is a fun and comfortable environment filled with hands-on, experimental learning." Her beginning of Core comments and rating from the self-evaluation provided information about her professional experiences and perceptions of her understanding of the ASTL Core outcomes.

After the first four months in the program, during the first reflection, Roberta reported an important change in herself.

> At this point in the Core, I feel I have grown tremendously as a teacher and a learner. When I entered the Core in May, I was kind of taking my job for granted. It was a lot of fun to be a preschool teacher; basically, I got paid to

play all day. After teaching preschool for six years, however, I began to feel stuck. As I wrote about in countless journal entries and reflections before this, I was feeling uninspired and unmotivated to change anything about my practice, even if it meant better serving my students. Once I began the Core, however, my outlook changed. Through everything we've done thus far, I have learned that I am the one who can change the way I teach and how my students succeed—and it is not an impossible task. For me, that is quite a powerful realization.

Roberta reiterated her increased confidence and motivation and its influence on her students in subsequent reflections. In the middle of the Core coursework she shared, "a higher level of confidence and the feeling that I can understand my children and my own teaching if I just stop for a minute and ask the right question." As Roberta transitioned into a leadership position at the end of the Core, she commented, "I feel I am better prepared now to take on my new role as leader in my school and I have the school and the knowledge to recruit my learning community to do the same." On her end of the Core self-assessment, Roberta acknowledges the role of the ASTL program in her learning. She rated her level of understanding each ASTL learning outcome as strong, similar to her beginning of core responses. For the learning outcome student learning, Roberta expresses a sense of renewal when she states, "Commitment is something I have plenty of. ASTL has given me greater skills to enhance my teaching."

During her last early childhood class at the end of her master's degree, Roberta frequently referred to the core outcomes of student learning, monitoring student learning, systematic inquiry of practice, and change agent. Her commitment to students and her practice continued after she completed the program, as evident in a post-program interview conducted one year after she completed the program. Roberta described the changes in her practice as a result of her experiences in the ASTL program, "I feel like after doing all of that, I really started being a lot more intentional with my teaching, kind of knowing why I was doing what I was doing and really focusing on the kids as opposed to what's easiest for me and what we did to cover this skill last year. . ." and highlighted her effects on student learning when she shared, "I pay a lot more attention now to each individual student, and not that I didn't before, but maybe I'm noticing it more now. I feel like I take a lot more time to get to know them and, um, kind of see what they're interested in and run with that."

This synopsis of Roberta's professional journey through ASTL highlights how the program uses multiple forms of evidence to evaluate teachers' learning and how program faculty are studying their own practices. Effective assessment practices that provide concrete evidence of teacher education graduates' knowledge has become an increasingly significant issue (Cochran-Smith, 2001; Darling-Hammond, 2006). As an integral part of the ASTL program, we have investigated ASTL students' understanding of the program learning outcomes using multiple measures. That is, our work has focused on obtaining a more comprehensive view of what teachers learn and what the program can contribute to their performance (Darling-Hammond, 2006). Although grades earned during coursework provide some information about ASTL students' professional learning, we contend that measures used to evaluate their understanding of learning outcomes may provide a more comprehensive understanding of teacher development. Since program evaluation has been a critical component of the program's design from the outset, we continue to use the visions of teaching and learning that guide our program to develop and refine coursework as well as to evaluate the program's overall impact on our teachers' learning (Darling-Hammond, 2000; Zeichner, 2006).

In this chapter we focus on using outcomes to assess program effectiveness. We describe the findings from three different types of programmatic evidence that have helped us determine the program's effect on students' understanding of our outcomes. As we mentioned in chapter 2, program evaluation was a guiding principle when the program was conceptualized and has informed our efforts over the last ten years. The three examples of data we have included in this chapter represent different types of evidence collected and analyzed at specific points in time to inform us about ASTL students' learning in relation to the outcomes. These three examples include: (1) a summary of a published study in which different measures of program outcomes were used with particular groups or cohorts of students; (2) a recent follow-up study using interviews with teachers in one particular concentration, physical education; and, (3) our latest endeavor to obtain feedback through an electronic questionnaire from teachers who have graduated earlier in the program. Although we have used these different types of evidence to seek a better understanding of how teachers change during the core sequence of coursework and how program outcomes may or may not be achieved, we continue to consider how we can intentionally incorporate additional measures that can be used systematically with all current and former students.

USING OUTCOMES TO ASSESS PROGRAM EFFECTIVENESS

As with many master's degree programs for experienced teachers, teachers enrolling in ASTL coursework begin the program with varying backgrounds, years of experience, and different needs and goals. We recognize the importance of understanding the unique professional development needs of experienced teachers to obtain one of our overarching goals, helping teachers move toward thoughtful actions. Consequently, we have systematically followed Cochran-Smith's (2001) suggestion that using standards to indicate what teachers know and can do leads to productive examination of teacher practices. Since the design of the ASTL program incorporates NBPTS standards as the foundation for our practices, we use the NBPTS propositions along with our three additional standards to provide a consensual, research-grounded view of what teachers should know and be able to do (Darling-Hammond, 2006). We believe that the eight program outcomes provide a path toward establishing evidence-based assessment systems that can incorporate multiple measures for examining teacher practices during and upon completion of the ASTL program. In addition, we have used the assessment of outcomes as a way to examine teacher educators' efforts for ongoing program improvement, including changes in curriculum and pedagogy (Darling-Hammond, 2006; Fox & White, 2010; Fox, White, Kidd, & Ritchie, 2008).

While there are research studies that compare the experiences of credentialed teachers with those who either earned alternative certification or none at all (Shoho & Martin, 1999; Turley & Nakai, 2000), and research that examines the usefulness of formal teacher preparation for those with prior teaching experience (Kunzman, 2003), there are fewer studies on master's degree programs for experienced teachers (Tom, 1999). In 1999, Tom called for more research on successful master's degrees and argued that, "the paucity of the research literature on innovative programs is a major barrier to the overall reform of Master's degree study for experienced teachers" (p. 251).

Unfortunately, more than a decade later only a few research studies on innovative master's level degree programs for teachers exist. In a study conducted by Manfra and Bolicks (2008) it was found that an emphasis on ongoing professional development, cohort grouping, student learning, and the use of technology responded to the unique circumstances of social studies teachers enrolled in an M.Ed. program. Manfra and Bolicks (2008) conclude that these experiences provided social studies teachers with the pedagogical content knowledge and resources necessary to become change agents in their schools. Wenzlaff and Wieseman (2004) studied cohort-based, interdisciplinary master's degree programs and conclude that the curriculum in programs for experienced teachers should provide opportunities to discuss learning theories, introduce teachers to use research-informed practices, and provide opportunities to participate in professional learning communities. Moreover, the authors found that active, situated learning with multiple opportunities to apply learning in teachers' respective classrooms encouraged teachers to improve their practice. Wenzlaff and Wieseman (2004) contend that a collaborative culture comprised of teachers from different levels of schooling and content areas as well as different district contexts can help teachers broaden their perspectives about teaching, learning, and educational systems.

While there continues to be a scarcity of research specific to innovative master's degree programs for experienced teachers, the evidence-based education movement, which holds that decisions about practice and policy should be made on the basis of empirical evidence about outcomes, has gained a firm foothold (Cochran-Smith & Boston College Evidence Team, 2009). According to Cochran-Smith and Boston College Evidence Team (2009), a culture of evidence and inquiry builds the capacity within teacher education programs to assess progress and effectiveness, shifts accountability from external policy to also include internal practice, and generates knowledge used both in local programs and more broadly. That is, an inclusive academic culture of research, rigorous standards, and respect for evidence provides for a self-correcting and continually improving teacher education program. In ASTL, adhering to these principles and recognizing that using multiple data sources involve ongoing efforts, rethinking, and mechanisms to sustain evidence-based decision making (Cochran-Smith & Boston College Evidence Team, 2009).

The ASTL faculty also refer to research specific to effective professional development in school settings that is not focused on university graduate education. We rely on this literature to guide our use of evidence to evaluate how program outcomes may or may not be achieved. For example, we have considered the importance of the contexts ASTL students bring to our classes and the need to consider not only teachers' own contexts but also the program's demands on teachers and how those demands can be met within their school contexts (Desimone, 2009). We have also considered the importance of coherence in terms of ASTL students' interpretations of how well aligned the professional development activities are with their learning for PK–12 students and themselves. We acknowledge that a professional development activity is more likely to be effective in improving teachers' knowledge and skills if it forms a coherent part of a wider set of opportunities for teacher learning and development (Desimone, 2009; Garet, Porter, Desimone, Birman, & Yoon, 2001). Consequently, the evidence used to investigate ASTL students' understanding of program learning outcomes has been derived from data embedded in the Core classes. By using data, such as ASTL students' reflections, we have examined their interpretations and understanding of the learning outcomes across the Core classes. Specifically, we seek evidence that can inform us about whether the ASTL students perceive a sense of coherence between their learning experiences and the program learning outcomes. Similarly, we use self-assessments and follow-up interviews to focus on the application of course content and learning experiences to ASTL students' own professional contexts during and after they complete program coursework. The following three programmatic research summaries provide evidence specific to ASTL students' understanding and application of learning outcomes that have been collected over time with multiple cohorts of ASTL students.

EVIDENCE DERIVED FROM STUDIES USING MULTIPLE MEASURES OF PROGRAM OUTCOMES

In the multiyear study, "Investigating Teachers' Professional Learning in an Advanced Master's Degree Program" (White, Fox, & Isenberg, 2011), we examine specific data within and across multiple cohorts of ASTL students to document the changes in their professional learning. The study focuses on: (1) pre- and post-program self-assessments of how ASTL students rated their experience level and understanding of the eight program learning outcomes prior to and following the Core; (2) prompted reflections, the way the ASTL students' reflective writings demonstrated growth and change in reflection related to program learning outcomes as they progressed through the Core; and (3) the ASTL students' perceptions of how they have sustained the program learning outcomes one year after completing the Core. Eighty-nine ASTL students ranging in one to twenty-two years of teaching experience in PK–junior college participated in this study. These participants represented three cohorts or groups of students enrolled in the ASTL program over a period of three years. Twenty ASTL students were selected from the original pool of participants for follow-up interviews.

We used three data sources in this study: (1) pre- and post-program self-assessments, (2) five sets of prompted reflections written at specified points during the education Core, and (3) follow-up interviews. Data were collected from the participants using the pre- and post-program assessments and prompted reflections that referred to specific program learning outcomes. The follow-up interviews were conducted one year after participants completed the Core. We designed the interview questions to ascertain perceptions about coursework in relation to program learning outcomes.

Data were analyzed using qualitative research methods, particularly coding and categorizing (Glesne, 1999; Maxwell, 2005). Pre- and post-program self-assessments that measured participants' perceived level of understanding of each program learning outcome were tabulated, compared, and connected to teachers' comments regarding these outcomes. Each set of prompted reflections were first hand-coded and analyzed by learning outcome and emergent themes (Maxwell, 2005). Further, a count of the number of times each ASTL student mentioned any of the eight learning outcomes was recorded for each reflection set. A content analysis of cross-program reflections was conducted to look for evidence of change in ASTL students' reflective writing, such as changes that occurred in their language, references to course readings, and relevance of examples drawn from their teaching settings. The interviews with twenty ASTL students were recorded and transcribed; researchers coded the interviews for connections to the learning outcomes using passage counts and allowed additional themes to emerge. We summarize the findings for each of the three data sources; pre- and post-program self-assessments, prompted reflections, and follow-up interviews separately, and then discuss the findings across the three data sources.

Pre-Program and Post-Program Self-Assessments

The self-assessments asked participants to evaluate their level of experience and understanding of the eight learning outcomes at both the beginning and the end of the education Core. Participants used a four-point scale from zero to three (i.e., zero indicates no understanding of the outcome; three indicates strong understanding) and explained why they rated themselves this way. Across the three groups, the participants expressed a moderate or strong understanding of the majority of outcomes during the pre- and post-program self-assessments, with a shift toward the strong level of understanding by the end of the Core. The results indicated that 40 percent of the average of the responses across the outcomes was at the strong level of understanding on the pre-assessment. The level of understanding increased 20 percent on the post-program self-assessment, with nearly 60 percent of the average responses indicated a strong level of understanding. The majority stated that they possessed a moderate or strong understanding of each outcome at the beginning of the program.

Qualitative analysis of participants' comments regarding their understanding of each learning outcome revealed several differences among the participants' applications to their classrooms in the pre- and post-program self-assessments. Initial self-assessment data indicated ASTL students' understanding of the importance of the different outcomes, defined what the outcome meant, and described their beliefs about the outcome. Many of the participants' responses began with "I believe" or "I think" when commenting on particular outcomes. In contrast, the comments on the post-program self-assessments focused on applying the outcome to participants' own teaching and included rich examples drawn from their classrooms.

A detailed analysis of differences between and among the three cohort groups highlighted the extent and nature of the participants' knowledge of each of the eight learning outcomes. The majority of group I teachers reported their level of understanding as strong for six outcomes, excluding systematic inquiry of practice and technology. Group II participants expressed a moderate level of understanding for five outcomes: content and pedagogy, monitoring learning, systematic inquiry of practice, diversity, and change agent. Of the group III participants, the majority indicated a strong understanding of just two outcomes, student learning (the strongest area across the three cohort groups), and learning communities. The majority of group III participants reported a moderate level of understanding for diversity, monitoring student learning, and change agent on the pre-program self-assessment. Across groups, the outcomes of student learning and learning communities had the greatest percentage of respondents rating themselves as having a strong understanding. The outcomes technology, systematic inquiry of practice, and change agent had the highest number of participants in the three groups who reported a minimal level of understanding at the beginning of the program.

Prompted Reflections

The five sets of prompted reflections written to an ungraded guided prompt at specified points during the education Core for the three different groups provided general trends across cohorts. We identified changes that occurred across the program from early to later prompted reflections by analyzing the number of times (reported in percentages) participants discussed one or more of the eight outcomes. For example, in reflection one, using the total group average, the number of times participants mentioned *systematic inquiry of practice* accounted for 22 percent of the mentioned outcomes across the three cohorts. The next most frequently mentioned outcomes were diversity (19 percent), monitoring student learning (15 percent), and student learning (14 percent). The least frequently mentioned outcomes were change agent at 4 percent, technology at 7 percent, and content knowledge and pedagogy at 8 percent. These percentages correspond to the content of the two courses that were taken at the beginning of the program when participants completed the first reflection.

Using the total group average, a similar pattern in reflections two, three, and four was found. For example, in reflection two, in which systematic inquiry of practice remained the most frequently referenced outcome (20 percent), the course corresponding to reflection two focused on analyzing assessment and instruction. At reflection three, it was not a surprise that diversity was mentioned in 25 percent of the reflection passages because the course preceding that reflection focused on the role of culture and diversity. At reflection four, written after the course on teachers as change agents, the change agent learning outcome represented 28 percent of the reflection passages.

The synthesis reflection, written at the end of the course sequence, asked participants to reflect on their learning across the program and to comment on each of the eight learning outcomes. The reference to learning outcomes in this reflection corresponded less to the content in particular courses and provided a more retrospective reference to those outcomes addressed at the close of program coursework. Using the total group average, the most frequently mentioned outcomes at the conclusion of the course sequence were content knowledge and pedagogy (19 percent), change agent (18 percent), diversity (15 percent), student learning (13 percent), and systematic inquiry of practice (13 percent). Monitoring student learning was mentioned in 10 percent of the synthesis reflections while learning community was mentioned in 9 percent of the passages and technology was the least referred to outcome. In comparing individual group percentages, for the content knowledge and pedagogy outcome there was higher variation among the groups than in other outcomes. For this outcome, group II referred to content knowledge and pedagogy in 26 percent of the synthesis reflections whereas group I mentioned it in 11 percent of the reflections.

Following the coding of the eight learning outcomes and analysis of the program outcome frequencies, the data were then analyzed qualitatively to determine the nature of the content for each prompted reflection. Analysis of the narrative data in the prompted reflections indicated that participants' provided a deeper understanding of the meaning of the outcomes as well as how the outcomes could be applied to their classroom practice. The reflections across all coursework demonstrated a trend in the sophistication of participants' use of language. A comparison of reflections from the beginning of Core coursework to those at the end of coursework indicated a change in language from more superficial statements to statements that included more specific examples and clear references to course content at the end of coursework.

Follow-up Interview Data

In-person interviews using open-ended questions were conducted with program graduates one year after they completed study in the education Core. Data for eight participants were available from both groups I and III with four participants from group II. Questions focused on the eight learning outcomes to examine the ways that participants might continue to apply knowledge and skills learned in the education Core in their teaching. Interviews were recorded and transcribed and coded for learning outcomes, and then for emergent themes.

The overall responses across the three groups were very similar. For example, across the groups, diversity appeared to have a substantial impact on participants as reported in the interviews. Group I interview responses related to diversity comprised 17 percent of the responses; group II responses made up 31 percent while group III responses about diversity totaled 23 percent. Many of the participants mentioned that upon entry into the program they were unaware of the complexity of diversity, how "culture" is a key piece of this concept, not merely skin color or language. Through the interviews, it became evident that participants talked about how they began looking at each individual student, "The biggest impact was recognizing the diversity of learners, and of course you see them in the classroom . . . but realizing that you know they don't really, some kids aren't intrinsically motivated and don't enjoy school" (respondent 32). Overall, the percentages for diversity were highest at an average of 23 percent.

Student learning comprised the second highest total for the learning outcomes, with 9–26 percent of the responses. The overall average response rate for this outcome was 18 percent. The data suggest that the education Core coursework influenced how participants view student learning. For example, respondent 18 said,

> [T]rying to see the patterns in their learning and the progression of where they're at and having a clear understanding of where they were . . . and hopefully developing a plan of where they eventually will be.

Content knowledge was another outcome that resulted in a higher number of responses. The overall average response rate for the content knowledge outcome was 15 percent. Respondent 32 said,

> My knowledge of how you learn to read went from zero to so much more because I don't remember being taught to read. I don't remember how people learned to read from school. I didn't know any of the terminology or what the learning awareness meant, because my teaching had been with the older kids and didn't have to do any of that. So how can kids learn how to read? That was huge for me.

The learning community outcome also resulted in a higher number of responses with the response rate ranging between 15 and 16 percent. Participants discussed the importance of working together both within their content areas and across the Core. Respondent 30 shared her experience with some research she had completed at her school when she stated, "I got to share the outcomes and the individual strategies and the readings actually with [a colleague]. We did a lot of collaborative work together."

The final four learning outcomes were mentioned much less frequently than the previously mentioned program outcomes. Monitoring student learning and systematic inquiry of practice passage counts for all three groups averaged just over 7 percent. Comments related to being a change agent varied the most with group I at 5 percent, group II at 16 percent, and group III at 8 percent. Participants did not consistently articulate an understanding of their own leadership, and often the interviewees did not appear to understand fully the meaning of the term "change agent." Finally, the technology outcome was rarely mentioned in these interviews. Since technology was referred to infrequently throughout all of the interviews, it appears as if it were not one of the more pervasive outcomes impacting participants' practices one year after leaving this degree program.

After coding for the eight learning outcomes, the language and terminology used to describe the participants' understanding of the outcomes was analyzed. Five broad themes emerged from the interview data: reflection, increased self-confidence/empowerment, life-long learning, leadership, and self-awareness of pedagogical choices. These five themes were found to articulate participants' incorporation of the learning outcomes as part of their professional practice.

Reflection was discussed often by almost all participants. Respondent 18 summarized the overall sense of all of the participants when she said, "But the main thing that—for me I wouldn't even choose a specific principle. It's just more being reflective and aware of my teaching practices." Leadership was another theme that the participants discussed. Interview data suggested that participants felt more empowered after having completed the program, to assume leadership roles. Respondent 9 illustrated the serious changes in leadership for her.

> I've become more vocal about things that I want to see happen in the building. I've taken on more leadership roles. I am team leader this year for my team. We had to write a grant for that class and I got my grant, so I am pumped up about that.

The analysis of interview data resulted in a unique view of how this program affects the beliefs and practices of its participants. It is apparent that some of the outcomes continue to influence the ASTL students and their teaching one year after completing coursework. Other learning outcomes appear to have a less powerful impact.

Summary of Multiple Measures Research

Our research examining the use of multiple measures to consider ASTL students' understanding of program outcomes yielded three primary implications:

(1) multiple measures can be used to examine a program's effects on teacher learning; (2) prompted reflections can provide evidence of a program's influence on teacher thinking; and (3) program structure and content are important elements to consider when designing and assessing programs for experienced teachers. Our findings suggest that advanced programs can use multiple measures to examine a program's effects on teachers' professional learning. These findings reflect Darling-Hammond's (2006) suggestion that the use of multiple measures aligned with teacher education outcomes can lead to a more comprehensive view of what teachers know and are able to do and what a program contributes to their professional learning.

As seen in the opening vignette, Roberta's self-assessments, reflections, and follow-up interview responses provide a more complete picture of a teacher's understanding of program outcomes before, during, and after the Core courses. Although we would like to consider teachers such as Roberta as representative of most if not all teachers who complete the program, our data tells us otherwise. For example, we find in most cohorts that there are teachers who do not demonstrate a pathway of growth and change from the beginning to end of the Core. These teachers often do not reflect as deeply as Roberta, do not articulate as much awareness of their influence on students' learning, nor do they indicate a willingness to assume responsibilities as change agents. Consequently, data from our multiple measures evidence have influenced how we consider different characteristics of our students such as years of teaching experience and previous teacher education coursework when planning and teaching Core courses. For example, when placing ASTL students in small groups we strategically establish groups that are comprised of students with different years of experience to consider how Dewey's levels of reflection apply to prompted reflection excerpts the ASTL students have written. We have also become more cognizant of building background knowledge when presenting classics such as Dewey's writing about reflection or Piaget's theories of cognitive development. When considering critical periods of development on adolescents' learning, we ask ASTL students who have previous coursework in child development to scaffold others in their group on Piaget's developmental ages and stages when developing content for a scenario designed to develop points for professional colleagues to address pupils who do not demonstrate abstract reasoning. Additionally, we've learned that it is important to explicitly address the purpose, importance, and relevance of the program learning outcomes in all of the Core classes. For example, we explain the importance of the ASTL program learning outcomes in each of the Core classes as we discuss the role of assessment in standards-based instruction. The multiple measures evidence continues to inform our own practices as we gauge our teachers' changes in their understanding and application of the program learning outcomes.

EVIDENCE DERIVED FROM FOLLOW-UP INTERVIEWS WITH ONE CONCENTRATION: PHYSICAL EDUCATION

Interviews with six elementary and secondary physical education ASTL students were conducted one year after they completed the program as the first group of students to complete the physical education Concentration. These post-program interviews provide an example of program evaluation from the perspective of program participants in a specific Concentration area. The feedback from the participants provided valuable information on their learning and professional development as a result of the new program Concentration. The analysis of the data highlighted the unique experiences of this cohort of program completers as the eight program learning outcomes did not capture the experiences reported in the interviews. Instead, five emergent themes were identified based on an iterative and collaborative coding process conducted by several researchers. The emergent themes were diversity, technology, obstacles, increased professional confidence, and assessment/differentiation. While some overlap between the program learning outcomes, particularly with the themes of diversity and technology, were evident, the other three themes emerging from the data analysis suggested that the ways in which the ASTL physical education students apply their learning in their current professional settings differed from program completers in other Concentrations.

A content analysis within these themes revealed distinct ways that the participants discussed each theme. Overall, the interview participants most frequently discussed their increased professional confidence, particularly in terms of their increased capacities to provide choices to PK–12 students and to differentiate their instruction based on students' needs and abilities. For example, a high school physical education teacher reported,

> [S]tudents have more ownership and more involvement in the learning process and have leadership opportunities. . . . Every student's given kind of a task with their own team so you see all the students engaged, whereas teaching team sports without the sport education model, some students never get a chance to shine.

This quotation reflects similar comments by other participants, indicating that they applied content from the physical education coursework to meet the needs of a wide range of PK–12 students, including culturally diverse students and students with disabilities. An elementary school physical education teacher shared her growth in the area of diversity when she stated,

In the past, I tried to talk when I look into the eye of the students. Now I know there are certain cultures that don't think it's polite. . . . I try to think about that as I'm talking with the students and think about what in their culture is appropriate and what is not.

The participants referred to content addressed in the program regarding how different instructional approaches can be used to meet PK–12 students' individual needs, including the use of assessment and teacher research as tools for differentiation.

The participants also mentioned an increased self-confidence or sense of empowerment one year after completing the program. One elementary school physical education teacher said that the ASTL program "gave me more confidence. I really do know what I'm talking about. I'm a good teacher and I can do this. I'm knowledgeable about my subject area. I can show that to somebody. I can help them in any way." Other examples of empowerment that the participants discussed were increased abilities to collaborate with colleagues, working with student teachers, or serving as a lead or mentor teacher, leading professional development for other teachers, writing curriculum, initiating new programs or instructional models, and applying for grants. A high school physical education and health teacher provided evidence of the leadership roles she had assumed when she noted, "I have been a department chair; this is my second year at the high school level. I was also department chair at the middle school level, so I've always kind of been engaged in improvement and change in the department." Interestingly, at the same time as the participants underscored their increased professional confidence, they also discussed a variety of obstacles related to their practice.

The discussion of obstacles primarily referred to the identification of a variety of barriers to implementing practices they had learned about during the ASTL program. In discussing the implementation of a new elective model, a high school physical education and health teacher described her frustrations, "But it's hard because then there's a couple of periods that I teach with teachers who don't want to do the electives. . . . It's pretty hard." While this ASTL student is confident in the new approach to provide PK–12 students with more choices to better meet their needs, the fact that she isn't able to obtain cooperation from all of the physical education teachers in their schools is a significant obstacle.

The resistance to change by their peer physical education teachers, and by other teachers and administrators in their school buildings, was echoed by interview participants at the elementary and secondary levels. Participants mentioned a variety of barriers to implementing practices addressed in the ASTL program, such as limits within the school based on schedules and the PK–12 student population, limited resources including technological resources or support, fixed or rigid curricula, and demands and pressures on the teachers. In describing the logistical obstacles related to participating in professional learning communities, an elementary physical education teacher expressed, "They do give us a lot of information, but not enough for putting into our P.E. program. . . . There's just no time. I'm not free when they meet for the learning community. So it kind of makes it difficult." This conflict between the practices presented during the program and constraints found in school contexts, especially in relation to aspects of practice such as learning communities or technology advocated by the ASTL program was evident in many of the interviews. The interview participants reported both their increased professional confidence to carry out high quality instruction in physical education and health and the constraints found in their practice.

The follow-up interview data derived from ASTL students in the physical education Concentration encouraged us to carefully consider the coherence of content knowledge and the Core program learning outcomes. As a result of the follow-up interview data, we are working with physical education Concentration faculty to incorporate assignments in the Core that are viewed by physical education teachers as relevant to their practice (tailoring assignments such as videoing one's teaching in different spaces such as a gymnasium or outside with larger groups of PK–12 students). Similarly, we began conversations about the alignment of specific assignments between the physical education Concentration and Core courses. For example, we are discussing how a grant proposal assignment found in both the physical education Concentration and the Core can be tailored to the content and contexts of the Core in different ways than in the Concentration. The follow-up interview data from the physical education Concentration has provided opportunities for faculty teaching in the Core and Concentration to engage in focused discussions regarding content knowledge and pedagogical content knowledge based on the data found in these ASTL students' follow-up interviews.

As the ASTL faculty have become accustomed to reviewing and discussing different types of qualitative evidence, the need to collect evidence from a larger numbers of former ASTL students became apparent. This need has also been driven by external accreditation requirements to collect data on students' satisfaction with the ASTL program.

EVIDENCE DERIVED FROM ASTL FOLLOW-UP SURVEY

Our most recent effort to examine our ASTL students' learning after they leave the program is the distribution of an electronic survey. Since we had not previously collected data from our program graduates, a survey was developed to provide feedback regarding program quality and relevance to ASTL students who had completed the program over a ten-year period. We sent out the ASTL student survey in 2010 seeking evidence regarding the influence of the program on former ASTL students' professional roles and practices, specifically in relation to the program learning outcomes. One hundred ten former ASTL students who completed the graduate program from 1999 to 2009 responded to the survey. Study findings related to the professional experiences of program graduates indicated that the vast majority, 94 percent of respondents, are currently working in a school or school division in a public education setting (84 percent). Respondents are teaching at a variety of levels with 2 percent working at the preschool level, 49 percent working at the elementary level, 17 percent working at the middle school level, 22 percent working at the high school level, 3 percent working in a K–12 resource position, and 7 percent in another position in education. The range of years as an educator reported were from two to forty years in 65 percent suburban, 17 percent urban, and 9 percent rural settings.

Respondents evaluated the extent of the influence of the program on their skills and knowledge for the learning outcomes student learning, content knowledge, and effective pedagogy, monitoring student learning, systematic inquiry of practice, diversity, and technology. They rated the level of impact on a scale of 1 to 4 where 1 is not at all, 2 is very little, 3 is very much, and 4 is a great deal. In Figure 6.1, the majority of graduates indicate that their experiences in the ASTL program increased their professional capacities. In an average across the six outcomes, more than three-quarters of respondents (77 percent) reported that the ASTL program enhanced their abilities very much or a great deal. The highest percent of participants reported a great deal of influence for the learning outcomes content in knowledge and pedagogy (44 percent) and student learning (31 percent), followed by the outcomes monitoring student learning (29 percent) and diversity (25 percent). The lowest percentage of respondents reported a great deal of influence for the learning outcomes technology (14 percent) and systematic inquiry of practice (2 percent).

Table 6.1 provides evidence that the respondents assumed significant professional leadership and collaborative roles upon program completion. The highest percent of program completers indicated that they were team leaders or department chairs or mentored novice teachers. In terms of future plans, 65 percent planned to continue in their current positions, while 25 percent of students had begun or planned to begin doctoral studies, and 18 percent planned to move to a specialist position. In addition, 23 percent planned to apply for National Board Certification, and 5 percent had already become a NBCT. These findings especially highlight the impact of the program learning outcomes learning community and leadership. The ASTL student survey provided a useful avenue for feedback from program graduates.

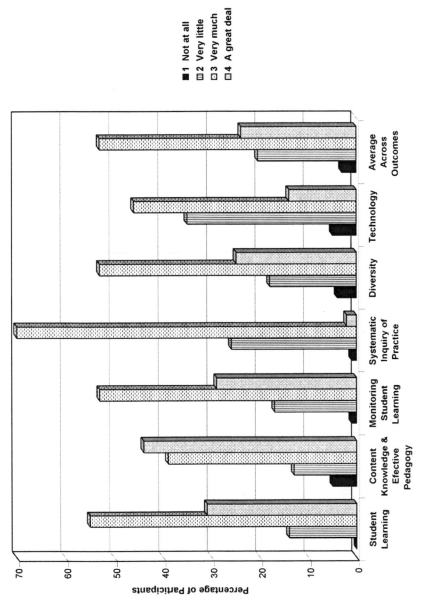

Figure 6.1 Extent of impact of ASTL program (learning outcomes).

Table 6.1 Top Five Professional Roles Identified by ASTL Graduates

Activity	Percentage of Respondents
Team leader or department chair	51
Mentor for a novice teacher	50
Trainer providing professional development for other teachers	42
School representative on a division-wide committee	22
Cooperating teacher or clinical faculty member	18

Survey respondents also provided a variety of suggestions for improvement based on their professional experiences since completing the ASTL program. Overall, the respondents reported that their learning experiences were positive and contributed to their professional growth. For example, a respondent reported, "The program was great. Wonderful professors and really prepared me for my PLC at work and for continuing education." Another former ASTL student shared,

> I felt I gained a lot of experience as a student in the ASTL program. It does teach us to be more reflective practitioners [sic] and to "own" our lessons, making them rich and relevant to our students. I enjoyed the class discussions and feel our professors overall enjoyed their job and enjoyed exchanging their knowledge with us. . . . I have highly recommended the program to fellow teachers looking to obtain their M.Ed.

Critical comments largely related to suggestions for changes or improvements to specific courses, assignments, or critical feedback regarding particular instructors. Regarding a course in the Core, a respondent commented that the course "needs to be re-vamped. Better scaffolding, better focus, more relevant products." A former ASTL student whose Concentration area was literacy stated, "In the core for Reading Teachers, you must include more writing courses, something on guided reading and word study. There was too much emphasis on research and not enough on teaching strategies." The comments also provided feedback about areas of additional focus or additional learning experiences within the areas of assessment, technology, opportunities to share successful practices in the classroom, specific strategies to teach within a content area, and the collaborative teaching process. The comments from former ASTL students reflected strengths and areas of improvement found in both the Core and Concentration courses and provided a range of perspectives from program completers.

Both the survey comments and item response results provide us with additional evidence of program effectiveness. The survey data, in particular, has generated faculty discussion about potential changes to be part of our continuous program improvement efforts. For example, the survey response indicates that technology is perceived by program graduates as one of the least influential outcomes and suggests to the faculty to reconsider the role of technology in the program. Our ASTL students' prior experiences with technology, as well as the types and uses of technology in the schools, have changed dramatically since we established technology as a learning outcome at the outset of the program. Faculty discussion of these results has focused on whether technology should remain a program learning outcome as we consider the different experiences with technology across core courses. By examining the survey data in relation to other data sources such as reflections collected during the program we have been able to compare and synthesize data results to determine patterns found across the data sources. In the instance of technology we are finding similar results across different data sources (such as the prompted reflections) which provides a stronger case for decisions the faculty make regarding continuous program improvement.

CONCLUSION

By building the program around measurable outcomes and then examining the results through multiple measures, we have attempted to develop an understanding of ASTL students' learning. As we ask ASTL students about their understanding of program outcomes and how they situate the program's outcomes in their own teaching, we are concurrently engaging in research on our own practices. Drawing upon the original ASTL design of evaluating ASTL student feedback, we are becoming more sophisticated in the types of evidence we collect and analyze and what we do with that evidence. At the same time, we acknowledge that we can improve our own practices regarding the evidence we use to evaluate program effectiveness. For example, we are increasingly mindful of the need to conduct research in more robust and rigorous ways. That is, we realize the need to build multiple and overlapping structures that systematize and institutionalize a data-rich environment in which quantitative, qualitative, and mixed-methods assessments and studies inform programmatic decisions (Cochran-Smith & the Boston College Evidence Team, 2009). We also acknowledge that we face challenges of building a stronger culture of evidence with less than optimum resources to support this effort. It is also important to recognize that the evidence on program effectiveness that we have studied over time has yielded negative as well as positive findings. We strive to use all of the evidence as we consider ways to improve our own practices as well as improve our program.

7

Evidence of Effectiveness

Portfolio as Program Pedagogy

The room was filled with faculty and program teachers, who had completed their coursework and were there to share their program portfolios. Each of the roundtables consisted of a faculty member and five ASTL students who were finishing their program and giving a ten-to fifteen-minute portfolio presentation. Each teacher shared his areas of greatest growth during the program and also talked about some professional plans. When it was Mary's turn to share her portfolio, she distributed a colorful page that was covered with pictures, flow charts, bulleted summaries, coursework titles, and a list that captured her salient learning during the program. It was entitled "Portfolio Presentation 2008, Learner and Teacher Coming Together," and it included information about her growth and development during the program.

Mary began by sharing that the photo in the center was of her twin nieces, pictured there with their arms intertwined in a smiling bear hug. The picture was labeled "Core and Concentration, ASTL and Literacy: The Learning Community." Under the picture was the legend stating: Teacher-Researcher: Twin Endeavors. The program's eight learning outcomes were clearly listed on the left. Although she reported that all of the learning outcomes were important to her and were intertwined, she felt that two stood out to her. Systematic inquiry of practice was the learning outcome in which she had grown the most and had provided the greatest effect on her students' learning. The area of diversity she was targeting was ongoing professional development. As she explained her thinking, she said that "as greater numbers of students with diverse cultural, linguistic, and cognitively diverse backgrounds enroll at my school, it is important that no one is overlooked or disenfranchised." Her plans for the next school year highlighted "inclusion for students with autism" and learning Spanish so that she could communicate better with groups of Spanish speaking parents and students.

Mary explained that after teaching for nineteen years, she had been stuck in a mindset where "I didn't think there was any compelling need to question my methods. I didn't know what I didn't know." She explained that as she began her courses, she learned that through research and self-reflection of her teaching practice, new understandings about theory, and teacher research, she could actually provide greater freedom to her students as she became "less rigid about teaching and learning." Now, as a result of the coursework and a new area of expertise in literacy, she reported that she welcomes other teachers into her classroom to observe and co-teach, she has students routinely lead the learning activities, and she has truly become the "guide on the side." This role of facilitator, who approaches her classroom learning environment through the lens of inquiry, has also enabled her to reach beyond her classroom to effect change with her teaching team, with other faculty in the building, and to even help her reach beyond her immediate building setting.

Portfolios are powerful learning tools. Although they require careful thought and planning, if they are integrated well, program portfolios have the potential to provide a rich source of evidence for the individual preparing the portfolio. Portfolios can also provide candidates an opportunity to engage in a highly individualized learning process. When individuals engage in the development process, portfolios have the potential to provide powerful data for individual and program analysis. Portfolios should not be considered as a quick, "slam-dunk" program addition, but should be incorporated carefully.

This chapter presents the concept of the professional portfolio as program pedagogy. The first section explains how portfolios have been implemented in the ASTL program as performance-based assessment tools for all participants. The second section focuses on programmatic research that has been conducted by faculty using ASTL students' portfolio data. These studies have specifically focused on portfolios as evidence of ASTL students' approaches to inquiry and the growth of their reflective practice during the program.

DEFINING THE ASTL PROFESSIONAL PORTFOLIO AND ITS PURPOSE

The purpose of the ASTL professional portfolio is twofold. First, in documenting learning, it encourages ASTL students to develop their teaching practice to its highest level. This is accomplished through evidence of targeted reflection, presentation of pedagogical and content-based knowledge, action research skills as they inform teaching practice and a synthesis of professional knowledge and skills. Secondly, it provides performance-based evidence to ASTL students and faculty about the degree to which program goals have been met. As both a formative and summative document, the ASTL professional portfolio articulates the principles of NBPTS and the three additional ASTL learning outcomes, other content-specific standards, and the mission and goals of the CEHD at George Mason University.

All ASTL students in the program create a professional portfolio that is clearly aligned with the program's eight learning outcomes. The ASTL professional portfolio is a performance-based document that provides concrete evidence of student professional development throughout the program and is one of several factors considered in determining an ASTL student's successful program completion. See Appendix F for the full ASTL portfolio guidelines. By incorporating course performance-based assignments, PK–12 student work samples, and ASTL students' prompted reflections that focus on applying course content, the portfolio provides evidence of how ASTL students connect their program assignments to their educational practice. The portfolio provides ASTL students with the opportunity to synthesize and reflect on their learning as they progress through the program coursework and the opportunities to document the connections between their coursework and daily encounters with PK–12 student learning in the context of school-based experiences. It is comprised of evidence from both Concentration and Core coursework and includes a synthesizing reflection that the ASTL students write to a prompt asking them to articulate the salient aspects of their learning across the entire program as they bring content and pedagogy together. See Figure 7.1, Overview of the Components of the ASTL Portfolio, which shows how these two program components are conceived.

Two primary goals of the ASTL program are to encourage ASTL students to become critical, reflective practitioners and to use reflection-based inquiry in their classroom practice. The portfolios used in our program encompass two types: (1) a program portfolio that supports the growth and development of ASTL students' critical reflective practice, and (2) a portfolio used by program faculty to determine the outcomes attained by ASTL students during program coursework. The portfolio is also professional evidence to their schools in support of an articulated professional development plan.

The ASTL Portfolio: Its Context and the Role of Reflection

Since the early 1990s, an increasing number of teacher education programs in the United States and in many other countries began to include portfolios among their program requirements. Related literature in the field addresses

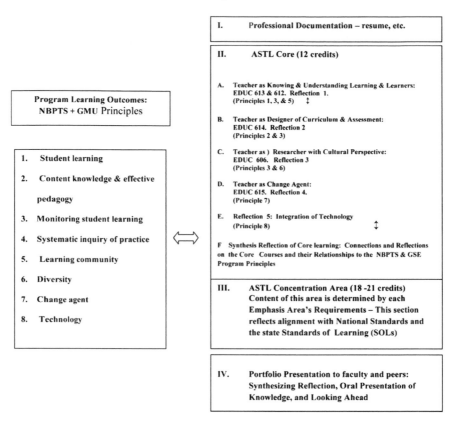

Figure 7.1 Overview of the components of the ASTL portfolio.

the various purposes of portfolios in both preservice and in-service programs. For example, portfolios may be used as an assessment tool (Carroll, Potthoff, & Huber, 1996; Hammadou, 1996; Mokhtari, Yellin, Bull, & Montgomery, 1996) and as an opportunity for program candidates to provide evidence of the ways they are applying theory to practice in their classrooms (Barton & Collins, 1993; Fox, 1999). Portfolios may also be used as a forum for documentation of directed reflection to form the basis for professional growth and development (Hammadou, 1998; Meyer, Tusin, & Turner, 1996; Wade & Yarborough, 1996).

There are many different types of portfolios that programs might implement (e.g., showcase, developmental, formative, or summative) to provide evidence of what their students have learned and can do. Because of the many possible types of portfolios with unique contents and completion timelines, teacher education programs should clearly articulate their expectations about the purposes and goals of the portfolio they require (Francis, 1995; Hammadou, 1998; Winsor & Ellefson, 1995). There is also an ongoing need for faculty to conduct targeted research on the specific skills and abilities these portfolios measure, as well as the degree to which their program candidates meet specified goals and standards (Darling-Hammond, 2006).

Reflection in Program Portfolios

The ASTL program draws from the NCTAF (1996) statement about reflection that says teachers should be able to think systematically about their practice and learn from experience (National Board for Professional Teaching Standards, 1989a). According to the NCTAF statement, teachers must be able to "critically examine their practice, seek the advice of others, and draw on educational research to deepen their knowledge, sharpen their judgment, and adapt their teaching to new findings and ideas" (1996, p. 75). Our ASTL portfolio includes examples of a student's engagement in reflection. Reflection is systematically integrated into both the portfolio and throughout program coursework requirements.

Schön (1983) states that the best teachers actively incorporate reflection into their practice and take time to reflect in many ways not only on their teaching but also to consider the results of their teaching on learners. As teachers build on their understandings about teaching and learning, they stand to profit from deep reflection that connects their development to the larger context of professional learning theory and professional practice (Brookfield, 1995; Rodgers, 2002). In other words, scaffolding and building reflective capacity can serve to strengthen teachers' practice by helping them personalize and individualize professional learning experiences into their practice.

Reflection must have meaning to serve a purpose in informing personal growth and change. If it is developed well, the process of reflection that teacher education programs work so hard to help establish can serve as a conduit through which teachers examine their practice. The growth of critical reflection is an integral component of our program and the program portfolios created by the ASTL students. As we developed and refined our definition of critical reflection, we applied the levels of reflection Carol Rodgers (2002) synthesized from John Dewey to provide a framework for encouraging teachers to attain deeper levels of thinking. Rodgers explains that critical reflection involves the following levels: (1) "presence to experience," attention is drawn to an event or an experience and take note of it; (2) "description of experience," follows awareness where teachers describe the experience and their perceptions of the details; (3) "analysis of experience," collect and analyze data to determine a need for change; and (4) "intelligent action/

experimentation," take action to apply some aspect of change as a result of analyzing and interpreting data (p. 856). Our research in ASTL (Fox, White, & Kidd, 2011) has defined a fifth level of reflection for practicing teachers: (5) "implications of classroom inquiry beyond the classroom" where in-service teachers extend their inquiry beyond their immediate classroom setting and share what they have learned.

This research shows that such engagement has spearheaded collegial exchanges of ideas, helped our ASTL students identify areas in need of improvement at the team, department, or school level, and caused them to consider other professional issues beyond the immediate inquiry. It is in this fifth stage of reflection that ASTL students articulate how they have become teacher leaders. This level also connects ASTL student reflections to ASTL's sixth learning outcome, teachers as change agents and teacher leaders, by providing additional evidence of the ways ASTL students have come to talk about their work as leaders and agents of change.

The portfolio reflective framework can support ASTL students in taking an active role in looking critically at their practice and connecting their instructional decisions to research and theory. Moreover, according to Dewey (1933, 1998), engaging in systematic inquiry suggests that an individual holds the belief to provide evidence. Systematic reflection requires active, ongoing, and attentive examination of that belief (Lyons, 2006). Dewey also suggests that inquiry implies a need for a scaffold to sustain engagement in reflective inquiry over time (Lyons, 2006).

Recent research in the area of reflection by Korthagen and Vasalos (2005) "builds on the assumption that by nature people reflect on their experiences, but that systematic reflection often differs from what teachers are accustomed to doing" (p. 48). Korthagen and Kessels (1999) also examine carefully the process of reflection in and on practice as teachers develop their capacities to reflect meaningfully about their classroom interactions and take action as a result of their reflective practice. In the preservice domain, teacher education programs increasingly focus on the development of reflective practice in their coursework and fieldwork, and research has shown that there may be an assumption in the profession that practices in reflection that began during preservice teacher education coursework will carry over into one's professional teaching life (Borko, Michalec, Timmons, & Siddle, 1997; Carroll, Potthoff, & Huber, 1996; Delandshere & Arens, 2003; Freidus, 1996; Morin, 1995; Wade & Yarborough, 1996; Winsor & Ellefson, 1995). Our research supports these findings and provides evidence that calls for opportunities that support targeted development of teachers' reflective capacity.

In a study on portfolio development (Fox, Kidd, Painter, & Ritchie, 2007), we found that when ASTL students beginning the Core course sequence were asked to comment about their reflective practice, many replied that they "reflect all the time." Similar to findings by Lyons (1998) and Korthagen and Vasalos (2005), these ASTL students' reflections included only elemental or surface-level components of the reflective process. Consequently, it cannot be assumed that self-evaluation and reflection have actively extended from preservice into a teacher's professional classroom life (Borko, Michalec, Timmons, & Siddle, 1997; Lyons, 1998; Wade & Yarborough, 1996), nor that these practices are systematically used to redirect practice or activate change (Lyons, 2006). In fact, many highly experienced teachers may actually be novices at reflective practice (Rodgers, 2002; Ross, 2002) and thus require specific experiences such as critical conversations and collaborative inquiry in a supportive environment to move beyond descriptive thought and writing (Lyons, 1998).

Zeichner and Wray (2001) report that portfolios can capture teachers' knowledge and skills while also providing an avenue to examine teachers' reflections. Since reflection in the portfolio involves a process of interpreting experiences, this can foster a mental process that occurs while a portfolio is created (Winsor & Ellefson, 1995). Thus, the portfolio can become a type of learning environment supporting reflective development: a space where teachers reflect on single experiences, on experiences that encompass different events and contexts, on connection of experiences, on approaches to problematic situations, on changes of views and beliefs, and on the process of producing the portfolio itself. In this way, the portfolio houses teachers' changing thoughts and perceptions, providing a cognitive space where they and others might examine the nature of their growth and consider their learning as it relates to their teaching practice.

PROCESS AND PRESENTATION OF THE ASTL PORTFOLIO

Since the ASTL portfolio is compiled over the span of the ASTL students' graduate program, it has the potential to serve as both a formative and summative document. This process allows the ASTL students to articulate perceptions and reflections that enable them to examine their growth over time; the process also provides in-progress evidence to program faculty about what ASTL students are learning during coursework. With prompted reflections written at the conclusion of courses and then revisited at post-program when they write their synthesizing reflection, ASTL students can consider any changes in understanding and depth of knowledge that have occurred during program coursework. Critical reflection is part of each course in the Core courses and is incorporated into each section of the portfolio. At the conclusion of program coursework, each ASTL student writes a synthesizing reflection and engages in a summative portfolio presentation. This portfolio reflection not only provides closure for the ASTL student, but also provides program faculty with an opportunity to consider the areas where the student has excelled and those where development was not as significant. Figure 7.2 contains the guidelines and oral reflection prompts we provide to ASTL students to help them prepare for their final oral portfolio presentations.

—— ∞∞ ——

GUIDE FOR THE
ASTL ORAL PORTFOLIO PRESENTATION
Portfolio Presentations: 10 minutes per candidate

Part IV of the **ASTL Professional Portfolio** is an oral presentation to peers from the ASTL learning community and the ASTL Core Faculty. This presentation is to serve as both a synthesizing reflection and a time to look forward. The presentation should consist of a thoughtful presentation by the ASTL student that focuses on: (1) the pedagogical learning experiences that occurred in the Core, (2) a synthesized overview of what and how the ASTL student learned, and (3) the impact of the ASTL student's learning on the PK–12 students in his/her classroom, or educational setting. ASTL students should address the following questions during the presentation.

Content of the Presentation: Think across the eight program principles/learning outcomes (see below) and consider the learning experiences provided in the ASTL Core and your Concentration courses. At the beginning of your presentation please provide a **brief overview** (2–3 minute) of your portfolio. Please touch on any major aspects or messages that you would like for the attendees to focus on, or point out a theme you adopted.

1. **Choose one principle (learning outcome)** in which you feel you have experienced the most growth during the Core. Tell about *what* growth has occurred and connect it to P–12 student learning. Please reflect on *why* this has been your area of substantial growth and *why* you feel it has had an impact on your students' learning.

2. Of the eight Core principles (learning outcomes), which one did you not achieve to the degree you would have liked? Present/share your **action plan** for addressing this principle.

3. For **Program Completers**, please provide a brief overview of the evidence you have included from your area of Concentration and comment on the

development of your Content knowledge. Point out insights you have gained in your content area expertise (Concentration) as a result of your work in *both* the Concentration and Core classes. This reflection should provide an overall synthesis of your Concentration and Core knowledge.

Figure 7.2 Portfolio presentation guide.

In her final portfolio presentation, Mary shared that she successfully brought together theory and practice and her growth of understanding over the course of her program. Thus, at the conclusion of her program, Mary's portfolio was summative, providing culminating evidence to school- and university-based stakeholders of her successful achievement of "praxis." While her final portfolio presentation was a summative moment concluding her program coursework, the portfolio presentation was also a formative moment in the sense that it provided a forum for identifying areas she would like to focus on for professional development. As a program faculty, we have investigated both the contents and oral presentations of ASTL students' portfolios to help us understand the nature and scope of their growth as a result of program coursework.

PROGRAM RESEARCH: UNDERSTANDING TEACHERS' LEARNING THROUGH PROGRAM PORTFOLIOS

As teacher education institutions have become increasingly accountable for the quality of their graduates, there is an identified need to find effective ways of providing concrete evidence of teachers' knowledge (Cochran-Smith, 2001; Darling-Hammond, 2006; Zeichner, 2006). Professional development programs have also been called upon to deepen their understanding of the visions of teaching and learning that guide their programs; they should be able to articulate the nature and results of coursework, as well as its effects on teachers and teaching (Darling-Hammond, 2000; Tom, 1999; Zeichner, 2006). By examining teachers' portfolios, several studies have documented that teacher educators can gain insight into understanding teachers' growth to determine to what degree teachers are meeting professional standards (Fox & Galluzzo, 2006; Kimball & Hanley, 1998) and applying theory to practice in their classrooms (Barton & Collins, 1993; Fox, 1999; Winsor & Ellefson, 1995). Other studies have shown that portfolios can be implemented into programs as a forum for promoting critical reflection of teachers and examining the growth of teachers' critical reflection over time (Foote & Vermette, 2001; Fox, White, Kidd, & Ritchie, 2005). We summarize here two studies that were conducted using portfolio data from recent cohorts of ASTL students in which we sought to understand dimensions of teachers' growth that occurred during program coursework.

Inquiry Stance Study

The growth of critical reflection was the focus of the study, entitled "Program Portfolios: Documenting Teachers' Growth in Reflection-based Inquiry" (Fox, White, & Kidd, 2011). This qualitative study examined the portfolio reflections of fifty-one ASTL students enrolled in the program. By analyzing ASTL students' reflections included in their program portfolios, we sought to examine how cohorts of students grew and changed in their approach to inquiry as a result of coursework taken during a professional development master's degree program. As previously stated one of our principal program goals is to help ASTL students become critically reflective educators and engage actively in inquiry. We should understand if our students were able to engage in systematic reflection, learn from and apply their experiences in the coursework, and draw on educational research to drive decisions in their classrooms (National Commission on Teaching and America's Future, 1996).

In this study, analysis of the ASTL students' reflections included in their program portfolios revealed that their incorporation of inquiry changed as they proceeded through the coursework. To understand the nature of their growth, we first used the four levels of reflection as defined by Rodgers (2002) to analyze ASTL students' critical reflection as they progressed through the coursework sequence: awareness of inquiry, beginning to act on one's inquiry, middle stages of inquiry, and full engagement in inquiry. A fifth level emerged from our data analysis, which we have labeled implications of inquiry beyond one's own classroom. These five levels provided a framework for analyzing and reporting the findings. A coding guide was developed based on these five levels, with definitions and examples of ASTL students' statements that provided evidence of their incorporation of inquiry into their critical reflections. The following results focus on ways that teacher education programs can utilize components of portfolios, such as critical reflections, to analyze program participants' change and development during program coursework.

Results

The content of ASTL students' portfolio reflections written to prompts at specified times during coursework appeared to capture changes in the scope and depth of their critical reflection during program coursework. This analysis provided both expected and different applications of the levels of inquiry. For example, ASTL students' reflections did show that they all engaged in critical reflection; however, the reflections also indicated differences in how they applied inquiry in their educational setting. Through the analysis of these changes, we identified specific patterns found in the ASTL students' reflections which revealed how they engaged in inquiry as they compiled evidence from their classrooms, searching for solutions to their puzzlements.

As ASTL students progressed through the program, patterns analyzed in their portfolio reflections also indicated that as they developed inquiry skills, they appeared to progress through five identified levels of inquiry. These levels ranged from awareness of the inquiry process to full engagement in inquiry, resulting in actions taken within and beyond the classroom. Students who reached full engagement in the inquiry process seemed to view themselves as teacher researchers capable of effecting changes that influenced teaching and learning in their classrooms and beyond.

The study provided evidence to advance our program's understanding about how portfolio data can be used as one tool to examine the effects of our coursework and learning experiences on ASTL student development. Though our engagement in inquiry focused on program outcomes relying on students' portfolio reflections and content, such as the data analyzed in this study, we determined that it was possible for faculty to gain insight into the nature of ASTL students' growth of inquiry through portfolio content and reflections. In addition, through targeted portfolio research on students' reflections, the faculty gained insight into ways to interact more effectively with cohorts of students participating in the program. This study also set the stage for more targeted research on individual ASTL students, as we sought to understand not only overall cohort trends but also how to best meet the needs of the individual students in our program.

Case Studies of Three Teachers

As part of our longitudinal research, we have used a case study methodology (Yin, 2003) to examine the growth and change of individual teachers. In "Delving into Teachers' Development through Program Portfolios: Case Studies" (Fox, White, Kidd, & Ritchie, 2008), we considered aspects of our program's effects on teachers and their application of program content in their classrooms. Three ASTL students were purposely selected as representative of the teachers in our program. Specifically, we examined the written reflections submitted in their program portfolios and transcripts from their exit presentations to identify connections to program learning outcomes and to gain insight into the scope and nature of the change of the students during the program. Pam, Adam, and Matthew (all names are pseudonyms) were three ASTL students from a cohort that reflected a range of experiences and number of years in the classroom setting, varying backgrounds and teacher preparation programs, and different teaching disciplines.

Previous research and faculty discussion helped us determine that program completers seem to gather into three principal categories, or clusters. We defined the clusters as follows:

Cluster 1: ASTL students who consistently demonstrated the ability to synthesize and apply course content to their practice during the program and completed the program with clear and consistent connections to program goals and learning outcomes;

Cluster 2: ASTL students who showed steady and significant growth along the program, and completed it with evidence of having made strong connections to program goals and learning outcomes; and

Cluster 3: ASTL students who demonstrated weaker writing skills and did not appear to progress along the same pathway as the other two groups during the program, but who completed the program by providing adequate evidence of attaining program goals and learning outcomes.

For purposes of this study, Pam was selected to represent cluster 1; Adam represented cluster 2; and Matthew, cluster 3.

Results

In this study, nine themes emerged from analysis of the reflection data: Teaching Practices; References to Self; Teacher/Action Research; Reflection; Culture; Learners, Learning, Learning Communities; Leadership; Technology; and other uncategorizable statements. These themes provided a framework for analysis of the growth and change of these three ASTL students: Pam, Adam, and Matthew. We examined the ways that each of the common themes emerged in the ASTL students' portfolio reflections and exit portfolio presentations through individual and cross-case analysis of the three participants. Similar to Lyons (1998) and Fox, White, and Kidd (2011), our findings related to the three teachers' individual portfolios provided further support for the idea that teachers engage in different levels of critical reflection (Rodgers, 2002).

Pam's reflections, for example, showed clear connections between theory and practice and included additional discussion about how she was implementing new practices in her classroom, as well as her perceptions about their effects on her elementary students' learning. Her portfolio provided evidence of strategies and tools she used in her teaching, her advocacy for individual students' needs, and the studied changes she implemented in both her teaching and her school. Because Pam was the most experienced of these three participants, it was important to recognize the extensiveness of her experience may have influenced her ability to reach deeper levels of reflection and connections from coursework to classroom practice. Pam appeared to be representative of ASTL students who take a broader perspective on their teaching (Borko, Michalec, Timmons, & Siddle, 1997).

Adam, a cluster 2 teacher, wrote reflections that were more concrete in nature at the outset of his coursework. He saw the value in reflection and introspection and stated that it provided him with a more informed basis for classroom decision-making and instructional practice. While Adam actively sought to apply new theories in his classroom, his reflections were more concrete than Pam's, and he viewed teacher research and reflection as having a positive effect on his teaching in the areas of culture, leadership, and teaching practice. His progress by the end of the program was apparent through his discovery that reflection could, and did, play an important role in deepening his understanding of his students and his own teaching practice.

Matthew, a cluster 3 teacher, wrote reflections that seemed to remain at a more descriptive, concrete level. His more closed ideas at the outset of the program appeared to undergo change as he became more aware of how course content could be connected to his classroom practice. At the beginning of the program, Matthew's reflections tended to be descriptive and indicative of one who does not value reflection. Although he focused primarily on specific assignments and articulated concerns about how he would find time beyond the scope of the coursework to conduct research in his classroom, his reflections did show a level of growth and development over the course of the program. At the end of Core coursework, his reflections articulated a depth of awareness that was not evident at the program's outset. For Adam and Matthew, the portfolio provided "evidence of their thinking, learning, and performance" (Darling-Hammond & Snyder, 2000, p. 536).

A cross-case analysis allowed us to compare and contrast the portfolios from the three ASTL students. Although Pam, Adam, and Matthew were at different levels of reflection at the conclusion of the program, all three demonstrated individual growth across the program, and their reflections were linked to course content. A comparison of the portfolio reflections provided additional insight into the degree to which these three ASTL students met our program standards (Fox & Galluzzo, 2006; Kimball & Hanley, 1998) and applied theory to practice in their PK–12 classrooms (Barton & Collins, 1993; Fox, 1999; Winsor & Ellefson, 1995). The three case studies also provided a source of in-depth data to address program-level questions about how we might best meet the varying needs of teachers who enter our program.

CONCLUSION

When portfolios as a program-level performance assessment are carefully implemented, they can provide rich data for faculty. This source of multiple data points can be used to examine ASTL students' learning during program coursework and to consider the ways they seek to apply new knowledge in their educational settings. For ASTL students like Mary, the PK–12 teacher highlighted at the outset of this chapter, portfolio presentations provide ASTL students an opportunity to articulate their ideas about their growth and learning during the program coursework. It is also possible for faculty to consider the evidence provided in the program portfolios to study the program and its effects on our students. ASTL students' connections from theory to practice can be found in the portfolio which can also provide a window into the learning and application of their knowledge in the PK–12 setting.

In the study focused on inquiry, we found changes in the scope and depth of ASTL students' critical reflection during program coursework through analyzing the content of their portfolio reflections. The patterns analyzed in the ASTL students' portfolio reflections indicated that as they developed inquiry skills, they appeared to progress through five identified levels of inquiry. The case studies of individual students allowed us to examine more closely the individual differences exhibited in the three identified clusters of students who participate in our program.

These studies provided evidence to advance our program's understanding about how portfolio data can be used as one tool to examine the effects of our coursework and learning experiences on teacher development. Using these results to guide decisions about programmatic content and structure has resulted in several course-level changes. For example, portfolio data have helped us identify when specific assignments or readings need to be changed or augmented. As we continue to implement program changes and study their effects on ASTL students, portfolios provide important qualitative data that can be used by program faculty to understand the different learning needs of the ASTL students enrolled in the program. Using data in this manner directly responds to Tom's (1999) suggestion that "[t]he issue of program substance is best addressed in relation to the characteristics and needs of particular teachers and school settings" (p. 252).

III

New Discourses

It is clear that master's degree programs for practicing teachers must respond to the same influences that are prompting changes in K–12 schools. Just as the role of teachers has changed in the era of school reform, so has the role of the academy regarding the development of practicing teachers. Those of us responsible for professional development for practicing teachers face increasing attention to accountability, to faculty roles and responsibilities, and to student and university expectations.

Parts 1 and 2 of this book focus on program design and evidence. In part 3, we attend to new discourses in the academy based on challenges that differ from those we have faced in the past. We build on the previous sections to elevate the conversation about new forms of accountability, new faculty roles, and new approaches to working with our practicing teachers. These three chapters comprise our collective perspective in re-envisioning the role of the academy in the development of practicing teachers. The final chapters are intended to generate dialogue, questions, and further investigation, rather than a set of answers, about the development of practicing teachers—a group often omitted from the conversation in teacher education. We hope that these insights will help those who are responsible for master's degrees for practicing teachers to be better prepared to face today's challenges of teachers' professional development.

These final three chapters on new discourses convey the ideas, perspectives, and practices that have worked for us in our institution for more than a decade. Hopefully, they will enable you to build a stronger degree program, to imagine new possibilities, and to be better positioned to act on them at your respective institutions.

8

New Dimensions of Accountability

We have started the chapters in this volume with vignettes designed to give the reader an inside look at how ASTL runs. This chapter is more about the challenges we face, and rather than beginning with a vignette conveying the challenges we and most other teacher educators face when it comes to measuring program effects in an era of high stakes accountability, this chapter begins with an observation drawn from the National Academy's study of NBPTS (Hakel, Koenig, & Elliot, 2008).

Measures of outcomes for students, such as their academic achievement, do provide a means of evaluating teachers' job performance, but it is enlightening to consider what this would mean if extrapolated to other fields. For example, this is similar to evaluating the validity of a medical certification test by collecting information about the outcomes for patients of a board-certified physician or evaluating the validity of the bar exam by considering the outcomes for clients of a lawyer who had passed the bar exam and been admitted to the bar. Outcomes for patients reflect many factors other than the skills and knowledge of the physician who provides services, such as the severity of the illness being treated and the degree to which the patient adheres to the professional advice given. Likewise in law, the outcome for the client depends on such factors as the nature of the legal problem, the record of prior legal problems, and the extent to which the client follows the [lawyer's] advice. Furthermore, should the outcomes for a high-priced lawyer, who can select his clients, be compared to the outcomes for a public defender? While data are available that might be used in such evaluations (e.g., rates of death or guilty verdicts) and several such studies have been conducted, many factors can contribute to the outcomes, making interpretation of the relationships very tricky (p. 25).

Throughout this book, our goal has been to bring the reader inside our program to see our fundamental values, the nature of the program, its goals, and how we strive to achieve them. Along the way, we hope the reader gets a sense of how we conceive a master's degree that strives to be professional development in an essentially traditional university coursework setting. The reader has seen: the context in which the ASTL program was created and its ties to the propositions of NBPTS; the belief that all teacher education programs should be a campus-wide commitment to improving teacher content knowledge; the premise that what a teacher does all day prior to coming to class is a laboratory for studying themselves, their students, their effects, and the school in which each works. In chapters 5 through 7, the reader has also been invited into our conceptions of accountability and of evidence in accomplishing the goals of the program and how and why selected data are collected at both the individual teacher level, the course level, and the program level. We have worked diligently not to stray from our fundamental values of the program unless the evidence warranted it, which was also described earlier in this volume where an entire Core course was revised, and assignments and tasks in others completely redesigned to hew more closely to the program's goals.

However, in practice the endpoint in ASTL has been changes in the teachers who complete the program, which is to say that we have not included student achievement as one of the effects of our program. A proposal was taken to the school division from which most of the teachers have enrolled in ASTL to study the effects of the teachers' preparation on the achievement of the students. Unfortunately, the school division declined to give us access to the teachers' personnel records and their students' test scores, so those data have yet to be examined for the effects that ASTL might have on PK–12 student achievement. This point is raised here because of the shifts that have occurred in the decade that ASTL has been in existence. When we began the program, our interests were in changes in teachers' self-perceptions of their skills from matriculation to graduation, and we designed a series of short scales to assess that (Fox & White, 2010). As described in chapter 5, we used one of these scales for many years to get a sense cohort by cohort how well the program was working in the eyes of the students. However, from 1999 until the writing of this book in 2011, the pressure on education schools to demonstrate the value they add to a teacher's repertoire and skill has increased both from those outside the profession as well as those within the profession (Boyd, Grossman, Lankford, Loeb, Wyckoff, 2009; Crowe, 2010; Harris & Sass, 2009). There are at least three sources of external pressure on education schools to demonstrate their effects: one that is federal, one that relates to institutional accreditation, and one that relates to professional accreditation.

NO ESCAPING THE AFTERMATH OF FEDERAL REGULATION

As noted throughout this volume, ASTL was created prior to the passage of the No Child Left Behind Act of 2001. It was not created with the anticipation that there would be a significant and continuous march in the policy community toward measuring teachers' effectiveness through the use of standardized test scores for preservice teachers initially, and now for practicing teachers earning a master's degree. At the time, the concept of "value-added" was in its earliest days (Sanders & Rivers, 1996; Wright, Horn, & Sanders, 1997), and was, and in many instances remains, widely seen by the education community as not resulting in valid judgments of teachers (Adams, Heywood, & Rothstein, 2009; Winerip, 2011). We admit to subscribing to this view at the time we designed ASTL. The general proposition we adopted was that if teachers became more knowledgeable about the content they teach, more skilled in teaching it, and more thoughtful about why they do what they do, then we were accomplishing our goals. We did not expect the contemporary calls, most visibly from the Bill and Melinda Gates Foundation, or the expectations for the reauthorization of the Elementary and Secondary Education Act as proposed by President Barack Obama and U.S. Secretary of Education Arne Duncan (United States Department of Education, 2010) for assessing the value-added by teachers to students' achievement. Nor could we have anticipated the bipartisan interest in removing the salary increases given to teachers who earn a master's degree and replacing it with a performance pay scheme based upon gains made by students on standardized achievement tests (Cavanaugh, 2010; Glazerman, Goldhaber, Loeb, Staiger, Raudenbush, & Whitehurst, 2010; Klein, 2011), and that are now policy in the Commonwealth of Virginia (Virginia Department of Education, 2011). As such, like most education school faculty, we are being asked to consider how we can widen the lens on the program's outcomes to address the value-added by our program to the growth on the pupils our students teach, and then to tie that to the education schools that the teachers attended.

We have given this topic some serious thought, but have not yet found the right equation nor the right dependent measure that would isolate the effects of the program on student achievement. Part of the problem is the equation itself. As Winerip (2011) notes, there are still many imperfections in these analyses, regardless of what the creators of these equations believe (Sanders, Ashton, & Wright, 2005). Quantifying the effects of a teacher earning a master's degree over a two- to three-year period requires accepting a series of assumptions about the: (1) comparability of the students they teach from one year to the next; (2) acquisition of reliable pre-test data in any given year; (3) assumption that the teacher will remain in the same school for the entire time it takes her to complete the master's degree; (4) the stability of teacher behavior from one year to the next; (5) state tests that report more than the percentage of students passing those tests; and many others. In our estimation, the current array of multilevel models for estimating teachers' effects fails to take into consideration any one of these assumptions, thus rendering the application of such methods misguided. As such, the ASTL program continues to use the teachers' themselves as the unit of analysis in an ever-evolving pre/post design of the program's effects. This should not be taken to mean that we are not interested in understanding our effects more broadly, but it does denote our determination that the statistical models are not yet developed well enough to overcome the natural variations in schools, in student testing, in teachers' mobility, and the like to trust the findings from this approach to accountability.

In addition to this foregoing argument, the intervening years have also brought a rise in other expectations for accountability, including regional accreditation and professional accreditation. Each of these accreditation agencies is expecting the influence on students to be a part of institutional and unit review, respectively.

Regional Accreditation

Our university receives its regional accreditation through the Southern Association of Colleges and Schools (SACS). We are now acutely aware that SACS has reoriented its historic focus on inputs (e.g., number of volumes in the libraries, faculty qualifications, quality of campus life) to include measures of student accomplishment. SACS does now ask that institutions implement some type of performance-based assessment system for students across all units or programs. To meet this expectation, the ASTL faculty are in the early stages of identifying three areas of programmatic impact: (1) our students' knowledge of content; (2) our students' planning; and (3) the program's effect on their PK–12 students' learning, for which we have written scoring rubrics.

These new expectations have caused us to reexamine what we want from our students, and have raised some interesting challenges that we are now facing. The first one is documenting the development of teachers' content knowledge, and how it implicates the structure of the program. As we described in chapter 1, our program has been the linking of two separate pieces: the Core and the Concentration. Students, regardless of their Concentration, proceed through the Core as a cohort in a twelve-month cycle. All twelve credits of the Core are completed during this time. Some students simultaneously take a course or two in their Concentrations, but they are not integrated formally. With the new expectations for assessing what our students know in the discipline (their Concentration), we now see our program's structure as a barrier to gathering evidence about content knowledge of some students. This happens because when some students complete the Core, they are still taking classes in their Concentration, thereby making judgments about the skills and knowledge, in say, history or mathematics, prematurely.

As of fall 2011, we are rethinking course scheduling. One option under consideration separates the last course of the Core, EDUC 615: Educational Change, from the other four Core classes. This particular course will become a capstone course for the entire program, which will culminate in the students completing a final portfolio of their accomplishments in the entire program, in contrast to those who completed the Core, but not their Concentration. Simultaneously, we are also working with the content fields in our Concentrations to ask each of them to require a capstone experience that will give the students an opportunity to demonstrate the new knowledge they have gained in these content areas. This marks a shift away from students simply completing the eighteen credits without some form of consolidating exercise that can create deeper insights into the content. Another option is to have all students complete their Concentrations before beginning the Core. We have discussed these options with the ASTL Advisory Council and have their support that any change that would culminate in a richer evaluation of the program's effects is one worth undertaking.

This approach to program design for improved assessment is completely new territory for us, and as the literature suggests, for the field. Extensive literature searches have not uncovered the advanced content knowledge teachers need and that is gained in a master's degree program. This is likely because there are not many master's degrees for practicing teachers that require collaborations with departments outside the school, college, or department of education. This form of teacher education program evaluation is a nascent field, and we are challenged regularly by our program and our students to continue practicing the collaborative reflection that advances a program closer to its goals. Regional accreditation, in our case, in the form of SACS, has impelled us to think more deeply about how to assess what practicing teachers learn in their master's degree programs. At the same time, that SACS accreditation is causing new conversations about accountability; we are also looking at the standards for professional accreditation to be sure we are addressing those, as well.

Professional Accreditation

Our education unit at George Mason University has been accredited by the NCATE for decades. Throughout this time, we have continued to try and stay abreast of NCATE's expectations for quality processes, and now outcomes, in achieving accreditation. Each program in the unit has a conceptual framework. Each program has program outcomes. Each program has students post their course products on an electronic learning management system. Each course has a scoring rubric that reflects the goals of the course and each student receives feedback based on that rubric. As an "advanced program" in the NCATE jargon, there are four standards that speak directly to the changes in our conversations about accountability.

Content Knowledge

Standard 1A states, "Candidates in advanced programs for teachers are recognized experts in the content that they teach." As noted in the previous discussion regarding regional accreditation, we must and now do work more closely with our colleagues in the departments that offer the Concentrations (e.g., history, mathematics, literacy). The new dimensions of accountability that include deeper content knowledge are changing the structure of the program to make it easier for us to gather data on how well the faculty members in the Concentrations rate the students' expertise in the areas they teach.

Situating this expectation within our own conceptual framework, we see this as the second Core proposition of NBPTS, "Teachers know the subjects they teach and how to teach those subjects to their students." Assessing teacher content knowledge and pedagogical content knowledge is a new conversation for the ASTL faculty and those who teach in the Concentrations, as until recently, we operated on the general principle that "good outcomes come from good processes" and now, to address the first half of this proposition, we are shifting to a focus on the verification of content knowledge by the content experts themselves. These colleagues, spread across our university, are now devising capstone experiences for making more holistic judgments about content knowledge. As we continue to talk with them, we ask the faculty members in each Concentration to design the most fitting culminating assessment for the ASTL students that would allow them to demonstrate their conceptual understandings of the content in the Concentration. For some, it might be a comprehensive examination and for others it may be a culminating project. How each Concentration faculty seeks to assess content that the students are "recognized experts" is a choice each makes. The approach we are taking in this area is one that is predicated on maintaining the trust of these colleagues and their belief that the ASTL program is consistently honest about increasing and improving teachers' knowledge of the content they teach. We have learned that maintaining this trust is essential to the program's success. People change. We work with new colleagues in these disciplines.

We strive to keep the expectations as constant as possible so relationships can build.

But these are hard conversations. In the traditional academic disciplines, the thesis has historically served as the measure of program completion. As we'll discuss next, content expertise is a necessary but not a sufficient condition for teaching effectiveness. Thus, there are historical barriers that must be approached and handled in thinking about how a future professor of history in a master's level class and how a teacher of high school history in the same master's level class should be evaluated. As we prepare this volume, this is one of the conversations we are having and it has led us to moving the last class in the Core to the last class in the entire program, where we can begin pilot-testing samples of our own ASTL students' work in the disciplines and developing new metrics for assessing the quality of teacher content knowledge.

Pedagogical Content Knowledge

The second half of the Board's proposition focuses on the teacher's ability to teach the content. NCATE's standard 1B states that "candidates in advanced programs for teachers have expertise in pedagogical content knowledge and share their expertise through leadership and mentoring roles in their schools and communities. They understand and address student preconceptions that hinder learning. They are able to critique research and theories related to pedagogy and learning. They are able to select and develop instructional strategies and technologies, based on research and experience, that help all students learn." In our work, this important standard is so multifaceted and multidimensional that it enlightens as much as it confounds. We treat this NCATE expectation as the second half of the Core proposition addressed previously. However, in this case, the focus is on "the ability to teach the content." To this we can add two of our three "program Core propositions," specifically, that teachers attend to the diversity in their classrooms when planning, teaching, and assessing; and that teachers use learning technologies to facilitate students' learning.

The standard is enlightening in that it recognizes the interplay between what a teacher knows and how a teacher teaches, as well as how a teacher conceptualizes what students know, and how a teacher makes informed instructional decisions. It also implies that teacher pedagogical content knowing (Cochran, DeRuiter, & King, 1993) is a body of knowledge developed over time and improved upon in a master's degree program. The implications for a program such as ASTL are vast, primarily because of its expectation that studying in a Concentration is something more than a continuation of undergraduate content. Rather, it relies on the teacher's practical experiences and the wisdom gained therein and graduate-level content that is intended to augment and deepen the teacher's understanding of that field. In addition, the Core should simultaneously be developing the teacher's sense of repertoire and purpose. However, it is up to the teacher to reconstruct his own PCK, and that is where new dimensions of accountability are needed.

Perhaps one of the best attempts at researching this is the work of Deborah Lowenberg Ball and her colleagues, and arguably best captured by Hill, Ball, and Schilling (2008). In a study of mathematics teachers' PCK, they expose just how challenging it is to measure this construct that is comprised of content and pedagogy, and how teachers put them together. They found that the teachers in their study did possess knowledge that is situated between the content field and the teaching of the content field. One specific area they cite is teachers' knowledge of students' conceptions of mathematics, a specific enabling understanding that can lead to more focused instruction and feedback. At the same time, they also found it very challenging to measure that knowledge with precision. These findings are even more problematic when we think about applying them to the education of teachers, and this is where the new conversations about program accountability must occur. We know PCK exists and we know it has multiple dimensions, and the challenge for the ASTL Core faculty is to help the content experts in the disciplines, who often don't study teaching, begin to understand how the content they require the teachers in the Concentration to master develops the students' PCK, in addition to their content knowledge. This is a challenge that falls between the structure of a program that includes faculty outside the education school as well as the time-bound course-taking patterns of students, which is confounded in Concentrations that are merely a collection of courses, rather than a coherent whole. In some Concentrations, there is a specified set of interrelated courses that are intended to form a "whole cloth"; in others, it remains a collection of courses pieced together by the students. As gratified as we are to engage our colleagues in the traditional academic disciplines at the advanced level, there remain many further discussions of how to know how well the ASTL students are mastering that content and then for the Core faculty to design methods of ascertaining how well they then teach that content to classrooms characterized by student demographic diversity, as well as the instructional decisions they make to use learning technologies to create multiple learning environments that will appeal to and attract their pupils to improved learning habits. These become our goals as we continue to improve upon the quality of our program.

Additionally, we can place NBPTS' fourth Core proposition within this NCATE standard, which expects teachers to "think systematically about their practice and to learn from experience." In ASTL, the students prepare multiple reflections for each course in the Core. Many of these reflections are opportunities for the faculty to enter into a one-on-one relationship with each student to get to know each of the ASTL students and their teaching settings more intimately, and to encourage them to continue reflecting on their students, themselves, and the content that brings them together. In many instances, these reflections have served as papers presented at professional annual meetings and as publications (Fox & White, 2010; Galluzzo & Hilldrup, 2005; Lukacs, Holincheck, Fuhrman, & Galluzzo, 2007). These analyses then feed back to the program for possible revisions in design, outcomes, and assessments. Reflection is now an expectation in teacher education. We treat it as a process goal to be achieved and assessed through journal entries on a weekly basis that tie course content to instructional practices with regular feedback designed to help our students continue to hone this important dimension of teaching.

In sum, it is reasonable to hold an education unit accountable for developing teachers' PCK in an advanced program. The ongoing work of initiating and sustaining conversations about the intellectual development of teachers is much harder, and the challenge is compounded because PCK is hard to measure. In the end, we don't know whether our content expert colleagues in the disciplines will acknowledge this literature without more substantial evidence, and therefore we don't know whether they teach for it and make it an outcome in the Concentration. So we need to tread lightly but with intention to continue to talk about how to assure ourselves that our students are making progress on this important outcome for an advanced program for teachers.

Pedagogical Knowledge

NCATE's standard 1C states, "Candidates in advanced programs for teachers develop expertise in certain aspects of professional and pedagogical knowledge and contribute to the dialogue based on their research and experiences. They take on leadership roles in the professional community and collaborate with colleagues to contribute to school improvement and renewal."

ASTL, given its moorings in the NBPTS' Core propositions, has always been focused on helping teachers see themselves as more than teacher leaders who contribute to their schools' improvement. The program's faculty members have the goal of going beyond the teacher leader concept and more toward teachers as agents of school change in these times when closing achievement gaps is a school-by-school proposition. To become those change agents, the Core faculty requires the teachers in the program to become skilled inquirers about teaching and learning through child study and action research, as well as understanding the influences of culture on teaching, learning, teachers, children, and schools. It also requires the teachers to widen their repertoire to include more indirect teaching strategies that open more doors for their students. Lastly, it expects the teachers to demonstrate their skills to think creatively about the school in which each works, to suggest changes, and to have the skills to acquire resources to make change happen for the students in their school. This is our interpretation of NCATE 1C. How well we do that continues in this chapter, and subsequently we find ourselves engaging in conversations not often found in the literature. When we think about these outcomes, we find ourselves discussing how to discover whether our teachers have these skills. For example, how do we hold ourselves accountable for preparing teachers who are agents of their schools' change? We do this by asking the ASTL students to engage their school leadership in a change effort that is based on the school's performance data. In one school, the teacher might notice that students for whom English is a new language are not performing on early literacy assessments equal to their peers. As part of an ASTL requirement, the teacher undertakes a project with the school's leadership to prepare a grant proposal submitted to philanthropic organization for funding to create the proper conditions to increase literacy skills for ELLs. The decision about what the intervention is to be is left to the teacher, her peers, and the school's leadership. It might include funding for specific materials, or an initiative that reaches into the home to help the parents become better teachers of reading, or whatever change the people in the school feel would address the puzzlement. Our goal is to teach the teachers how to be advocates for their students and for making their schools into the best environments possible for the nature of the student body that walks in its doors every day.

The field of teacher education has also not been very enlightening on this matter. Returning to the report from the National Academies concerning NBPTS, its remedies are not particularly realistic for ASTL. Hakel, Koenig, and Elliott (2008) recommend that NBPTS and education researchers interested in the Board conduct longitudinal studies to assess how well it achieves its goals. In a one-year timeframe for documenting one's teaching, this may be more possible because of the stability of student enrollment in the Board candidate's class, but in a master's degree program that takes some students three to four years to complete, the evaluation methods aren't able to address the numerous validity issues that arise from the question, such as the teacher staying in the same building or even the same grade in the same building; or, the teacher using her knowledge and skills in the ASTL program to move into the position of a school-based literacy coach, or department chair. As noted earlier, we have approached a local school district with a proposal to study our students by merging personnel records with student achievement and were denied that request. Given these ongoing hurdles, we have decided, so far, and we fully acknowledge that it is a controversial decision, not to measure the quality of our programs based upon the standardized test scores of the pupils our students teach. While we have work samples in our students' final portfolios, so far they have not been particularly revealing in terms of PK–12 student academic achievement on Virginia's SOL examinations. Rather, we strive to teach our students to become much more mindful of how they look at each student, but we cannot reliably estimate this for a cohort of our students. So, our microscope into this important dimension of teaching focuses on one teacher-student dyad. That's all we think the culture will allow methodologically. We see no easily implemented assessment protocol at this point that doesn't come with costs our institution can support. As it looks to us, ASTL and any other teacher education program would have to become a research and development center with funding large enough to conduct studies in the classrooms of our students, and be broad enough to appeal to the policy and philanthropic communities, who have not been interested in institutional research. The best we can offer from our experiences is that each teacher education program faculty must necessarily wrestle with the extent to which it wants to be held accountable for its program's quality, whether it is focused at the level of teacher candidate or the candidates' pupils; we've opted for the former to date. As stated in various parts of this text and chapter, we are not convinced by the current value-added models for revealing the kind of learning we believe our program seeks to foster in children.

But NCATE has continued to evolve its conception of an accredited program by including performance expectations, which may include the value that our graduates add to their students' achievement. In other words, the kind of assessing brought forward with passage of the No Child Left Behind Act of 2001 is seen in the latest expectations of our professional accreditation agency. Studying the gain scores is now a new challenge, and as a faculty we have to consider the degree to which we believe there is enough good science to suggest this is a viable path to pursue and whether it is worth the expense toward program improvement (Bill and Melinda Gates Foundation, 2010). In essence, we must now wrestle with the question derived from the title Glazerman, Goldhaber, Loeb, Staiger, Raudenbush, and Whitehurst (2010) gave to their essay, namely that value-added models may not be perfect, but are they worth it? In short, we remain skeptical, along with Newton, Darling-Hammond, Haertel, and Thomas (2010), and the Economic Policy Institute (2010) who found, that the contexts in which teachers teach exert tremendous influence on the amount of value a teacher adds to a student's achievement. Moreover, we must also wrestle with how many resources answering this question takes and what other valuable information about program effects and effectiveness we might not gather that would provide even better feedback to the program faculty.

Assessment

NCATE standard 1D states, "Candidates in advanced programs for teachers have a thorough understanding of assessment. They analyze student, classroom, and school performance data and make data-driven decisions about strategies for teaching and learning so that all students learn."

This standard raises important questions for the ASTL Core faculty. In April 2009, we conducted a study of all ASTL graduates over the first ten years. One of the main findings was that we do not address student assessment enough. We have taught our students to write and test scoring rubrics, but our data suggest that our graduates are caught between the heavy emphasis policymakers and school leaders are placing on test preparation, and the teachers' desires to provide more useful feedback about more than memorization and mastery. In preparing for an accreditation review, we have become more mindful of finding the balance between the testing regime that influences so many of the decisions our students must make concerning instruction, and helping them discover how to take the material they are expected to teach in Virginia's SOL and develop assessment mechanisms that can help them provide feedback to students that encourages growth independent, yet supportive of, content mastery.

CONTEMPLATING THE NEXT STEPS

ASTL is an intentionally collaborative act among the faculty who teach in it that is predicated on the fundamental value that it must be a master's degree that combines scholarly thought with professional development. In our experience, it demands more from us than any other program in which we teach. We have found that cohorts take much more care than students enrolled in any class we teach outside ASTL. Also each cohort changes our instructional dynamics in some subtle, and sometimes explicit, ways. Like the NBPTS on which we predicated our conceptual framework, we often feel we're learning to fly the plane once it's in the air.

Perhaps nowhere are we more challenged than in considering the future, both our roles and how we hold ourselves accountable. We know we are not where we can and should be when it comes to accountability, but we are quite far along, nonetheless. We have evidence, as presented in chapters 5 through 7 that our program is changing our students' conceptions of teaching and what it means to teach and be a teacher. Our students' portfolios reveal a tremendous amount of growth, which was captured again in a decennial follow-up study of all cohorts to identify what the program does well, and those areas that still require attention. Ideally, ASTL would be our only assignment, but it is not. We teach in other programs, both preservice and doctoral. The time we devote to ASTL, while more than we devote to any of our other programs, is still not enough to maintain a robust research and development agenda that informs the field about how to use the master's degree to graduate teachers who approximate the Core propositions of NBPTS. In our experience, it is a challenge for our university to allow us to give all of our time over to ASTL, as it has other needs for our time. So, as we look to the next steps forward, it is developing that robust research agenda about evidence of accountability.

One of the challenges in program design in teacher education is the struggle to keep our eyes on what we want for our students and what our external reviewers want from us. NCATE keeps changing, as it should, and we are busy trying to study our program as we prepare for the ultimate accountability of a professional school, accreditation. But even that forces new challenges to consider, for example, how do you stay true to your history when external conditions force changes away from what you're trying to accomplish? In this instance, it is the continuing expectation that we will use PK–12 students' test scores as an indication of the program's effects and effectiveness. As noted previously, we side with the skeptics regarding the wisdom of this.

A second challenge, though, is expanding our own evidence about effects. As discussed earlier in this chapter, we are unable to measure teachers' thinking and planning as results of the program. It is not how students attend academic programs. Perhaps by moving the final class in the Core, Educational Change, we would open the doors to better program inquiry. We currently can't measure program effects across Core and Concentration to assess PCK because they remain isolated from one another. A new form of accountability is to hook the two together in culminating projects that try to address both ASTL's eight Core propositions and the NCATE standards in unison. Then, once we have identified the major products we want our students to demonstrate as they complete the program, we can design pre-program assessments that give us more than their self-evaluation of their skills upon entry; we can actually gather data on how they might plan a lesson, consider the influences of teaching in diverse classrooms, implement a strategy that requires the use of learning technologies, think about themselves as agents of school change, and more. Over these first ten years of ASTL, we've learned that expectations for teachers, and therefore teacher education, will never be static. The landscape has changed and now becoming comfortable with uncertainty is all the more reason for each program to chart its own path to accountability.

We continue to practice our collaborative reflection as a faculty. We locate fissures where we once saw continuity. We talk about the data we have on our students. We discuss what the data from any cohort means for the next one. Books are changed; assignments are changed; instructional activities are changed to fit the needs of the evolving landscape of teacher education. As we stand back and reflect about our goals for the program, the challenge is to ensure we design the program to provide our students with the analytic tools necessary to put themselves on a path of self-renewal. Perhaps, in the end, ASTL is the foundation for a career of self-directed professional development that does not require them to "go back to school" to learn more. Rather, we hope they find their own ways to demonstrate their effects on their own pupils in a collaborative reflection environment that they helped to shape in their schools.

9

New Roles for Education Faculty

It's so hard to be a program, meaning striving to achieve conceptual holism, when the norm in higher education is that programs are often a collection of courses. As off-putting as that statement appears, we learned some very important lessons about how working closely together as a program faculty changed how we approached our work as professors, and added a new role to our professional lives: data analyst.

It was a damp and cold Friday in February when the ASTL faculty met in a peer-oriented, open forum initiated by the dean to improve cross-program communication and collaboration among the college's faculty. Entitled the Collegial Program Seminars, this initiative asked the faculty in each program area to prepare an overview of the program and then to present data on its effects or effectiveness to a group of peers from other programs in the college.

On this particular Friday, the ASTL faculty were making their presentation to be discussed by their peers. Two of the ASTL faculty attended the seminar with both the requisite program description and with the data to share. Because both of these professors had taught at other institutions some years earlier, such a format was not something we had experienced; we had to adopt our new role to fulfill our obligation.

As we prepared, we quickly realized that in addition to the teaching, scholarship, and service roles with which most professors are accustomed, we found ourselves as data analysts. We had to compile many of the pieces of course and program data we've described throughout this volume. We walked our peers through the purposes of ASTL, our goals for our students, and the data that we believe demonstrates our effects and our effectiveness. The exercise proved quite valuable for the program faculty as it had to determine what evidence best-represented the program's accomplishments. We worked for some days to make the best presentation possible—one that was both transparent as well as invitational to those in the room.

In many ways that experience propelled us to prepare this volume. We learned that through collaboration and reflection, two of our program's Core propositions, we could begin to see our own story. We became committed data analysts as a result of this experience and have tried, with some degree of success, to let the data on our students tell the story of ASTL.

Each year, education professors teach thousands of practicing teachers who enroll in a variety of master's degree programs. Nearly one-quarter (23.8 percent) of all graduate students are enrolled in a master's degree program in education (Council of Graduate Schools, 2005, p.12), such that in 2008–2009, the field of education awarded the highest number of master's degrees offered by any field. Faculty teaching graduate-level courses for practicing teachers and other education professionals are being pressed to provide experiences that address the real concerns of professionals in the workplace and to offer worthwhile ongoing professional development as defined by such standards setting and accrediting organizations as NBPTS, NCATE, and the Teacher Education Accreditation Council (TEAC).

Education professionals seek advanced study for a variety of reasons. They may want to prepare for a new scholarly or professional career, improve their practice to better facilitate student learning, increase their salary, or satisfy a need for further learning. The advanced degree they earn not only serves their needs but also serves our schools and other educational organizations. Education professionals with advanced degrees hold positions as leaders and contribute to the nation's educational well-being, thus making good use of the leadership, clinical, and applied research skills gained from their graduate program (Council of Graduate Schools, 2005).

Since the 1990s, many research reports and policies have pressed colleges and universities providing master's degrees to prepare better graduates (Hakel, Koenig, & Elliot, 2008; Holmes Group, 1995; National Council for the Accreditation of Teacher Education, 2008b; Wayne & Young, 2003). Higher education today is defined more and more by pressures to promote excellence through accountability, to define what college graduates should know and be able to do across degree levels (Cibulka & Leibbrand, 2010; Dilworth & Cleveland, 2010; Lumina Foundation for Education, 2011), to better measure the skills and knowledge they impart to students, and to address an increasing focus on learning outcomes for degree students. These pressures are also influencing the way faculty define themselves and their roles.

To address the steadily increasing demand to document what their graduates know and can do in the workplace, the ASTL faculty reexamined their traditional roles and responsibilities regarding its program in the context of increased standards of good practice. Much of the content of this chapter is based on the collective experiences of four faculty members who have collaborated on this degree program for more than a decade. This chapter addresses the changing roles the ASTL faculty experienced by first providing an overview of traditional faculty roles followed by changing faculty roles based on a shifting landscape in the academy, schools, and our own CEHD. It concludes with questions that our faculty is examining as we make decisions for the future.

TRADITIONAL FACULTY ROLES

Traditional faculty roles are closely tied to the central functions of higher education—teaching, research, and service. This triad is the cornerstone of the academy although the emphasis upon each one often differs by institutional type and across institutions. From the outset of American higher education in 1636, college and university faculty have undertaken research, teaching, and service roles to carry out the academic work of their respective institutions. Each of these roles enables faculty to generate and disseminate knowledge to a variety of audiences and is discussed in the following.

The Teaching Role

Teaching is a central mission of institutions of higher education. As discipline experts, faculty are expected to remain current in their field, disseminate and impart basic or applied knowledge to their students, and examine their students' learning and application of knowledge. This traditional view of teaching assumes the faculty member is the content expert and students are regarded as learners or novices to the academic discipline or field of study.

The teaching role is the most widely shared among faculty across institutional types. During the 1980s and 1990s the teaching role came under increased scrutiny through the Wingspread Group on Higher Education (1993) and the publication of Boyer's *Scholarship Reconsidered* (1990), among others. These publications questioned the emphasis of teaching as dissemination as not fulfilling the educational mission of the institution. Boyer (1990), for example, was instrumental in turning the academy's attention to student learning and emphasizing effective pedagogies. The shift from teaching as disseminating content to teaching with a focus on what degree students are learning reflects the paradigm today—that of faculty as facilitators of learning.

The Research Role

University faculty members engage in research, thereby contributing to the knowledge base of their subject area. Like the teaching role, the context, mission, and type of institution largely determine the extent of a faculty member's research role. Faculty with active research agendas are more often than not part of a research-oriented institution. The research role also includes expectations that faculty contribute to the discipline through publishing scholarly articles, presenting research findings, and disseminating knowledge to a variety of internal and external constituencies within their content areas.

The Service Role

Faculty members are also expected to provide service both internally and externally to the institution and to be good citizens. In comparison to teaching and scholarship, the service role is often considered less critical for tenure and promotion. Service activities that are internal to the college or university include work at the department, college, and university levels; external service includes work in the local, state, regional, and national communities, and to professional associations. With the foregoing establishing the traditional definition of the three roles that professors assume, we turn our attention to the newer roles that we have found ourselves having to play.

CHANGING FACULTY ROLES

As the academy and teacher education have evolved, so have faculty roles. The increased attention to the rising expectations for program effectiveness, including accreditation, a greater emphasis on degree students' learning outcomes, and a focus on the twenty-first-century skills of collaboration and teamwork all necessitate a look at faculty roles for the future. To adapt to these changing roles, there is a need for faculty to re-interpret these traditional roles to fit today's higher education environment while maintaining the integrity guaranteed and protected by academic freedom. Faculty also revisited the multifaceted work that goes into current views of effective teaching and create authentic curricular pathways through which students gain the competencies and skills they need—developing a true scholarship of teaching (Boyer, 1990; Glassick, Huber, & Maeroff, 1997).

The ASTL faculty works in a college that is organized programmatically, not departmentally. This distinct structure allows faculty to reach across the disciplines to create a myriad of curricular opportunities for students as well as to collaborate in their research efforts. For example, faculty in the literacy program may collaborate with faculty in other college programs in research or course offerings and not be constrained by the need to generate departmental student full-time equivalencies in enrollment. Like most education faculty in the ever-changing world of education, our roles are changing, dynamic, and innovative.

Apart from the organizational structure of the college, the four of us have established a collegial culture that has assisted us in adapting to the changes while maintaining our own integrity and that of the program. The real transformation began with the way we worked together to create and maintain a vital, relevant professional development degree program for practicing teachers who want to remain in the classroom. Specifically, the ASTL faculty had to become committed to one another as colleagues as well as to the students in the program. This commitment strengthened the program's coherence, one of the most challenging programmatic elements to accomplish in teacher education (Buchmann & Floden, 1992). Coherence, which Buchmann and Floden call a "rebel angel," is the ability to form a unified whole that allows for many kinds of connectedness. Educational reformers have often called for program coherence "as a central principle and even as the primary indicator of curricular worth" (Buchmann & Floden, 1992, p. 4). Building coherence continues to be viewed as a critical determinant for ongoing professional development (Holmes Group, 1986; Learning Forward, 2011).

To achieve coherence meant that our work was predicated on knowing what our students in the Core had done prior to teaching them in our successive classes. Through regular, monthly meetings, our conversations centered on what was happening in each course so that each faculty member developed a full picture of what was happening with a particular cohort. That level of open communication is rare but essential in providing a coherent program of experiences for our students. Our collective and individual contributions enabled us to accomplish what we did in a culture of collegiality based upon respect for one another's professional knowledge and expertise. Yet these changing roles have also been influenced by an increased emphasis on new accountabilities, such as a higher bar for NCATE or TEAC accreditation, data usage for program improvement, and faculty development, as discussed in many of the other chapters in this volume.

New Accountabilities

According to the authors of *Tomorrow's Schools of Education* (Holmes Group, 1995), "the increasingly ambitious goals of the schools necessitate a more ambitious responsibility by the university" (p. 87). While progress has definitely been made, most universities find it impossible to implement fully the worthy goals that they have endorsed for the education of school professionals. Why, then, are the objectives of reform so hard to attain? And how have ASTL faculty been influenced by a higher standard of accreditation, its concomitant requirement to be more intentional to program quality, and its effects on student learning? How have ASTL faculty balanced this new accountability with the traditional roles of teaching and research?

Accreditation is a lever for strengthening education overall and assuring quality learning for those pursuing careers in schools and education schools. The current NCATE (2008a) accreditation criteria are testimony to this statement. NCATE explicitly states that programs for the continuing education of teachers use the NBPTS propositions. Notable for ASTL faculty is the language used in the NCATE definition of *conceptual framework* that has been a catalyst for moving the ASTL faculty to a level of ensuring the highest quality program and student quality that is possible. NCATE defines a conceptual framework as "an underlying structure in a professional education unit that gives conceptual meaning to the unit's operations through an articulated rationale and provides direction for programs, courses, teaching, candidate performance, faculty scholarship and service, and unit accountability" (NCATE, 2008a, p. 85). ASTL's eight learning outcomes stated with a collaboratively written conceptual document form the program structure that obligates faculty to remain on the same page so that the program has coherence and is not dependent on particular faculty. In the next section, we examine how the ASTL faculty is learning to integrate new accountabilities into the fabric of their shifting roles while remaining accountable to the triad of teaching, research, and service.

Shifting Faculty Roles

For ASTL faculty, there has been a shift in three primary roles that were not initially obvious to any of us. The first relates to how the ASTL faculty used the forum of Collegial Program Seminars, our college's forum for program reflection, as an opportunity to examine its program and faculty roles explicitly in the context of intentional reflection and collegial dialogue. The second shift is associated with how faculty are modeling best professional practices in teaching, research, and service amidst a rapidly changing academic culture. And the third shift refers to acculturating new faculty into the program's values and practices.

Examining Faculty Roles in the Context of Intentional Reflection and Collegial Dialogue

Using the college's five Core values of collaboration, ethical leadership, innovation, research-based practice, and social justice to unify the college, the dean of CEHD initiated a three-year reflective process of planned professional conversations entitled Collegial Program Seminars. The seminars were designed to share each program's implementation of the college's five Core values. They were based on the premise that through intentional reflection on these and other Core values combined with thoughtful collegial conversation and feedback, the quality, delivery, and outcome of individual programs could be enhanced. These seminars were a manifestation of the college's commitment to the value of intentional, reflective dialogue and feedback, program improvement, and accountability to the CEHD Core values.

The Collegial Program Seminars were intended to extend each program's opportunity to reflect on itself and its relation to the college and the profession. They were also to serve as an exemplary reflective process that complemented the accreditation processes and to communicate what individual programs were doing. Each program responded to seven key questions ranging from ways the Core values were reflected in their program, to the specific values that a program prioritizes and manifests, and the program's challenges in meeting the CEHD Core values. At the outset of these faculty seminars, however, the process was explicitly not part of accreditation, which led to a wide variation in the depth and quality of the faculty commitment to engage in a high level of intentional reflection and collegial conversation.

Given the opportunity to study our own practice, what did the ASTL faculty learn about new faculty roles? As can be seen from this chapter's opening vignette, we have consistently studied ourselves, taken our struggles seriously, and have been open about which program areas were strong and which ones needed to be addressed or reconfigured. Studying our own practice has provided us with a lens into how the ASTL faculty adapted to new roles in teaching, research, and service that we describe next.

New Teaching Roles

In looking back at more than a decade of experiences, we find ourselves in three new teaching roles: (1) focusing on collaboration, (2) preparing courses differently, and (3) using a co-teaching model. First, because of the ASTL cohort model, we often teach the same section of a course next door to our faculty peers. Our students expect the same experiences, content, and quality regardless of the section they are in or the faculty member who is teaching it. What has happened because of students' expectations, along with the faculty striving for coherence across the courses, is a changed dynamic. We find ourselves teaching the same course in a different way each time because of our teaching peers and a different set of students. That is, while we have always modified our courses each time we teach them, we are now modifying them in a different way; we are no longer teaching alone. We teach in partnership with a peer, either a full-time faculty member or an adjunct. This dynamic has led to the second new teaching role—that of preparing courses differently.

The way ASTL faculty prepare to teach each course has also shifted. At the outset of this program, we operated in a traditional way. That is, we had an approved syllabus and shared that syllabus with the faculty members teaching the course. From that point on, the faculty member taught students on her own, according to the syllabus. Because we now teach in partnership with our faculty peers, what has shifted for us is the reality and necessity of keeping in close contact with one another about not only meeting students' needs, but also opening ourselves to new ways of thinking about providing course content and course experiences as a result of increased collaboration. Our students expect this from each course and we have shifted our focus to be more open to new ways of teaching. Moreover, we are increasing our attention to different assessment data derived from our performance-based assessments and systematic feedback from students. As a result, we are understanding the shift in focus from teaching as knowledge dissemination to teaching as scaffolding student learning.

Finally, we are using a co-teaching model to mentor our doctoral students planning to enter the field of teacher education. For example, to address the continuing challenge of finding and supporting faculty who meet accreditation requirements for qualified faculty, doctoral students have completed an "internship" in the ASTL Core classes. During the internship, the doctoral student assists in planning for the course, observes during each class, leads particular activities, and assists the full-time faculty member with evaluating student reflections and grading other assignments. We are currently working with doctoral students to assume full responsibility for teaching a Core class under the supervision of a full-time faculty member after successful completion of an internship.

New Research and Program Evaluation Roles

Probably the single most changed role for ASTL faculty in the research area is that of program analyst (i.e., faculty members who have adopted an inquiry stance to teaching and program evaluation as well as research). To illustrate, we use a variety of types of data collection, such as starting each cohort with an operational self-assessment, analyzing course products, such as the individual case study project that specifically addresses our student learning outcome and analyzes the final portfolio at the end of the Core. We use data from each of these artifacts for program improvement, such as course level products from the Core and from Concentrations. We engage in critical conversations based on student and faculty feedback around assignments, program learning outcomes, course focus, and relevancy. We now explicitly align coursework and its effectiveness on student learning outcomes and are moving to review student performance data systematically to inform alignment of assignments within and across coursework. Naturally, this move necessitates faculty development on how to review and discuss varied data sources to inform decision making. As we add or have added data sources and different types of data, management and organization of the different data sources needs to be developed so we can efficiently and systematically review and consider what the data are saying. Faculty need to work on development of how to align coursework and make decisions using more comprehensive and varied qualitative and quantitative data sources.

New Service Roles

Our roles in both internal and external service are also shifting. Internally, our most current efforts include meeting with all Concentration faculty to review overall program successes and challenges and recommend procedural changes, such as course scheduling and tightening the connections between our assignments and assessments. Faculty have also assumed active roles in the Alumni Advisory Council in an effort to obtain feedback from former students on their perceptions of the program from one to five years after finishing. Part of the Advisory Council work for faculty has also involved obtaining input from former ASTL students on topics ranging from specific assignments to course sequencing to course content.

The overarching lesson the ASTL faculty can offer in the context of intentional reflection and collegial dialogue is this: Practice what you preach. We teach practicing teachers who bring to us questions and issues regarding what they are expected to do in the schools with their students. We, in turn, are engaged in this same approach to inquiry in our program.

Modeling Best Practices in Teaching, Research, and Service

The newly revised Standards for Professional Learning (Learning Forward, 2011) delineate the characteristics of professional learning that promote effective teaching, leadership ability, and improved student learning. The standards clearly delineate the important role that educators have in their own learning and the equally important role that professional learning providers have in focusing on professional learning for educators that will lead to learning for their students. Three current best practices that most teachers are using to inform student learning in their schools are professional learning communities (PLCs), data-driven decision making, and collaborative learning. Those practices have greatly influenced our faculty roles and helped us to live our Core propositions through collaborating in our own PLC.

Professional Learning Communities

In today's schools, increasing attention is being given to teachers as members of learning communities and to using PLCs as a vehicle for deepening teachers' pedagogical knowledge (Dufour, Dufour, Eaker, & Many, 2006; Tom, 1999). For teacher educators to support these practices, their university coursework must be community and collaboration oriented. Providing the context for learning as a member of a community means providing emotional, physical, and intellectual safety, promoting intellectual camaraderie and healthy attitudes toward learning, building on the learning of others, fostering excitement in learning, and promoting connections to the outside community (Bransford, Brown, & Cocking, 1999; Maslow, 1999). Collaborative learning is more achievable when faculty embed workplace collaboration skills within coursework and fieldwork so practicing professionals can further experience these attributes and have a basis for transferring them into their own settings.

Our own shifting faculty teaching roles related to PLCs can best be illustrated by how we attend each other's classes when students are completing a course or courses prior to beginning the course we are teaching. As part of the transition from course to course, we observe our students as they present their performance-based assessment for the ending course. We also confer with each other regarding student performance across Core classes, not just our own, and participate in the culminating portfolio presentations at the end of the Core. Moreover, we deliberately seek feedback from each other before changing course readings, assignments, or assessments because we realize the effects that changes in one course have on the courses that precede and that follow. Moreover, we have become our own PLC through studying our own practices, deepening our interest in student learning and program integrity, and disseminating information culminated in this book. The link between our own learning and that of our students is increasing the likelihood that our ASTL students' learning is also contributing to their PK–12 students' learning.

Data-Driven Decision-making

Influenced by the new accountabilities and accreditation, our faculty have been collecting, analyzing, and using data that ranges from knowledge generation to evaluating the effectiveness of a teaching approach. The nature and content of the data we collect and have collected has changed over time. For example, we have moved from the initial point of obtaining feedback on student perceptions of coursework, to studying their reflections in depth, and now examining more specific aspects of teacher learning and change, such as the cultural projects and teacher efficacy studies discussed in chapter 5. Consequently, the results of different data collection efforts have informed the program and simultaneously prompted us to respond to student needs, outside accreditation and accountability needs, and influence faculty direction in their own research. We continue to write and publish about the program, to give research presentations locally, nationally, and internationally, to write and publish with students, and to lead dissertations.

Collaborative Learning

Collaboration, the third practice that has affected our new faculty roles, is increasingly being recognized as a critical skill that is necessary for success in the complex life and work environments of the twenty-first century. According to the Partnership for 21st Century Skills (2004), collaboration requires the ability to: (1) "work effectively and respectfully with diverse teams, (2) exercise flexibility and willingness to be helpful in making necessary compromises to accomplish a common goal, and (3) assume shared responsibility for collaborative work and value the individual contributions made by each team member" (p. 4). Teaming and collaboration, essential ingredients of the twenty-first century workplace, are the norm for a workplace that is different from today's workplace and require the cooperative interaction between and among members of a team as they work to be productive and achieve a goal (Pink, 2005). Developing the necessary collaborative skills requires those who prepare professional educators to integrate twenty-first century skills across all subjects, grade levels, and human development professions so that students will learn collaboration skills as they learn the content necessary for their respective disciplines. Although inconsistent, our collaboration with education and arts and sciences faculty is becoming increasingly paramount to address how we measure student content knowledge. In effect, we continue to learn as we go.

The ASTL faculty collaborates regularly and systematically with PK–12 practitioners and with faculty in other college or university units. We are actively engaged in a community of learners. As such, we provide leadership in the profession, schools, and professional associations at state, national, and international levels. Examples include changes made to assignments and readings based on student performance and post-program feedback as discussed under new service roles and in greater length in the next chapter.

Acculturating New Faculty: Faculty Development for the Twenty-first Century Academy

Because there are so few faculty "dedicated" to ASTL, acculturating new faculty into the program has been difficult and very challenging. We may only have a full-time faculty member teaching one class a year and so we use a co-teaching model with new faculty to do some of the scaffolding needed for them to teach on their own in subsequent years. Although we continue to be more successful with part-time faculty and doctoral students as they co-teach with us, we infrequently have this opportunity with our full-time faculty peers. In addition to scaffolding new faculty in a particular course or courses they are learning to teach, we intentionally discuss how the courses fit with other courses and program components such as the portfolio. We have found that the eight program learning outcomes and corresponding performance assessments can and do provide a structure for understanding how the different program components fit together. As the program has changed over time based on our use of programmatic data, we continue to reflect on specific ways to more effectively acculturate new faculty.

A Systematic Look at Learning Outcomes

As the ASTL faculty enters the second decade of its program in advanced professional development, we continue to engage in systematic reflection of our changing faculty roles within a traditional academic framework. It is standard practice for us to look back to our original ASTL learning outcomes, which have informed our decisions about program improvement and continue to guide programmatic changes. This reflective process has been critical in helping us adapt to changing roles.

To meet the increased complexity and diversity of faculty roles at our institution, the ASTL faculty engaged in critical conversations about the best ways to assume and execute these roles. At the time, we may not have realized how this represented a shift in faculty roles and responsibilities. As we engaged in more serious conversation, we were actually living a change that, retrospectively, we now can see. For example, while one ASTL faculty member was actively engaged in programmatic research, she was also keenly aware of the importance of using data to examine systematically the results of the ASTL faculty work. We continue to take a systematic look at our learning outcomes to help us stay true to the program Core while simultaneously thinking through the new roles we are assuming.

Looking and Thinking Ahead: New Decisions

We, like most advanced programs, are a context-specific program and operate as such according to our college and university missions, the standards of NBPTS, and our accrediting bodies. In many ways, we were ahead of the curve twelve years ago by designing this program around the Board's propositions. If you are faculty in an advanced program today and are accredited by NCATE or TEAC, or will become accredited by the Council for the Accreditation of Educator Preparation (CAEP), the 2012 expected consolidation of NCATE and TEAC that will serve as a single accrediting body for reform, innovation, and research in educator preparation going forward, you are encouraged to use the NBPTS propositions to define your program. For our faculty, the flexibility of these propositions coupled with our commitment to collaborate and work as a team makes addressing the new questions and decisions a very natural way to operate. Our continual examination and reexamination of new roles have taken us beyond our initial program conceptualization to a place where we can now retrospectively look at the changing roles we have assumed. Some of the new decisions we are facing are reflected in the following questions and will require adapting roles as well as practices. These questions consider the uniqueness of faculty who work with advanced educator preparation:

- How can faculty overcome that there are few incentives for excellent teaching and little preparation for effective teaching?
- How can working collaboratively be recognized as an effective form of effective teaching and professional growth?
- How can efforts to build communities of learners among faculty be sustained for the long term and to what end?
- What is the role of professional faculty in school reform?
- What is the role of teacher education faculty in helping teachers confront the achievement gap and address the increasing role that culture and language play in our classrooms today?
- How can faculty in advanced programs accommodate the limited foundational knowledge teachers from alternative programs and other backgrounds bring to the advanced program?
- How can we sustain the intents and purposes of the program as its original leaders move on to other leadership positions?

CONCLUSION

In visioning what tomorrow will entail for ASTL faculty roles, we ask ourselves what we expect and how we get there. Recall Alice's adventures in wonderland when she asks the Cheshire cat which path to take, to which he responded, "That depends a good deal on where you want to get to." The lesson learned here is that while we will encounter challenges and setbacks along the way, we do need to know where we are going. Even as we write this book, several structural and organizational changes are occurring in our college that affect faculty roles. How we navigate the shifting waters will depend, in part, on how we view our own shifting faculty roles.

10

Looking Back and Looking Ahead

It is a typical Monday morning and the ASTL faculty holds its monthly meeting. They are a small group; sometimes as few as five, and rarely more than eight. When it is small, you're looking at the Core faculty, and when it is larger, some of the faculty from the concentrations attend, but that is rare.

The topic for this meeting is an assignment in the Core. For the first five years of the program, the students in the course Educational Change, which is designed to teach the skills of teacher leadership and change agency, were required to complete a review of an innovation in education that could be useful to their school. Each student reads thoroughly about the innovation (defined as "new to you") and the research that supports it, and then prepares a presentation intended for peers to encourage them to consider making a similar change in their school. Each of these was submitted to the professor who then compiled them into a bound collection and gave all students about twenty different reviews of innovations that each student could take back to his school to share with peers. This was the signature assignment in this course to help teachers learn to find new thinking in the field. The topics were often curricula (e.g., Read Naturally, Mathematics Investigations, Project-based Learning).

After five years, the professor followed up with some of the students to find out what had happened with each one's innovation project and the compendium. From the feedback, it was evident that it sat in a desk somewhere. While the project was reported as a valuable learning activity, the products did not always find their way into the schools.

At the ASTL faculty meeting, the discussion is "what can we do to make the change assignment more meaningful, more active?" Two of the professors were proposing teaching the skill of grant writing and requiring the students to work with their peers and administrators on identifying a problem the school can address, if it has the funds to do it. The other faculty members were engaged in the discussion and walked the line between academic freedom and program fidelity with the Core propositions of ASTL. One of the faculty members asked, "what proposition(s) will this new assignment achieve?" The response was, "I see us working on the same ones as before, of course, 'teacher as change agent,' but also, 'member of the learning community and reflective practitioner,' which are new with this change." After an hour of additional analysis by the ASTL faculty as a collective and much discussion of how all three propositions can be included in the assignment, it was agreed to make this change in the program. The new assignment would require the teachers in the course to examine their school's data on the aspect they'd like to change—for example, student achievement scores, attendance rates, reading skills, learning English as a new language. They would then meet with their principals to discuss the area and to plan an innovation that might help the school change its profile in this one area. Once they reached an agreement, the teachers would locate a philanthropic organization and then prepare a grant proposal for funds to begin initiating a change. It could be a new supplemental program, professional development for the school's staff, the implementation of a "take home" reading or math program to engage parents in their children's education, a behavior management protocol, and many others. The goal of the new assignment is to teach the ASTL students to reflect on their school's performance, work with their building's leadership, propose a solution, and learn the skills of seeking grant funding to make change happen.

The foregoing is but one example of how the ASTL faculty members attend to the program as much as to their courses. As a program faculty, we strive to keep all of us included in all decisions, even those that lean hard against the academic freedom we experience in other courses we teach in other programs, where this kind of program integrity is not as high. We also collectively considered the role this new assignment might have on the teachers and how it might better contribute toward the achievement of the overall program learning outcomes.

This introductory vignette, while admittedly brief in its capturing of the discussion, is one example of the degree to which we believe that course decisions, which are usually the prerogative of individual course faculty, are also program decisions that affect what the program is trying to accomplish. In a sense, course readings are program readings, and course assignments are program assignments. ASTL is the sum of its parts, but it is also the interrelationships among the courses, assignments, and the faculty. Periodically throughout this text we have used the expression "collective reflection." It is not an overstatement; the faculty meetings do include more in-depth discussions of courses as described previously to maintain a fidelity to one another, to create coherence for us and for our students. We have not seen this as an impingement on our academic freedom; rather, we see it as striving for coherence and a commitment to accomplish program goals. In a sense, the program, not the course, is the unit of change. As the vignette suggests, courses can and will be changed, but they are changed in the context of the eight Core propositions of the program.

As the title of the chapter suggests, we are using this space to reflect on what we've learned in the last ten years. Our students have taught us many lessons about teacher education, and we've tried to be astute learners. We've taught ourselves many lessons through the data we collect on our students. As a specific example, our old habits of being assigned a course by a department chair without much regard for what comes before and after were challenged immediately in our more "threaded" curriculum. The notion of professor as an individual intellectual entrepreneur had to be reconceived as the faculty members themselves participate in their own reflective learning community.

This final chapter represents our collective reflections on what we've learned about the master's degree as teacher professional development, and the inherent balance between a university's traditional and regulatory expectations, such as, promotion and tenure, scheduling classes, and our institution's transition from a teaching-oriented institution to one that is research-oriented and the tension it has created. We also want to share what we've learned about what our relatively new teachers, or "second stage teachers" (Donaldson, Moore Johnson, Kirkpatrick, Marinell, Steele, Szczesiul, 2008) need to stay in the field and become the leaders and change agents we set as one of our Core propositions, and we firmly believe school reform requires.

In the day-to-day management of the program, we can easily slip into attending to all of the details of our students' concerns or the university regulations or the malalignment of the school calendars with the university calendars or our teaching assignments, and the myriad unpredictable minutiae that we must elevate to a level of importance because of their immediacy. Surrounding these issues are the typical lives of professors who have other courses to teach in other program areas, an expectation for presenting and publishing, the service work of professors to the college, university, and the broader communities that we inhabit. Like any program, ASTL is situated within the lifestyle of professors, and reflecting on what we've learned and want to share from our experiences form the substance of this chapter.

LESSONS LEARNED OVER TEN YEARS

To strive to create as much transparency as possible, we're dividing this chapter into sections to focus the lessons on particular aspects of ASTL. Those areas are: students, faculty, the university, and considerations for the future.

Students

After many years of gathering data using a variety of scales, including teacher efficacy, one's orientation toward becoming an agent of change, job satisfaction, other personality inventories, as well as reading across the portfolios, and examining outcome data, the first lesson we learned about students is that no two cohorts are the same. In other words, with each new class, we are always starting anew. We acknowledge this important contextual variable and do all we can to get to know the students well in the first Core course if we hope to accomplish our goals. As such, we are now obligated to differentiate instruction by cohort. Admitting a student into the program is not the same as admitting a student into a cohort. Each cohort develops its own personality. The students in ASTL stay together for the first twelve months of the Core, and the faculty members "rotate" in to teach. In many ways, the faculty member is the outsider in the group and quickly has to establish her identity and credibility in an already established group. The farther the students go into the Core, the more likely it is that each new professor they meet must quickly become a member of the group. This can be a daunting task for professors whose experiences are that courses are typically designed with them at the center and it's the students who must adjust. Our experiences are precisely the opposite. As such, each summer, when new cohorts start, we have had to become better at identifying ways to understand the nature of the teachers in the cohort at the beginning, and not just retroactively, and to adapt instruction, readings, and experiences to meet students' needs. The tightrope we walk then is not to prejudice the faculty who will be working with these cohorts later in the year. We find that in our meetings we discuss the cohorts' personalities, as well as some students, but work hard not to predispose some faculty to "prepare themselves" for individual ASTL students, but to know the dynamics of the group prior to beginning, and to test ideas out on instructional arrangements that seem to work with each one. For example, one of the most popular concentrations is literacy and it is not uncommon to have a cohort where two-thirds of the students are "twenty-something" elementary teachers who are becoming leaders in the teaching of literacy. At that proportion and with that focus, it is very easy for the other third of the group to feel left out. In the next year, the cohort may be comprised of more senior teachers in a wide variety of concentrations with many who teach at the secondary level. We've learned that these are two distinct groups of students and that they need particular considerations in our design and instruction. It is safe to say that no two cohorts have been comparable in the ten years ASTL has been offered. Our failure to acknowledge the distinctions among cohorts mitigated the effects of our program against our goals. As such, we now strive to understand quickly the students in each new cohort and to keep an eye on its collective personality to reconfigure some activities in the program to maximize our impact.

A second lesson we have learned about students is that smaller-sized cohorts are better than larger ones. In the early years, we would admit a class of more than twenty students into one cohort, and then we'd watch as some of the students failed to achieve our Core goals as they proceeded through the program. Then, as the program gained visibility and prestige among the local school district leaders, we began to restrict a cohort to about seventeen or so students. Over the last few years, the evidence in the students' portfolios and on the scales suggests that we've found the optimal size for a cohort of ASTL students. This has proven beneficial for both the students and the faculty.

For the students, they are competing with fewer peers to participate in the very active learning environments in our classes. Given that we view their classrooms as laboratories for experimentation and the source for reflection, our time in class is essential for debriefing and reflecting. Large classes proved themselves not conducive to providing the time for Board-like reflection and feedback, nor did large classes allow us to know our students well. To balance the university's expectations for enrollment and our desire for maximum effect, we've found that two cohorts of approximately eighteen students are optimal for achieving our goals for these teachers.

It is also beneficial for the faculty because we value providing feedback to students prior to the next class session and many of the assignments we give to our students are large and include reflective essays. Teaching in the ASTL Core requires a daily commitment by faculty to keep the intense focus on improving the students' instructional practices, reflective habits of mind, and analytic stance on a growth trajectory. We fully understand that our students teach all day, and as noted throughout this volume, we tailor the assignments to fit into that laboratory. At the same time, we can become entrapped by the routines of our lives, and so can our students. Timely feedback has proven one very good way to keep the focus of ASTL in the minds of everyone.

Faculty

Perhaps the most important lesson we've learned through the ten years is that there is never enough communication. Remembering that many faculty members who teach in the ASTL concentrations are not in CEHD, our program coordinators must regularly meet with faculty colleagues in history, the sciences, mathematics, art, and geography, as well as with the faculty from concentrations within the college. As we look back, the commitment to ASTL of colleagues outside the Core faculty remains high. That is, each of these areas has professors who are interested in strengthening the content knowledge of teachers using this programmatic venue. They have designed these concentrations in a sincere interest to see that teachers' knowledge of content is developed further, such that the ASTL students can become leaders in their schools. As much as we should celebrate our colleagues' commitment to the program, we also have learned that their participation in the ongoing development of ASTL is low. This is something many of us who have worked in preservice teacher education know: making teacher education a university-wide commitment remains a challenge. In an effort to remain true to our goals, we now often use "back channel communications" with those who are the advisers in the concentrations. Of course, this means we aren't always working with people who are part of our ongoing discussions about the direction of the program. In other words, our desire to increase teachers' content knowledge and PCK is a conversation we do not have often enough with these colleagues. Rather, it places the Core faculty in the position of rethinking the structure of the program to approximate this goal better, which will be discussed next.

As noted, faculty communication remains an ongoing challenge in teacher education. Returning to the fundamental reasons for creating ASTL, one of them was to bring the disciplines back into teacher education, but in our case, at the post-baccalaureate level as professional development. It is not the purpose of this volume to propose organizational solutions to this, such as rewarding history or mathematics faculty for participating in ASTL or teacher education. Rather, our solution remains a commitment by the Core faculty to keep the communication channels as open and as frequent as possible to keep the participation of the concentration faculty in the program. Without this solution, fundamental values undergirding ASTL are in jeopardy of not being achieved.

University Expectations

Universities are their own systems with their own policies and processes. They also have the expectation that people will follow those processes and therefore comply with those unstated policies. But policies are blunt instruments designed to create norms, not scalpels that can be used to facilitate the many boutique programs found on their campuses. Where ASTL has run into the one-size-fits-all policies pertains to course scheduling.

As described in chapter 1, the ASTL Core is five classes totaling twelve credits. Clearly, some classes are not three credits. Specifically, there are three two-credit classes and two three-credit classes. Because these classes do not fit into the university's fifty-minute periods, in which students attend a class (in other disciplines) for one hundred fifty minutes a week in blocks of two classes or three classes per week, scheduling two-credit classes that meet for one half of a semester and four clock hours per week is not a priority in the university's scheduling system. Simply stated, the university's definition of a course and ASTL's definition of a course are incompatible. To make the ASTL courses "teacher friendly" (teacher here denoting our ASTL students), we've compressed the time, designed the instruction around that, and built our expectations, assignments, and outcomes into that format. It was then that we discovered that our courses could not be scheduled through the central offices of our university. Our solution is now to offer the Core in a local school district building. The Concentration classes, which all conform to the university's scheduling process, remain on campus in the normal campus schedule. However, we've found that we can teach our Core courses off campus, reduce the tuition by a substantial amount, thereby making the degree more affordable, and accomplish our programmatic goals. This was a growth process for us. Like any professor we wanted our courses near our offices rather than having to drive twenty minutes or more to a school, set up the technology we need, rearrange the furniture in a high school teacher's class, and attend to that delicate relationship. However, the lesson we learned is that our students prefer this arrangement. When one of us asked the students whether they would like to have class on campus, the answer was a resounding, "no." They prefer not to come to campus, scout for parking, and pay on-campus rates. For the faculty, what initially appeared to be a problem became a marketing strategy that gives us, in a sense, a geographical advantage the teachers prefer. The real change in this instance was in how we defined our teaching spaces. The Core faculty members are now quite comfortable with this arrangement. Once we accomplished that, the fact that we could not negotiate space on campus became an afterthought.

The lesson we learned is that being flexible in service to making the educational experience the best it can be for our students was worth learning. It opened doors for engagement with our students that facilitated our goals of having teachers participate in extended learning communities that ask them to confront their values with their peers. Because of the four-hour blocks of time, we can accomplish many varied activities, including problem-based learning, video analysis, cooperative activities, and many other activities that require focus, duration, and completion, all attributes of effective teacher professional development (Desimone, 2009).

Balancing a Healthy Future

This final section looks forward and considers what we'll be facing in the future as we find ways to balance our teaching, our scholarship, and maintain a program that in two separate follow-up studies continues to receive very high marks from teachers who graduated as far back as six years ago, and teachers who graduated as recently as one year ago.

As the Core faculty ages with the program and we seek new faculty to join the Core faculty, we face the reality that programs are a product of their time, place, and people who invest in them. Our program was created at the rise of NBPTS and was founded on its five Core propositions. The designers are still active in the program, as some new colleagues joined in the third and fourth years, and one joined us in the seventh year. All of us have remained committed to the program and its goals, and this is not to suggest we could not find similar commitments to programs made by faculty either here or elsewhere. However, as new faculty join, we have to find the balance between the core values and the innovations people bring with them. As the people change, the program will change. But what we've learned over these years is that a program is not a collection of courses; rather, a program is built on core values that strive to, in our case, accomplish school reform through enhanced content knowledge, improved teaching practices, reflection on practice, a disposition to include all learners in their classrooms, and by empowering teachers to lead change and be the agents of change. In the end, those core values are our touchstones, and by hewing to them and using them as our compass points, we make a program that maintains internal consistency at the same time new faculty bring new ways to think about and achieve those fundamental values. New faculty with new ideas can reshape and have reshaped the courses, the assignments, the evaluation of the students, and the like. They can even change the core values by participating in the community of program faculty. Someday, one of the core values may no longer be needed. But until the program faculty agrees to that, then each of us is committed to finding our own innovative ways of getting our students to achieve them.

Programs, and perhaps professional programs more than others, require constant tending. They can become dated and stagnant as the field continues to advance. In our view, data and transparency are the best antidotes. They compel us to reexamine often all that we do in the program, to practice as we've come to call it, collective reflection, at our program faculty meetings. We learn a great deal from the work of our students; they are our work samples of what our students are accomplishing. We can read across their final portfolios and locate pieces of work in the first courses that continue through the last course. We can seek patterns in how the ASTL students learn and what sense they make of the program as well as their own development as teachers. In addition, as part of that "tending," we have established an Alumni Advisory Council that convenes once each semester.

The ASTL Alumni Advisory Council guides us each semester as we contemplate the changes the evidence suggests should be made to the courses and to the program. This is a select group of teachers from whom we saw either tremendous growth in the program, or who entered already as high-performing teachers and who saw this program as a way to develop a content specialization to contribute back to his school. In short, these are teachers who took ASTL seriously and thoughtfully and from whom we'd want to hear feedback.

The Advisory Council is also our "ear to the ground." The members tell us what they are hearing and seeing in their schools. They keep us apprised of changes coming to their schools or of new needs emerging they believe ASTL should be addressing. As noted, we periodically conduct follow-up studies and in the last iteration, we asked the Advisory Council to interpret the survey data with us. We wanted to hear what they thought the data were telling us. As a specific example, it has become apparent that the lack of a close connection between the Core and the Concentration was showing itself more clearly in the use of new content knowledge as applied to the learning of new teaching strategies. In other words, our desire to improve teachers' PCK and reasoning as a teaching professional is a gap between these two parts of our program. Currently, we are facing the challenge of linking the pedagogy and content divide. As noted in chapter 4, maintaining close contact with colleagues around the university is essential for the program achieving its goals. We are reminded of the professor who challenged the dean in the opening vignette in chapter 1. He chided the dean for "selling undergraduate knowledge at graduate rates" on the grounds that master's degrees are not the place for teaching content knowledge. However, we have become convinced by our colleagues in the mathematics department who realized that elementary teachers need to see mathematics in new ways if they are to teach it well to their PK–12 students. We brought our data and our perception of the problem to the Advisory Council for their review and input. After some lengthy discussion among themselves, they offered a series of suggestions. The one that seemed to have the most support was to break up the Core from a contiguous entity of course offerings and to move the final class, Educational Change, to a capstone course in which the assignments will change to include a culminating activity that demonstrates PCK along the lines of the Board's assessment of the construct. As we look forward with this input, we see many other opportunities and a way to connect the Concentration faculty to the Core faculty in a presentation of this (eventual) project where the pedagogy faculty and the content faculty are both present to evaluate the students' work and portfolio. Without an Advisory Council to think about how this would work from the students' perspectives, it is likely we would not have come to this idea as quickly as they did, if ever. When we make this change, the capstone course will still include a change initiative for each teacher's school, and will add in a more robust portfolio activity that will be designed to capture PCK along the lines of the Board's assessments.

Another lesson we have learned goes beyond ASTL and speaks to the broader agenda of inquiry in teacher education. As we've demonstrated in this volume, we seek to review data on our program to inform our decisions about programmatic changes. We see it as our feedback loop. It has advantaged us in both the university's regional accreditation, and in our professional accreditation through the NCATE. Where our programmatic inquiry stalls is in our college-wide faculty review and journal publications. ASTL faculty members, on occasion, have received annual review feedback that suggests we're spending too much time writing about the program and the data we extract from it. This is a representation of a larger problem in teacher education, and that is the lack of top-tier journals in the field that will accept highly contextualized research and evaluation studies of a teacher education program. In fact, the leading journal in the field of teacher education, the *Journal of Teacher Education*, specifically states it will not review program evaluations. It is hard to imagine what will pass for research on teacher education if programmatic inquiry does not. Teachers are educated in about 1,200 institutions and many nonacademy-based settings, such as schools, Teach for America, the New Teacher Project, and others. To think that because the studies teacher education researchers conduct on their students and programs are bound by the settings in which they exist is enough of a weakness that it has no outlets is to state that teacher education is a field without a study. The reality, from our perspective, is that the education of a teacher is context-specific, and as we hope we've demonstrated in this volume it can be studied and the data can be used to make significant changes. But beyond that, it is that we can learn from one another, not so much for the sake of generalized findings, but for each program faculty to inquire into their programs and practices, improve them, and seek to use the master's degree as the "edge of the wedge" for school improvement through teacher professional development. Our own institution's faculty review procedures, our journals, and the general notion that for teacher education to be studied with validity it must be cross-institutional all inhibit program development as well as improving the field.

We have become a PLC and believe it has been essential to our goals. ASTL would not be ASTL if we didn't submit ourselves to the greater importance of the program.

Appendix A

ASTL Framework of Outcomes, Courses, Performance-Based Assessments, and NBPTS-Related Assessment Activities

George Mason University
College of Education and Human Development
Master's Degree Program in Advanced Studies in Teaching and Learning

I. Performance-Based Assessments in the ASTL Core Coursework

Principles and Candidate Outcomes	Courses	Performance-Based Assessments	NBPTS-Related Assessment Activities
1. Teachers are committed to students and their learning.	EDUC 612: Inquiry into Practice EDUC 613: How Students Learn	Performance-based assessments Multigenre autobiographical study with reflection Individual case study of a learner with rubric Critical journal responses with rubric	Write analytically and reflectively. Read critically from multiple perspectives. Apply theory into practice. Follow a learner over time.

Principles and Candidate Outcomes	*CoursesPerformance-Based Assessments*	*NBPTS-Related Assessment Activities*
2. Teachers know the subjects they teach and how to teach those subjects to students.	EDUC 614: Designing and Assessing Teaching and Learning Performance-based assessments Video of teaching containing written analysis of one's teaching practice and a sample of student work with rubric Rubric/performance assessment	Adapt and plan instruction for all learners. Write to prompts. Analyze students' work samples.
3. Teachers are responsible for managing and monitoring student learning.	EDUC 613: How Students Learn Performance-based assessments In-depth study of one student over time including recommendations for extending student learning (Case Study with rubric and Reflection) EDUC 614: Designing & Assessing Teaching & Learning Performance-based assessments Student Work sampling Analysis of videotape of one's classroom practice with rubric and Reflection	Analyze student work samples. Provide feedback to students. Adapt all instruction and recommending future lessons in specific learning, areas. Reflect on practice.

Principles and Candidate Outcomes	Courses Performance-Based Assessments		NBPTS-Related Assessment Activities
4. Teachers think systematically about their practice and learn from experience.	EDUC 612: Inquiry into Practice	Performance-based assessments Teacher action research proposal Multigenre study - Reflective Journal	Evaluate multiple perspectives on a research topic. Analyze and defend a scholarly position and reflect how it might inform classroom practice. Apply findings and recommenda- tions from scholarly articles to own practice. Utilize action research as a form of scholarly research.
	EDUC 606: Education and Culture		
		Performance-based assessments Culturally focused action research with emphasis on cultural dimensions in the educational setting (using peer support groups and following CIP)	
5. Teachers are members of learning communities.	EDUC 613: How Students Learn	Performance-based assessments Learning Theory Group presentations	Self-assess participation as members of cooperative learning groups. Document accomplishments of work with families, colleagues, and organizations outside the classroom.
	EDUC 606: Education and Culture	Performance-based assessments Teacher action research project with rubric— Critical reflection groups	
	EDUC 615: Educational Change	Performance-based assessments Group project Grant proposal based on contextual needs analysis	

Principles and Candidate Outcomes	Courses Performance-Based Assessments	NBPTS-Related Assessment Activities
6. Teachers account for the needs of culturally, linguistically, and cognitively diverse learners.	EDUC 613: How Students Learn Performance-based learning activity Case study of a learner Learning theorist group project EDUC 606: Education and Culture Performance-based assessments Culturally focused action research study	1. Analyze student work with attention to identifying misconceptions and extending student understanding. 2. Design, plan, and assess student learning from a cultural perspective.

Principles and Candidate Outcomes	CoursesPerformance-Based Assessments		NBPTS-Related Assessment Activities
7. Teachers are change agents, teacher leaders, and partners with colleagues.	EDUC 606: Education and Culture	Performance-based assessment Action research project with analysis of interventions and outcomes for change included Performance-based assessment Integrative case study and action plan for student and teacher Performance-based assessment Teaching video analysis	Critical writing addressing interpretive summaries of contributions to the teaching profession. Document accomplishments in the school and community arenas.
	EDUC 613: How Students Learn		
	EDUC614: Designing / Assessing Learning		
	EDUC 615: Educational Change - Explore roles as educational change agent both past and present		
		Performance-based assessments Team-project/ analyzing influences on educational change Grant Proposal focused on educational change	

Principles and Candidate Outcomes	*CoursesPerformance-Based Assessments*		*NBPTS-Related Assessment Activities*
8. Teachers use technology to facilitate student learning and their own professional development.	Performance-based Learning Experiences incorporated throughout in course products and weekly learning. Examples include: EDUC 612: Inquiry into Practice Electronic bulletin board (*Blackboard*) Teachers use technology in innovative and creative ways to create their multigenre study EDUC 613: How Students Learn Produce APA word-processed documents Use online and e-mail discussion groups Access electronic library reserves	EDUC 606: Education and Culture CIP website EDUC 614: Designing and Assessing Learning Wiki interactive learning Electronic sources for rubric and lesson planning EDUC 615: Educational Change External list serves and grant sources *ASTL Professional Portfolio created electronically*	Incorporates all NBPTS assessment activities via online and virtual learning communities.

Program Level Performance-based Assessment:
ASTL Program Portfolio and Presentation

See also Program Articulation Chart
and
Portfolio Guidelines in Appendix F

Program Website: http://gse.gmu.edu/programs/astl/

Appendix B

Rubric for Multigenre Assignment

George Mason University
College of Education and Human Development
Advanced Studies in Teaching and Learning Program
Performance-Based Assessment Rubric for EDUC 612, *Inquiry into Practice*

Multigenre Project	No evidence (Little or no evidence)	Beginning (Limited evidence)	Developing (Clear evidence)	Accomplished (Clear, convincing and substantial evidence)
100 points	F: <75	C: 75–79	B: 80–92	A: 93–100
Introduction **5 Points** Learning Outcome 4	No introduction is included, or the introduction is brief.	Introduction is included that presents the unifying theme but may not elaborate on two or more of the key elements.	Introduction is included that clearly presents the unifying theme but may not elaborate on one or more of the key elements.	Introduction included that contains clearly and substantially all key elements: Introduces the reader to the unifying theme. Provides a **roadmap** for the learning journey and explains how the theme will be carried through.

Multigenre Project	No evidence (Little or no evidence)	Beginning (Limited evidence)	Developing (Clear evidence)	Accomplished (Clear, convincing and substantial evidence)
Personal Beliefs Statement **10 Points** *Learning Outcomes 3 and 4*	***Teaching Beliefs statement*** provides little to no evidence about teachers' beliefs regarding: teaching, using inquiry to improve practice, focus on student learning, role of reflection—thinking systematically about your practice. Beliefs statement is abbreviated, or more than two of the key elements may be missing.	**Teaching Beliefs *statement*** provides limited evidence about teachers' beliefs regarding: teaching, using inquiry to improve practice, focus on student learning, role of reflection—thinking systematically about your practice. Beliefs statement is brief or two of the key elements may be missing.	***Teaching Beliefs statement*** provides clear evidence about teachers' beliefs regarding: teaching, using inquiry to improve practice, focus on student learning, role of reflection—thinking systematically about your practice. One of the elements may be missing.	***Teaching Beliefs statement*** provides clear and convincing evidence about teachers' beliefs regarding: teaching, using inquiry to improve practice, focus on student learning, role of reflection—thinking systematically about your practice.
Genres—Inquiry **20 Points** *Learning Outcome 4*	No description of a learning journey, or no theme is used to weave the genres together for the Multigenre Project.	Provides a ***learning journey,*** however it may lack elaboration on two of the elements. Project theme is present but doesn't clearly weave the genres together to contribute to the flow of the Multigenre Project.	Provides a clearly developed ***learning journey,*** that may lack elaboration on one of the elements. There is a clearly articulated ***theme*** that weaves the genres together and contributes to the flow of the Multigenre Project.	Provides a clearly and substantially developed ***learning journey,*** elaborates on self as learner, teacher, and teacher as inquirer. There is a clearly articulated ***theme*** that weaves the genres together and contributes to the flow of the Multigenre Project.

Multigenre Project	No evidence (Little or no evidence)	Beginning (Limited evidence)	Developing (Clear evidence)	Accomplished (Clear, convincing and substantial evidence)
Genres—Quantity **10 Points** *Learning Outcome 4*	Paper contains two or fewer genres, or limited to no excerpts from the personal reflective journal (two or fewer journal excerpts).	Paper contains three genres, one of which is multiple excerpts from the personal reflective journal (minimum of three journal excerpts).	Paper contains four genres, one of which is multiple excerpts from the personal reflective journal (minimum of four journal excerpts).	Paper contains **at least five genres**, one of which is multiple excerpts from the personal reflective journal (minimum of five journal excerpts).
Genres—Technology **5 Points** *Learning Outcome 8*	The presentation of the genres does not demonstrate that *technology* was effectively used. Project submitted on CD, jump drive, or via personal website.	The presentation of the genres demonstrates limited to little use of *technology*. Project submitted on CD, jump drive, or via personal website.	The presentation of the genres demonstrates effective or varied use of *technology*. Project submitted on CD, jump drive, or via personal website.	The presentation of the genres demonstrates effective and varied use of *technology*. Project submitted on CD, jump drive, or via personal website.

Multigenre Project	No evidence (Little or no evidence)	Beginning (Limited evidence)	Developing (Clear evidence)	Accomplished (Clear, convincing and substantial evidence)
Key Events and Application of New EDUC 613 Readings **15 Points** *Learning Outcome 5*	Project provides limited description or limited support of key events/people who shaped you as a learner. Limited references to EDUC 613 readings to articulate and support the statements you make about who you were/are as a learner and a teacher.	Project creates a focus around **key events/ people** who shaped you as a learner and incorporates at least two EDUC 613 readings to articulate and support the statements you make about who you were/ are as a learner and a teacher.	Project creates a focus around **key events/people** who shaped you as a learner and incorporates at least three EDUC 613 readings to articulate and support the statements you make about who you were/are as a learner and a teacher.	Project creates a focus around **key events/people** who shaped you as a learner and clearly incorporates at least four EDUC 613 readings to articulate and support the statements you make about who you were/are as a learner and a teacher.
Future Research **10 Points** *Learning Outcome 4*	Limited or no future teacher inquiry/research ideas are included, or lists fewer than two research questions.	Project includes limited ideas for future teacher inquiry/ research; lists two potential questions for research.	Project includes potential ideas for future teacher inquiry/research; lists three potential questions for research.	Project includes explicitly stated, potential ideas for future teacher inquiry/ research; includes list of four or more potential questions.

Multigenre Project	No evidence (Little or no evidence)	Beginning (Limited evidence)	Developing (Clear evidence)	Accomplished (Clear, convincing and substantial evidence)
Concluding Reflections (included at the end of MG project) **10 Points** *Learning Outcome 4*	**Concluding Reflection:** Reflection provides minimal connections to what was learned in the MG creation process, or reflection is not included.	**Concluding Reflection:** Provides a *reflection* about what the author has learned in the multigenre creation process. *Few connections of own learning to classroom practice.*	**Concluding Reflection:** Provides a critical *reflection* about what the author has learned in the multigenre creation process. *Connects own learning to classroom practice.*	**Concluding Reflection:** Provides a clearly articulated critical *reflection* about what the author has learned in the multigenre creation process. *Connects own learning to classroom practice.*
Referencing **10 Points** *Learning Outcome 4*	The project integrates three or fewer core (EDUC 612 and 613) readings, and/ or other current, relevant literature. References do not follow APA (6th edition) style.	The project integrates four core (EDUC 612 and 613) readings, and/or other current, relevant literature. References contain numerous APA (6th edition) errors.	The project integrates five core (EDUC 612 and 613) readings, and/or other current, relevant literature that are correctly referenced. References may contain minor APA (6th edition) errors.	The project integrates a minimum of six core (EDUC 612 and 613) readings and/ or other current, relevant literature that are correctly referenced. References adhere to **APA style (6th edition).**
Overall Style **5 Points** *Learning Outcome 4*	Contains many grammatical errors or error patterns.	Lacks in grammatical or stylistic form or contains many errors or error patterns.	Grammatically and stylistically written, but contains some errors or error patterns.	Grammatically and stylistically well written with few errors and no error patterns.

Appendix C

Rubric for Integrative Case Study

George Mason University
College of Education and Human Development
Advanced Studies in Teaching and Learning Program
Performance-based Assessment for EDUC 613, *How Students Learn*
Integrative Case Study Rubric

	No Evidence F	Beginning (Limited evidence) C	Developing (Clear evidence) B	Accomplished (Clear, convincing, and substantial evidence) A
Descriptive Discussion **15 points** *NBPTS—Learning Outcome 1* *ASTL—Learning Outcome 1*	Case study includes two or fewer descriptive elements listed under Accomplished	Case study includes three of the six descriptive elements listed under Accomplished	Case study includes three or four of the five descriptive elements listed under Accomplished	Case study includes: • Introduction • SES, ethnic, linguistic background (5 pts.) • Physical description • Background • Setting • Other significant information (5 pts.) • At least three learning factors that characterize your learner (5 pts.)

	No Evidence F	Beginning (Limited evidence) C	Developing (Clear evidence) B	Accomplished (Clear, convincing, and substantial evidence) A
Analytic Discussion	No analysis included	Case study includes three of the five elements OR Discussion includes only one learning factor	Case study includes cursory discussion of hypotheses, theoretical perspectives, learning factors, student's ways of learning, and recommendations **OR** Case includes only four of the five elements **OR** Discussion includes only two learning Factors	Case study includes thoughtful, thorough, and reflective discussion of:
35 points				• Introduction
				• Hypotheses about *why* the child learns this way
NBPTS— Learning Outcome 3				• Theoretical perspectives about student learning
ASTL— Learning Outcome 3				• How the three learning factors affect one another and influence the student's learning (15 pts.)
				• Student's ways of learning, learning challenges, learning strengths (5 pts.)
				• Research-based recommendations based on your understanding of this learner (15 pts.)

	No Evidence F	Beginning (Limited evidence) C	Developing (Clear evidence) B	Accomplished (Clear, convincing, and substantial evidence) A
Reflective Self-Evaluation 20 points *NBPTS— Learning Outcome 4* *ASTL— Learning Outcome 4*	No reflection included	Very limited discussion OR One of the four elements is missing	Cursory discussion of: • Your choice of this student • Lessons you learned • Your ideas and feelings • Changes in the way you teach, think about or relate to students as learners	Rich, thorough discussion of: • Your choice of this student • Lessons you learned about learning and yourself as a learner • Your ideas and feelings about learning (15 pts.) • Changes in the way you teach, think about, or relate to students as learners (Insights about yourself) (5 pts.)
Appendix 5 points *NBPTS— Learning Outcome 3* *ASTL— Learning Outcome 3*	No appendixes included	• Appendixes are included, but they do not relate to the descriptive, analytic, and reflective discussion • Appendixes do not include observational data and/or evidence that support your hypotheses and recommendations	• Appendixes show a weak relation to the descriptive, analytic, and reflective discussion • Appendixes are missing observational data or evidence that supports your hypotheses and recommendations	• Appendixes relate strongly to the descriptive, analytic, and reflective discussions • Appendixes include observational data and evidence that support your hypotheses and recommendations

	No Evidence F	Beginning (Limited evidence) C	Developing (Clear evidence) B	Accomplished (Clear, convincing, and substantial evidence) A
Draft Sections Submitted by Due Date **15 points**	No drafts submitted.	One draft submitted to instructor by due date.	Two drafts submitted to instructor by due dates.	All three drafts submitted to instructor by due dates.
Referencing **5 points** *NBPTS—Learning Outcome 4* *ASTL—Learning Outcome 4*	No evidence of references or References are not in APA style.	• Limited use of course readings and other current readings • References contain errors	• Course readings and other current readings are referenced. • References contain minor errors.	• The paper integrates course readings and other current, authoritative relevant readings that are properly referenced. • References are in APA style.

	No Evidence F	Beginning (Limited evidence) C	Developing (Clear evidence) B	Accomplished (Clear, convincing, and substantial evidence) A
Overall Style 5 points	Contains many grammatical errors or error patterns	Lacks in grammatical or stylistic form or contains many errors or error patterns	Grammatically and stylistically well written, but contains some errors or error patterns.	Grammatically and stylistically well written with few errors or error patterns.
NBPTS— Learning Outcome 4 ASTL— Learning Outcome 4				

Appendix D

ASTL Core Self-Assessment Questionnaire

George Mason University
Graduate School of Education
Advanced Studies in Teaching and Learning Program
Core ASTL Self-Assessment
2009–2010 Core Cohort

PART 1: KNOWLEDGE BASE AT THE BEGINNING OF THE CORE

Please think about and rate your experience level and understanding of the following eight items. The purpose of this self-assessment is to attempt to capture your experience level and skills in these areas at the beginning of your Core classes and has nothing to do with a grade or your final evaluation of any coursework. These eight areas correspond with the ASTL Program Core Learning Outcomes.

Following each rated outcome, please tell why you rated yourself this way. *Circle* your response using the 4-point scale adjacent to each objective.

I have <u>no</u> understanding of the learning outcome

Have a <u>minimal</u> understanding

Have a <u>moderate</u> understanding

Have a <u>strong</u> understanding

ASTL Learning Outcomes	Level of Understanding of this Learning Outcome
Student learning: Teachers are committed to students and their learning. _____ _____ _____ _____ _____	1 2 3 4
Content knowledge & effective pedagogy: Teachers know the subjects they teach and how to teach those subjects to students. _____ _____ _____ _____ _____	1 2 3 4
Monitoring student learning: Teachers are responsible for managing and monitoring student learning. _____ _____ _____ _____ _____	1 2 3 4
Systematic inquiry of practice: Teachers think systematically about their practice and learn from experience. _____ _____ _____ _____ _____	1 2 3 4
Learning community: Teachers are members of learning communities. _____ _____ _____ _____ _____	1 2 3 4

ASTL Learning Outcomes	Level of Understanding of this Learning Outcome
Diversity: Teachers attend to the needs of culturally, linguistically, and cognitively diverse learners. _____ _____ _____ _____ _____	1 2 3 4
Change agent: Teachers are change agents, teacher leaders, and partners with colleagues. _____ _____ _____ _____ _____	1 2 3 4
Technology: Teachers use technology effectively to facilitate student learning and their own professional development. _____ _____ _____ _____ _____	1 2 3 4

PART II: CLASSROOM CONNECTIONS AND YOUR IMPACT ON PPK–12 STUDENT LEARNING

1. As a result of your teaching experiences to date, please comment on how your teaching has impacted your own students' learning.

_____

_____

_____

_____

_____

_____

_____

_____

_____

_____

_____

_____

_____

_____

If you were asked to provide <u>documentation</u> of your impact on PPK–12 student learning, what evidence(s) might you provide?

_____

_____

_____

_____

_____

_____

_____

_____

_____

Please check current teaching setting or educational role:

For how many years have you been teaching? _____

Grade Level(s) currently teaching _____

Role(s) _____

Concentration Area _____

_____ Completed _____ To be taken _____In progress

_____ I am not currently teaching (please check).

Appendix E

Rubric for Culturally Focused Action Research Study

George Mason University
College of Education and Human Development
Advanced Studies in Teaching and Learning Program
Performance-Based Assessment for EDUC 606, Education and Culture

100 Total Points	No Evidence *Little or No Evidence*	Beginning *Limited Evidence*	Developing *Clear Evidence*	Accomplished *Clear, Consistent, and Convincing Evidence*
Puzzlement(s) and Background **9 Points** Learning Outcome 4	• States puzzlement(s) only implicitly • Presents little about "what is known" OR • Puzzlement is not stated • Information about "What is known" is missing	• States puzzlement(s), but not clearly • Information about "what is known" lacks clarity	• States puzzlement(s) clearly, but supporting details may be needed • Presents "what is known" clearly, but may not provide supporting details	• States puzzlement clearly and thoroughly, with many supporting details • Presents "what is known" clearly and thoroughly, with many supporting details

100 Total Points	No Evidence *Little or No Evidence*	Beginning *Limited Evidence*	**Developing** *Clear Evidence*	Accomplished *Clear, Consistent, and Convincing Evidence*
Cultural Questions **12 Points** *Learning Outcome 6*	• States cultural questions only implicitly or no cultural questions are stated • Provides limited or no discussion of relationship between cultural question(s) and puzzlement(s)/ what is known • Provides minimal or no rationale/support for choice of cultural question(s)	• States at least one to two cultural questions • May lack clear logical relationship between cultural question(s) and puzzlement(s)/ what is known • May provide partial rationale/support for choice of cultural questions(s)	• States at least one to two cultural questions clearly, with some details provided • Demonstrates logical relationship between cultural question(s) and puzzlement(s)/ what is known • Provides some rationale/support for choice of cultural question(s)	• States at least one to two cultural questions clearly and thoroughly, with many supporting details provided • Thoroughly demonstrates logical relationship between cultural question(s) and puzzlement(s)/what is known • Provides clear, consistent, and convincing rationale/ support for choice of cultural question(s)

100 Total Points	No Evidence *Little or No Evidence*	Beginning *Limited Evidence*	Developing *Clear Evidence*	**Accomplished** *Clear, Consistent, and Convincing Evidence*
Data Collection and Analysis **21 Points** *Learning Outcome 4*	• Link to cultural question(s) is unclear or missing • Presents minimal or no discussion of data collection and analysis methods • Presents little or no data related to cultural question(s) • Presentation of data is unclear or poorly organized • Demonstrates little or no attempt to understand puzzlement(s) from a cultural point of view	• Links to cultural question(s), but may be less than totally clear • Presents discussion of data collection and analysis methods, but less than complete or less than clear • Presents some data to address cultural question(s) • Presentation of data may lack some clarity or organization • Attempts to understand puzzlement(s) from cultural points of view, but may include some judgments	• Links clearly to cultural question(s) • Presents clear discussion of data collection and analysis methods • Presents solid data to address cultural question(s) • Presentation of data is clear and well organized • Attempts to understand puzzlement(s) from cultural point of views	• Links clearly and completely to cultural question(s) • Presents clear and complete discussion of data collection and analysis methods • Presents extensive and convincing data to address cultural question(s) • Presentation of data is clear, consistent, and convincing • Makes clear, consistent, and convincing attempts to understand puzzlement(s) from cultural point(s) of view

100 Total Points	No Evidence Little or No Evidence	Beginning Limited Evidence	Developing Clear Evidence	**Accomplished** *Clear, Consistent, and Convincing Evidence*
Interventions (Actual and Planned) **15 Points** *Learning Outcome 6 and Impact*	• Implements or describes few or no interventions • Link to cultural questions and data is unclear or missing	• Implements or describes some interventions • Link to cultural questions and data is less than totally clear	• Implements or describes several interventions • Link to cultural questions and data is clear	• Implements or describes many interventions in a clear, consistent, and convincing manner • Link to cultural questions and data is clear and complete
Monitoring (Actual and Planned) **9 Points** *Learning Outcome 6*	• Links to puzzlement(s) and interventions not clear or missing • Presents evidence to evaluate interventions with little or no clarity or in a poorly organized manner • Insufficient or no evidence presented to support evaluation decisions	• Links to puzzlement(s) and interventions, but less than totally clear • Presents evidence to evaluate interventions with some lack of clarity or organization • Some evidence presented to support evaluation decisions	• Links clearly to puzzlement(s) and interventions • Presents evidence to evaluate interventions clearly and in organized manner • Sufficient evidence presented to support evaluation decisions	• Links clearly and completely to puzzlement(s) and interventions • Presents evidence to evaluate interventions clearly and in a consistent and convincing manner • Clear, consistent, and convincing evidence presented to support evaluation decisions

100 Total Points	No Evidence / Little or No Evidence	Beginning / Limited Evidence	Developing / Clear Evidence	Accomplished / Clear, Consistent, and Convincing Evidence
Conclusions and Implications **6 Points** *Learning Outcome 7*	• Presents minimal or no statement of conclusions in relation to puzzlement(s) • Minimal or no discussion of broader implications (for own practice and/ or for other teachers, schools, etc.)	• Presents statement of conclusions in relation to puzzlement(s), but may lack some clarity • Explicitly discusses broader implications (for own practice and/ or for other teachers, schools, etc.) • May link to other research	• Presents clear statement of conclusions in relation to puzzlement(s) • Strong to Extensive discussion of broader implications (for own practice and/or for other teachers, schools, etc.) • Links to other research	• Presents clear, consistent, and convincing statement of conclusions in relation to puzzlement(s) • Explicit and extensive discussion of broader implications (for own practice and/or for other teachers, schools, etc.) • Clear, consistent, and convincing links to other research
Overall Style **9 Points** *Learning Outcome 4*	• Poorly organized across sections of report • Inconsistent "voice" used • Poorly written overall with many stylistic or grammatical errors and error patterns	• Generally well organized across sections, but has some organizational problems • Consistent "voice" used • May have minor problems with clarity of writing overall; may have stylistic errors or error patterns evident	• Well organized across all or most sections of report • Consistent "voice" used • Clearly written overall; very few errors evident	• Well organized consistently across all sections of report • Clear and consistent "voice" used • Clearly and convincingly written overall; no stylistic errors or error patterns

100 Total Points	No Evidence *Little or No Evidence*	Beginning *Limited Evidence*	**Developing** *Clear Evidence*	**Accomplished** *Clear, Consistent, and Convincing Evidence*
Literature and References **9 Points** *Learning Outcome 6*	• Connections to broader literature are not appropriate or are missing • Cites less than four sources (or < three not assigned for the course)	• Includes appropriate connections to broader literature • Cites four sources (with three not assigned for the course)	• Includes thoughtful connections to broader literature • Cites six sources (with three not assigned for the course)	• Includes thoughtful and thorough connections to broader literature • Clear, consistent, and convincing citation of more than six sources (with three not assigned for the course)
APA Format **6 Points** *Learning Outcome 4*	• Does not follow APA format for headings, citations, or references OR • No evidence of APA format	• Generally follows APA format for headings, citations, and references, but contains several errors	• Generally follows APA format for headings, citations, and references, but may have some minor errors	• Follows APA format for headings, citations, and references
Reflection **4 Points** *Learning Outcome 4*	• Does not include or minimal	• Includes • Does not address all three required areas	• Includes reflection section • Addresses the three required areas	

Appendix F

The ASTL Professional Portfolio

**Contents and Format of the ASTL Professional Portfolio
Reflecting Knowledge, Skills, and Dispositions
Related to the Program Outcomes**

The ASTL Portfolio consists of four parts. These are: I. Professional Documentation; II. Evidence of ASTL Core Knowledge; III. Evidence of ASTL Concentration Expertise; and IV. Portfolio Presentation: Synthesizing Knowledge and Looking Ahead. The Professional Documentation section, Part I, should be completed first. Either of Parts II or III is completed according to the sequence in which they are taken during the master's program (i.e., the Core courses may precede or follow the Concentration area completion). The final section, the Portfolio Presentation and Synthesis, Part IV, will be completed at the conclusion of the Core coursework and degree program.

There are two portfolio presentation completion possibilities, as follows:

1. Completion of Concentration Area first, Core second:
Participants who complete the Concentration, followed by the Core, will complete and present the full portfolio (Parts I–IV) at the conclusion of the Core coursework. Students will share portfolio contents with peers and faculty members and will include self-evaluation on growth, development, and change.

2. Completion of Core first, Concentration second:
  a. Participants who complete their Concentration following the Core coursework will complete and present Parts I–II and an oral presentation of the Core upon completion of the Core.
  b. Upon completion of the Concentration, students will share, or present, the completed portfolio contents with Parts III and IV added to the previously shared Core portfolio.

Guidelines and Suggested Format for the Reflection Points

Length: Aim to limit your response to two pages

Focus: Each Reflection Point should include a short description, but will focus on <u>interpretation</u> and <u>analysis</u> of learning by synthesizing knowledge from that learning module of the Core coursework.

Format: Each reflection point *describes*, *interprets*, and *examines* why and how the course product(s) provide evidence of the ASTL principles addressed in that learning module. Here you should also discuss the impact of this course/learning module on your teaching practice and its impact on P–12 student learning.

PART I: PROFESSIONAL DOCUMENTATION

A. Resume, or Curriculum Vitae
Suggested Professional Support Documentation
  Transcripts and scores
  Evidence of professional presentations or conferences attended
  Publications
  Other professional documentation, as determined by individual

PART II: EVIDENCE OF ASTL CORE KNOWLEDGE

Part II is divided into four major sections. Each section corresponds to a principle strand of the ASTL Core and suggests course products that could provide evidence of Core knowledge. Each section has a "Reflection Point" that connects the knowledge gained from the Core courses and course products to the NBPTS and GSE Principles. The final section is a comprehensive reflection of knowledge attained in the Program that is aligned with the program's stated learning outcomes (NBPTS and GSE Principles):

The Eight ASTL Core Principles

1. Student learning
Teachers are committed to students and their learning.

2. Content knowledge and effective pedagogy
Teachers know the subjects they teach and how to
teach those subjects to students.

3. Monitoring student learning
Teachers are responsible for managing and monitoring student learning.

4. Systematic inquiry of practice
Teachers think systematically about their practice and learn from experience.

5. Learning community
Teachers are members of learning communities.

6. Diversity
Teachers attend to the needs of culturally, linguistically,
and cognitively diverse learners.

7. Change agent
Teachers are change agents, teacher leaders, and partners with colleagues.

8. Technology
Teachers use technology effectively to facilitate student
learning and their own professional development.

Section A: Teacher as Knowing and Understanding Learning and Learners

This section will be completed at the conclusion of EDUC 612 and 613 and should include products from those two courses.

Reflection Prompt 1:
In this section, you will focus on how coursework, related readings, and products in EDUC 612 and 613 have led you to think more deeply about the

learning process and your own students, as well as your own learning. Please reflect on your own learning and your growth and change at this point in the Core. In your reflection, please address any of the applicable eight program learning outcomes and the ways in which the performance assessments included thus far in the Core provide evidence of your knowledge.

Suggested course products to be used as evidence of knowledge:

1. Multigenre Paper (EDUC 612)
2. Case Study of Learner (EDUC 613)
3. Handout from Learning Theory Group Presentation (EDUC 613)
4. Other item(s), as selected by individual (such as excerpts from reflective journal)

Section B: Teacher as Designer of Curriculum and Assessment

This section will be completed at the conclusion of EDUC 614 and will include products and learning experiences from that course.

Reflection Prompt 2:

In this section, you will focus on how coursework, related readings, and products in EDUC 614 have led you to focus more carefully on the teacher as designer of curriculum and assessment and how you are incorporating technology into your teaching practice and your Core experience. Please reflect on your own learning and your growth and change at this point in the Core. In your reflection, please address any of the applicable eight program learning outcomes and the ways in which the performance assessments included in this section provide evidence of your knowledge.

Suggested course products which may be provided as evidence of knowledge:

1. Video analysis of teaching practice with analysis of teaching and impact on student learning (EDUC 614)
2. Rubric/Performance/Alternative Assessments (EDUC 614)
3. Other, as selected by individual (be specific)

Section C: Teacher as Researcher with a Cultural Perspective

This section will be completed at the conclusion of EDUC 606.

Reflection Prompt 3:

In this section, you should focus on how coursework, related readings, and products in EDUC 606 have led you to focus more deeply on teachers as researchers with a cultural perspective. Please reflect on your own learning and your growth and change at this point in the Core. In your reflection, please address any of the applicable eight program learning outcomes and the ways in which the performance assessments included in this section provide evidence of your knowledge.

Suggested course products to be used as evidence of knowledge:

1. Teacher/Action Research Project and Paper (EDUC 606)
2. Selections from the Reflective Journal about research or cultural knowledge
3. Personal reflection (written to Okun Prompt)
4. Other, as selected by individual (be specific)

Section D: Teacher as Change Agent

This section will be completed at the conclusion of EDUC 615.

Reflection Prompt 4:

In this section, you will focus on how coursework, related readings, and experiences for the EDUC 615 have led you to think about yourself as a teacher leader in your school and in learning communities. Please reflect on your own learning and your growth and change at this point in the Core. In your reflection, please address any of the applicable eight program learning outcomes and the ways in which the performance assessments included in this section and in the Core provide evidence of your knowledge.

Suggested course products which may be provided as evidence of knowledge:

1. Grant Proposal Project (EDUC 615)
2. Selected journal/reflective responses from EDUC 615 or other Core coursework, as selected by teacher

Part III: ASTL Concentration Area

This section of the Portfolio should contain evidence of content area expertise and should include a description of the courses taken in your area of content, three or four selected performance-based or course products from the teacher's area of Concentration, and other evidences of content knowledge. You may include professional websites from your area of expertise or other professional affiliations aligning with your Concentration expertise. For some Concentrations in ASTL, this section may be comprised of its own content area Portfolio, if required by the program, and may include work samples from the area of concentration (four to six evidences are suggested).

PART IV: PORTFOLIO PRESENTATION: SYNTHESIZING KNOWLEDGE AND LOOKING AHEAD

Part IV is comprised of two parts: a written summative reflection and an oral presentation of the ASTL Portfolio.

Written Summative Reflection: Please describe your growth and change as you have progressed through the two components of the program: the Core and the Concentration. In your synthesis, please address the applicable eight program learning outcomes and the ways in which the performance assessments included in your coursework provide evidence of your growth and development as a professional. Please provide specific examples of how you are impacting student learning in your educational setting and what you will do to continue your professional development.

Oral Presentation to Faculty and Colleagues: Oral presentations will take place at the conclusion of the Core and Concentration areas, where Core only completers present their Core portfolio (I and II) and Program completers present full program portfolios with Parts I–IV. These presentations will provide the teacher an opportunity to share with program faculty and peers connections and conclusions drawn from coursework and teaching experiences while in the ASTL Program. The presentation should focus on the most powerful learning and change that have taken place during the degree program and the impact of a teacher on student learning. Candidates should articulate the connections made to the eight program learning outcomes.

Cohort Oral Presentations:

Date: As indicated to each cohort

References

Adams, S. J., Heywood, J. S., & Rothstein, R. (2009). *Teachers, performance pay, and accountability: What education can learn from other sectors*. Washington, DC: Economic Policy Institute.

American Educational Research Association. (2005, Summer). Teaching teachers: Professional development to improve student achievement. *Research Points, 3*(1).

Ball, A. F. (2009). Toward a theory of generative change in culturally and linguistically complex classrooms. *American Education Research Journal, 46*(45), 45–72.

Ball, D. L. (1991). Research on teaching mathematics: Making subject matter part of the equation. In J. Brophy (Ed.), *Advances in research on teaching, 2*, (pp. 1–48). Greenwich, CT: JAI Press.

Ball, D. L., & Cohen, D. K. (1999). Developing practice, developing practitioners: Toward a practice-based theory of professional education. In L. Darling-Hammond & G. Sykes (Eds.), *Teaching as the learning profession: Handbook of policy and practice* (pp. 3–32). San Francisco: Jossey-Bass.

Ball, D., Thames, M., & Phelps, G. (2008). Content knowledge for teaching: What makes it special? *Journal of Teacher Education, 59*(5), 389–407.

Barton, J., & Collins, A. (1993). Portfolios in teacher education. *Journal of Teacher Education, 44,* 200–210.

Belenky, M., Clinchy, B., Goldberger, N., and Tarule, J. (1986). *Women's ways of knowing*. New York: Basic Books.

Bill and Melinda Gates Foundation. (2010). *Working with teachers to develop fair and reliable measures of effective teaching*. Seattle, WA: Bill and Melinda Gates Foundation. Retrieved January 9, 2011, from http://www.gatesfoundation.org/learning/Pages/2010-reliable-measures-effective-teaching.aspx

Blackwell, P., & Diez, M. (1998). *Toward a new vision of master's education for teachers*. Washington, DC: National Council for the Accreditation of Teacher Education.

Blackwell, P., & Diez, M. (1999). *Achieving the new vision of master's education for teachers.* Washington, DC: National Council for the Accreditation of Teacher Education.

Borko, H., Michalec, P., Timmons, M., & Siddle, J. (1997). Student teaching portfolios: A tool for promoting reflective practice. *Journal of Teacher Education, 48*(5), 345–357.

Boyd, D., Grossman, P., Lankford, H., Loeb, S., & Wyckoff, J. (2009). Teacher preparation and student achievement. *Educational Evaluation and Policy Analysis, 31*(4), 416–440.

Boyer, E. (1990). *Scholarship reconsidered: Priorities of the Professoriate.* Princeton, NJ: Carnegie Foundation.

Bransford, J., Brown, A., & Cocking, R. (Eds.). (1999). *How people learn: Brain, mind, experience, and school.* Washington, DC: National Academy Press.

Brookfield, S. (1995). *Becoming a critically reflective teacher.* San Francisco: Jossey-Bass.

Brouwer, N., & Korthagen, F. (2005). Can teacher education make a difference? *American Educational Research Journal, 42*(1), 153–224.

Bruner, J. (1996). *The culture of education.* Cambridge, MA: Harvard.

Buchmann, M., & Floden, R. E. (1992). Coherence, the rebel angel. *Educational Researcher, 21*(6), 4–9.

Burroughs, R., Schwartz, T. A., & Hendricks-Lee, M. (2000). Communities of practice and discourse communities: Negotiating boundaries in NBPTS certification. *Teachers College Record, 102*(2), 344–374.

Carnegie Forum on Education and the Economy. (1986). *A nation prepared: Teachers for the 21st century.* Washington, DC: Carnegie Forum on Education and the Economy.

Carroll, J. A., Potthoff, D., & Huber, T. (1996). Learning from three years of portfolio use in teacher education. *Journal of Teacher Education, 47,* 253–262.

Cavanaugh, S. (2010, November 19). Bill Gates on school budgets: Cut wisely, change pay schemes. *Education Week.* Retrieved on January 13, 2011, http://blogs.edweek.org/edweek/state_edwatch/2010/11/bill_gates_on_school_budgets_cut_wiselyand_change_pay_schemes.html

Chappuis, S., Chappuis, J., & Stiggins, R. (2009). Supporting teacher learning teams. *Educational Leadership, 66*(5), 57–60.

Cibulka, J. G., & Leibbrand, J. A. (2010). Strengthening advanced teacher preparation and development: A systematic challenge for NBPTS and NCATE. In M. Dilworth and E. Cleveland (Eds.), *Accomplished teachers, institutional perspectives* (pp. 1–24). Arlington, VA: National Board for Professional Teaching Standards.

Cochran, K. F., DeRuiter, J. A., & King, R. A. (1993). Pedagogical content knowing: An integrative model for teacher preparation. *Journal of Teacher Education, 44*(4), 263–272.

Cochran-Smith, M. (2001). Constructing outcomes in teacher education: Policy, practice and pitfalls [Electronic version]. *Education Policy Analysis Archives, 9*(11). Retrieved July 1, 2006, from http://epaa.asu.edu/epaa/9(11).html

Cochran-Smith, M. (2004). *Walking the road: Race, diversity, and social justice in teacher education.* New York: Teachers College Press.

Cochran-Smith, M., & Lytle, S. (1999). Relationship of knowledge and practice: Teacher learning in communities. In A. Iran-Nejad & P. D. Pearson (Eds.), *Review of research in education* (pp. 249–305). Washington, DC: American Educational Research Association.

Cochran-Smith, M., & the Boston College Evidence Team. (2009). "Re-Culturing" teacher education: Inquiry, evidence and action. *Journal of Teacher Education, 60*(5), 458–468.

Cochran-Smith, M., Feiman-Nemser, S., McIntyre, D., & Demers, K. (2008). *Handbook of research on teacher education* (3rd ed.). New York: Routledge.

Cochran-Smith, M., & Zeichner, K. (2005). *Studying teacher education.* New York: Erlbaum.

Council of Graduate Schools. (2005). *Master's education: A guide for faculty and administrators.* Washington, DC: Council of Graduate Schools.

Crowe, E. (2010). *Measuring what matters: A stronger accountability model for teacher education.* Washington, DC: Center for American Progress.

Darling-Hammond, L. (2000). Reforming teacher preparation and licensing: Debating the evidence. *Teachers College Record, 102*(1), 28–56.

Darling-Hammond, L. (2006). Assessing teacher education: The usefulness of multiple measures for assessing program outcomes. *Journal of Teacher Education, 57*(2), 120–138.

Darling-Hammond, L., & Cobb, V. (1996). The changing context of teacher education. In F. Murray (Ed.), *The teacher educator's handbook.* San Francisco: Jossey-Bass.

Darling-Hammond, L., & Snyder, J. (2000). Authentic assessment of teaching in context. *Teaching and Teacher Education, 16,* 523–545.

Day, C., Elliott, B., & Kington, A. (2005). Reform, standards and teacher identity: Challenges of sustaining commitment. *Teaching and Teacher Education, 21,* 563–577.

Delandshere, G., & Arens, S. A. (2003). Examining the quality of evidence in preservice teacher portfolios. *Journal of Teacher Education, 54*(1), 57–73.

Delpit, L. (1995). *Other people's children: Cultural conflict in the classroom.* New York: The New Press.

Desimone, L. D. (2009). Improving impact studies of teachers' professional development: Toward better conceptualizations and measures. Educational Researcher, 38 (3), 181–199.

Dewey, J. (1933). *What is thinking? How we think.* Boston: D.C. Heath & Company.

Dewey, J. (1938). The meaning of purpose. *Experience and education.* New York: Collier Books.

Dewey, J. (1944). Experience in thinking. *Democracy in education.* New York: Free Press.

Dewey, J. (1998). *How we think: A statement of the relation of reflective thinking to the educative process.* (Original work published in 1933.) New York: Houghton Mifflin.

Dilworth, M., & Cleveland, E. (Eds). (2010) *Accomplished teachers, institutional perspectives* (pp. 1–24), Arlington, VA: National Board for Professional Teaching Standards.

Donaldson, M. L., Moore Johnson, S., Kirkpatrick, C. L., Marinell, W. H., Steele, J. L., & Szczesiul, S. A. (2008). Angling for access, bartering for change: How second-stage teachers experience differentiated roles in schools. *Teachers College Record, 110*(5), 1088–1114.

Dufour, R., Dufour, R., Eaker, R., & Many, T. (2006). *Learning by doing: A handbook for professional learning communities at work.* Bloomington, IN: Solution Tree.

Economic Policy Institute. (2010). *Problems with the use of students' test scores to evaluate teachers.* Washington, DC: Economic Policy Institute.

Fecho, B. (2004). *Is this English? Race, language, and culture in the classroom.* New York: Teachers College Press.

Feiman-Nemser, S. (1990). Teacher preparation: Structural and conceptual alternatives. In W. R. Houston (Ed.), *Handbook of research on teacher education.* New York: Macmillan.

Fendler, L. (2003). Teacher reflection in a hall of mirrors: Historical influences and Political reverberations. *Educational Researcher, 32*(3), 16–25.

Florio-Ruane, S. (2001). *Teacher education and the cultural imagination: Autobiography, conversation, and narrative.* Mahwah, NJ: Lawrence Erlbaum.

Foote, C. J., & Vermette, P. J. (2001). Teaching portfolio 101: Implementing the teaching portfolio in introductory courses. *Journal of Instructional Psychology, 28*(1), 31–37.

Fox, R. (1999). *This is who I am: The role of the Professional Development Portfolio in foreign and second language pre-service teacher education.* (Doctoral dissertation. George Mason University, Fairfax, VA, 1999). *Dissertation Abstracts International, 60-05A,* 1516. UMI Microform no. 9933323

Fox, R., & Galluzzo, G. (2006). Summative portfolio assessment. In S. Castle & B. D. Shaklee (Eds.), *Assessing teacher performance: Performance-based assessment in teacher education* (pp. 151–173). Lanham, MD: Rowman & Littlefield Education.

Fox, R., Kidd, J., Painter, D., & Ritchie, G. (2007). The growth of reflective practice: Teachers' portfolios as windows and mirrors. *The Teacher Educators Journal,* Spring, 13–25. Also available online (Fall, 2006) at www.ateva.org.

Fox, R., & Ritchie, G. (2003, November). *How higher education is improving teacher quality and raising student achievement.* Invited panel presentation for NCATE—NBPTS Higher Education pre-conference session, Washington, DC.

Fox, R., & White, C. S. (2006). Course-based performance assessments for advanced degree work. In S. Castle & B. D. Shaklee (Eds.), *Assessing teacher performance: Performance-based assessment in teacher education* (pp. 127–150). Lanham, MD: Rowman & Littlefield Education.

Fox, R. K., & White, C. S. (2010). Examining teachers' development through critical reflection in an advanced master's degree program. In E. Pultorak (Ed.), *The purposes, practices, and professionalism of teacher reflectivity: Insights for the 21st century teachers and students* (pp. 239–253). Lanham, MD: Rowman & Littlefield.

Fox, R. K., White, C. S., & Kidd, J. K. (2011, February). Program portfolios: Documenting teachers' growth in reflection-based inquiry. *Teachers and Teaching: Theory and Practice, 17*(1), pp. 149–167.

Fox, R., White, C. S., Kidd, J. K., & Ritchie, G. V. (2005, September). *Peering inside teacher dispositions: Program-based portfolios and teacher development.* Invited research presentation for the Accreditation, Accountability, and Quality: An Institutional Orientation and Professional Development Conference. Arlington (Crystal City), VA: AACTE and NCATE.

Fox, R., White, C. S., Kidd, J. K., & Ritchie, G. V. (2008, January). Delving into teachers' development through program portfolios: Case studies. *International Journal for the Scholarship of Teaching and Learning, 2*(1). Available online http://www.georgiasouthern.edu/ijsotl/issue_v2n1.htm

Fox, R., White, C. S., Muccio, L., & Tian, J. (2011). *Understanding advanced professional development of early career and experienced teachers through program portfolios.* Paper presented at the annual meeting of the American Education Research Association, New Orleans, LA.

Francis, D. (1995). The reflective journal: A window to preservice teachers' practical knowledge. *Teaching and Teacher Education, 11*, 229–241.

Freidus, H. (1996, April). *Reflection in teaching: Can it be taught?* Paper presented at the annual meeting of the American Education Research Association, New York, New York.

Galluzzo, G. R. (1997, November 17). *Proposal for a new advanced master's degree program.* Presented to the faculty of the Graduate School of Education, George Mason University, Unpublished document.

Galluzzo, G. R. (1999). *Aligning standards to improve teacher education and practice.* Washington, DC: National Council for Accreditation of Teacher Education.

Galluzzo, G. R., & Hilldrup, J. N. (2005, April). *Teaching teachers to be agents of educational change.* Paper presented at the American Educational Research Association, San Diego, CA.

Garet, M. S., Porter, A. C., Desimone, L., Birman, B. F., & Yoon, K. S. (2001). What makes professional development effective? Results from a national sample of teachers. *American Educational Research Journal, 38*(4), 915–945.

Glassick, C., Huber, M., & Maeroff, G. (1997). *Scholarship assessed: Evaluation of the professoriate.* San Francisco: Jossey-Bass.

Glazerman, S., Goldhaber, D., Loeb, S. D., Staiger, D., Raudenbush, S., & Whitehurst, G. (2010, December 15,). Value-added: It's not perfect, but it makes sense. *Education Week*, Retrieved January 8, 2011, http://www.edweek.org/ew/articles/2010/12/15/15whitehurst.h30.html

Glesne, C. (1999). *Becoming qualitative researchers: An introduction* (2nd ed.). New York: Longman.

Goldenberg, C. (2008, Summer). Teaching English language learners: What the research does—and does not—say. *American Educator,* 8–43.

Goodlad, J. I. (1990). *Teachers for our nation's schools.* San Francisco: Jossey-Bass.

Goodlad, J. I. (1998). Teacher education: For what? *Teacher Education Quarterly, 25,* 16–23.

Greeno, J. G., Collins, A. M., & Resnick, L. B. (1996). Cognition and learning. In D. Berliner and R. Calfee (Eds.), *Handbook of educational psychology* (pp. 15–41). New York: Macmillan.

Guskey, T. R. (1994). Results-oriented professional development: In search of the optimal mix of effective practices. *Journal of Staff Development, 15*(4), 42–50.

Hakel, M. D., Koenig, J. A., & Elliott, S. W. (2008). *Assessing accomplished teaching: Advanced- level certification programs.* Washington, DC: National Academies Press.

Hammadou, J. (1996). Portfolio design and the decision-making process in teacher education. In Z. Moore (Ed.), *Foreign language teacher education: Multiple perspectives* (pp. 123–150). Lanham, MD: University Press of America.

Hammadou, J. (1998). A blueprint for teacher portfolios: Concerns that need to be addressed when embarking on teacher assessment via portfolios. In J. Harper, M. Lively, & M. Williams (Eds.), *The coming of age of the profession* (pp. 291–308). Boston: Heinle & Heinle.

Hammerness, K., Darling-Hammond, L., & Bransford, J. (2005). How teachers learn and develop. In L. Darling-Hammond & J. Bransford (Eds.), *Preparing teachers for a changing world.* San Francisco: Jossey-Bass.

Harris, D., & Sass, T. (2009). *What makes for a good teacher and who can tell?* Washington, DC: Center for Analysis of Longitudinal Data in Education Research.

Hashweh, M. Z. (1987). Effects of subject matter knowledge in the teaching of biology and physics. *Journal of Teacher Education, 38*(3), 109–120.

Hill, H., Ball, D., & Schilling, S. (2008). Unpacking pedagogical content knowledge: Conceptualizing and measuring teachers' topic-specific knowledge of students. *Journal of Research in Mathematics Education, 39*(4), 372–400.

Hill, H. C., Rowan, B., & Ball, D. (2005). Effects of teachers' mathematical knowledge for teaching on student achievement. *American Educational Research Journal, 42*(2), 371–406.

Hole, S., & McEntee, G. (1999). Reflection is at the heart of practice. *Educational Leadership, 56*(8), 34–37.

Hollins, E. (2008). The deep meaning of culture. In *Culture in school learning: Revealing the deep meaning* (2nd ed.) (pp. 17–36). New York: Routledge.

Holmes Group. (1986). *Tomorrow's teachers.* East Lansing, MI: Holmes Group.

Holmes Group. (1990). *Tomorrow's schools.* East Lansing, MI: Holmes Group.

Holmes Group. (1995). *Tomorrow's schools of education.* East Lansing, MI: Holmes Group.

Houston, W. R. (Ed.) (1990). *Handbook of research on teacher education.* New York: Macmillan.

Hyland, N. E., & Noffke, S. E. (2005). Understanding diversity through social and community inquiry: An action research study. *Journal of Teacher Education, 56*(4), 367–381.

Interstate New Teacher Assessment and Support Consortium (INTASC). (1992). *Model standards for beginning teacher licensing, assessment, and development: A state resource for dialogue.* Washington, DC: Council of Chief State Officers.

Jacob, E. (1999). *The cultural inquiry process*. Fairfax, VA: George Mason University. Available online at http://classweb.gmu.edu/classweb/cip/index.htm

Judge, H. (1982). *American graduate schools of education: A view from abroad*. New York: Ford Foundation.

Kimball, W. H., & Hanley, S. (1998). Anatomy of a portfolio assessment system: Using multiple sources of evidence for credentialing and professional development. In N. Lyons (Ed.), *With portfolio in hand: Validating the new teacher professionalism* (pp. 189–201). New York: Teachers College Press.

Klein, J. (2011, March 12). What the school reform debate misses about teachers. *Washington Post*. Retrieved March 12, 2011 from http://www.washingtonpost.com/opinions/what-the-school-reform-debate-misses-about-teachers/2011/03/11/ABb2GSR_story.html

Knight, S. L., & Wiseman, D. L. (2005). Professional development for teachers of diverse students: A summary of the research. *Journal for the Education for Students Placed at Risk, 10*(4), 387–405.

Knowles, M. (1973). *The adult learner: A neglected species*. Houston, TX: Gulf Publishing.

Kohl, H. (2002). Topsy-turvies: Teacher talk and student talk. In L. Delpit & J. K. Dowdy (Eds.), *The skin that we speak: Thoughts on language and culture in the classroom* (pp. 145–161). New York: New Press.

Korthagen, F. A. J., & Kessels, J. P. A. M. (1999). Linking theory and practice: Changing the pedagogy of teacher education. *Educational Researcher, 28*(4), 4–17.

Korthagen, F., & Vasalos, A. (2005). Levels in reflection: Core reflection to enhance professional growth. *Teachers and Teaching: Theory and Practice, 11*(1), 47–71.

Kunzman, R. (2003). From teacher to student: The value of teacher education for experienced teachers. *Journal of Teacher Education, 54*(3), 241–253.

Lawrence, R. (2002). A small circle of friends: Cohort groups as learning communities. *New Directions for Adult and Continuing Education, 95,* 83–92.

Learning Forward. (2011). *Standards for professional learning*. Indianapolis, IN: Learning Forward. Available online at http://www.learningforward.org/standards/index.cfm.

Lukacs, K. S. (2009). Quantifying "the ripple in the pond": The development and initial validation of the Teacher Change Agent Scale. *The International Journal of Educational and Psychological Assessment, 3,* 25–37.

Lukacs, K. S., Holincheck, N., Fuhrman, C., & Galluzzo, G. R. (2007). *Exploring the ripple in the pond: Can early career teachers' attitudes toward educational change be explained?* Paper presented at the annual meeting of the American Educational Research Association, New Orleans.

Lukacs, K. S., Horak, A. K., & Galluzzo, G. R. (2010). Does teaching how to make a difference make a difference? A pre/post study of an Educational Change course. *Focus on Teacher Education, 10*(3), 7–11.

Lumina Foundation for Education. (2011). *Degree profile: A new framework for defining the learning and quality that college degrees should signify*. Indianapolis,

IN: Lumina Foundation for Education. Available online at http://www.luminafoundation.org/newsroom/news_releases/2011-01-25.html

Lyons, N. (1998). Reflection in teaching: can it be developmental? A portfolio perspective. *Teacher Education Quarterly, 25*(1), 115–127.

Lyons, N. (2006). Reflective engagement as professional development in the lives of university teachers. *Teachers and Teaching: Theory and Practice, 12*(2), 151–168.

Lytle, J. H. (2000). Teacher education at the millennium: A view from the cafeteria. *Journal of Teacher Education, 51*(3), 174–179.

Ma, L. (1999). *Knowing and teaching elementary mathematics: Teachers' understanding of fundamental mathematics in China and the United States.* Mahwah, NJ: Lawrence Erlbaum Associates.

Manfra, M. M., & Bolicks, C. M. (2008). Reinventing master's degree study for experienced social studies teachers. *Social Studies Research and Practice, 3*(2), 29–41.

Maslow, A. (1999). *Towards a psychology of being* (3rd ed.). New York: John Wiley & Sons.

Maxwell, J. A. (2005). *Qualitative research design: An interactive approach* (2nd ed.). Thousand Oaks, CA: Sage.

Meyer, D. K., Tusin, L. F., & Turner, J. D. (1996, April). *Preservice teachers' use of portfolios: Process vs. product.* Paper presented at the Annual Meeting of the American Educational Research Association, New York. ERIC Document Reproduction Service No. ED 396 000

Mokhtari, K., Yellin, D., Bull, K., & Montgomery, D. (1996). Portfolio assessment in teacher education: Impact on preservice teachers' knowledge and attitudes. *Journal of Teacher Education, 47,* 245–252.

Morin, J. A. (1995, July). *Portfolios: An effective tool used by prospective teachers to encourage self-evaluation and improvement.* Paper presented at the Annual Meeting of the National Evaluation Institute, Kalamazoo, MI. ERIC Document Reproduction Service No. ED 391 806

Muijs, D., & Harris, A. (2003). Teacher leadership-improvement through empowerment? An overview of the literature. *Educational Management and Administration, 31,* 437–448.

Murray, F. B. (1996). *The teacher educator's handbook.* San Francisco: Jossey-Bass.

National Board for Professional Teaching Standards. (1989a). *Toward high and rigorous standards for the teaching profession.* Arlington, VA: NBPTS.

National Board for Professional Teaching Standards. (1989b). *What teachers should know and be able to do.* Detroit, MI: NBPTS.

National Center for Education Statistics. (1999). *Teacher quality: A report on the preparation and quality of public school teachers.* Washington, DC: NCES.

National Commission on Excellence in Education. (1983). *A nation at risk.* Washington, DC: U.S. Department of Education.

National Commission on Teaching and America's Future. (1996). *What matters most: Teaching for America's future.* Washington, DC: NCTAF.

National Council for the Accreditation of Teacher Education. (2001). *Professional standards for the accreditation of schools, colleges, and departments of education.* Washington, DC: NCATE.

National Council for the Accreditation of Teacher Education. (2008a). *Professional standards for the accreditation of teacher preparation institutions.* Washington, DC: NCATE.

National Council for the Accreditation of Teacher Education. (2008b). NCATE to develop options within continuing accreditation, Washington: DC: NCATE. Available online at http://www.ncate.org/Public/Newsroom/NCATENewsPress-Releases/tabid/669/EntryId/72/NCATE-to-Develop-Options-within-Accrediting-Process.aspx

National Staff Development Council. (2001). *Standards for staff development, revised: Advancing student learning through staff development.* Oxford, OH: National Staff Development Council.

Newton, X., Darling-Hammond, L., Haertel, E., & Thomas, E. (2010). Value-added modeling of teacher effectiveness: An exploration of stability across models and contexts. *Educational Policy Analysis Archives, 18* (23). Retrieved May 23, 2011, from http://epaa.asu.edu/ojs/article/view/810

Okada, T., & Simon, H. A. (1997). Collaborative discovery in a scientific domain. *Cognitive Science, 21,* 109–146. doi: 10.1207/s15516709cog2102_1

Okun, B., Fried, J., & Okun, M. (1999). *Understanding diversity: A learning-as-practice primer.* Pacific Grove, CA: Brooks/Cole.

Partnership for 21st Century Skills. (2004). A framework for 21st Century Learning. Washington, DC: Available online at http://p21.org/index.php?option=com_content&task=view&id=254&Itemid=119

Pink, D. (2005). *A whole new mind.* New York: Berkeley Publishing Company.

Purcell-Gates, V. (2002). " . . . As soon as she opened her mouth!": Issues of language, literacy, and power. In L. Delpit & J. K. Dowdy (Eds.), *The skin that we speak: Thoughts on language and culture in the classroom* (pp. 121–141). New York: New Press

Putnam, R., & Borko, H. (1997). Teacher learning: implications of new views of cognition. In B. J. Biddle, T. L. Good, & I. F. Goodson (Eds.), *The international handbook of teachers and teaching* (pp. 1223–1296). Dordrecht, The Netherlands: Kluwer.

Putnam, R., & Borko, H. (2000). What do new views of knowledge and thinking have to say about research on teacher learning? *Educational Researcher, 29*(1), 41–45.

Rodgers, C. (2002). Defining reflection: Another look at John Dewey and reflective thinking. *Teachers College Record, 104*(4), 842–865.

Ross, D. L. (2002). Cooperating teachers facilitating reflective practice for student teachers in a professional development school. *Reflective Practice, 122*(4), 682–687.

Sanders, W. L., Ashton, J. J., & Wright, S. P. (2005). *Comparison of the effectives of NBPTS certified teachers with others teachers on the rates of student academic progress.* Cary, NC: SAS Institute.

Sanders, W., & Rivers, J. (1996). *Cumulative and residual effects of teachers on future student academic achievement.* Knoxville, TN: University of Tennessee Center for Value-Added Research and Assessment Center.

Schön, D. A. (1983). *The reflective practitioner: How professionals think in action.* New York: Basic Books.

Schön, D. A. (1987). *Educating the reflective practitioner.* San Francisco: Jossey-Bass.

Sherin, M. G., Linsenmeir, K. A., & van Es, E. A. (2009). Selecting video clips to promote mathematics teachers' discussion of student thinking. *Journal of Teacher Education, 60*(3), 213–230.

Shoho, A. R., & Martin, N. K. (1999, April). *A comparison of alienation among alternatively and traditionally certified teachers.* Paper presented at the annual meeting of the American Educational Research Association, Montreal, Canada.

Shulman, L. S. (1986). Those who understand: Knowledge growth in teaching. *Educational Researcher, 15*(2), 4–14.

Shulman, L. S. (1987). Knowledge and teaching: Foundations of the new reform. *Harvard Educational Review, 57,* 1–23.

Shulman, L. S., & Shulman, J. (2004). How and what teachers learn: A shifting perspective. *Journal of Curriculum Studies, 36*(2), 257–271.

Shulman, L. S., & Sykes, G. (1986). *A national board for teaching? In search of a bold standard.* New York: Carnegie Forum on Education and the Economy.

Sikula, J. (Ed.) (1996). *Handbook of research on teacher education* (2nd ed.). New York: Macmillan.

Sleeter, C. (2001). Preparing teachers for culturally diverse schools: Research and the overwhelming presence of whiteness. *Journal of Teacher Education, 52,* 93–106.

Sleeter, C. (2008). An invitation to support diverse students through teacher education. *Journal of Teacher Education, 59*(3), 212–219.

Sockett, H., DeMulder, E., Lepage, P., & Wood, D. (2001). *Transforming teacher education: Lessons in professional development.* Lewiston, NY: Edwin Mellen Press.

Sparks, D., & Hirsch, S. (1997). *A new vision for staff development.* Alexandria, VA: ASCD and Oxford, OH: National Staff Development Council.

Thames, M. H., & Ball, D. L. (2010). What mathematical knowledge does teaching require? Knowing mathematics in and for teaching. *Teaching Children Mathematics, 17*(4), 220–225.

Tom, A. (1997). *Redesigning teacher education.* Albany, NY: SUNY Press.

Tom, A. R. (1999). Reinventing master's degree study for experienced teachers. *Journal of Teacher Education, 50*(4), 245–254.

Turley, S., & Nakai, K. (2000). Two routes to certification: What do student teachers think? *Journal of Teacher Education, 51*(2), 122–134.

United States Department of Education. (2010). *A blueprint for reform: The reauthorization of the Elementary and Secondary Education Act.* Washington, DC: U.S. Department of Education.

Virginia Department of Education. (2011, April 28). Board of Education approves new model of teacher evaluation. Retrieved April 30, 2011 from http://www.doe.virginia.gov/news/news_releases/2011/apr28.shtml

Vygotsky, L. (1978). *Mind in society: The development of higher psychological processes.* Boston: Harvard University Press.

Wade, R. C., & Yarborough, D. B. (1996). Portfolios: A tool for reflective teaching in teacher education? *Teaching and Teacher Education, 12*(1), 63–79.

Wayne, A. J., & Young, P. (2003). Teacher characteristics and student gains: A review. *Review of Educational Research, 73,* 89–122.

Wei, R. C., Darling-Hammond, L., Andree, A., Richardson, N., & Orphanos, S. (2009). *Professional learning in the learning profession: A status report on teacher development in the U.S. and abroad.* Dallas, TX: National Staff Development Council.

Wenzlaff, T. L., & Wieseman, K. C. (2004). Teachers need teachers to grow. *Teacher Education Quarterly, 31*(2), 113–124.

Whitcomb, J., Borko, H., & Liston, D. (2009). Growing talent: Promising professional development models and practices. *Journal of Teacher Education, 60*(3), 207–212.

White, C. S., Fox, R. K., & Isenberg, J. P. (2011). Investigating teachers' professional learning in an advanced master's degree program. *European Journal of Teacher Education, 34*(4), 477–495.

Wilson, S. M., Floden, R. E., & Ferrini-Mundy, J. (2001). *Teacher preparation research: Current knowledge, recommendations, and priorities for the future.* Seattle: Center for the Study of Teaching Policy, University of Washington.

Wilson, S. M., Floden, R. E., & Ferrini-Mundy, J. (2002). Teacher preparation research: An insiders' view from the outside. *Journal of Teacher Education, 53*(3), 190–204.

Wilson, S. M., Shulman, L. S., & Richert, A. E. (1987). "150 different ways of knowing": Representation of knowledge in teaching. In J. Calderhead (Ed.), *Exploring teachers' thinking* (pp. 104–124). London: Cassell.

Wineburg, S. (2001). *Historical thinking and other unnatural acts: Charting the future of teaching the past.* Philadelphia: Temple.

Winerip, M. (2011, March 7). Evaluating New York teachers, perhaps the numbers do lie. *New York Times.* Retrieved March 7, 2011 from http://www.nytimes.com/2011/03/07/education/07winerip.html?pagewanted=1&src=un&feedurl=http://json8.nytimes.com/pages/education/index.jsonp

Wingspread Group on Higher Education. (1993). *An American imperative: Higher expectations for higher education. An open letter to those concerned about the American future.* Report of the Wingspread Group on Higher Education. Racine, WI: Johnson Foundation.

Winsor, P. J., & Ellefson, B. A. (1995). Professional portfolios in teacher education: An exploration of their value and potential. *Teacher Educator, 31*(1), 68–81.

Wiseman, A., & Fox, R. (2010). Supporting teachers' development of cultural competence through teacher research. *Action in Teacher Education, 32*(4), 26–37. doi: 10.1080/01626620.2010.549708

Wood, F. H., & Killian, J. (1998). Job-embedded learning makes the difference. *Journal of Staff Development, 19*(2), 52–54.

Wright, S. P., Horn, S. P., & Sanders, W. L. (1997). Teachers and classroom context effects on student achievement: Implications for teacher evaluation. *Journal of Personnel Evaluation in Education, 11*(1), 57–67.

Yin, R. K. (2003). *Case study research* (3rd ed.). Thousand Oaks, CA: Sage.

Zeichner, K. (2006). Reflections of a university-based teacher educator on the future of college- and university-based teacher education. *Journal of Teacher Education, 57*(3), 326–341.

Zeichner, K., & Wray, S. (2001). The teaching portfolio in US teacher education programs: What we know and what we need to know. *Teaching and Teacher Education, 17*, 613–621.

Index